FIFTH EDITION

KEYBOARDING/TYPEWRITING
FOR PERSONAL APPLICATIONS

BERLE HAGGBLADE

Professor, Information Management
California State University, Fresno

S.J. WANOUS

Professor of Education, Emeritus
University of California, Los Angeles

ISBN: 0-538-20730-2

Library of Congress Catalog Card Number: 84-52523

2345678H 2109876

Published by

SOUTH-WESTERN PUBLISHING CO.

T73

CINCINNATI   WEST CHICAGO, IL   DALLAS   PELHAM MANOR, NY   LIVERMORE, CA

PREFACE

The new title of this Fifth Edition, KEYBOARDING/TYPE-WRITING FOR PERSONAL APPLICATIONS, reflects the most recent changes that have occurred in the various types of equipment used to produce typed or printed copy. Today, the verb "type" has been supplanted to a large degree by the word "keyboard"; and the term "keyboarding" is now commonly accepted to indicate the method by which information is entered into a typewriter, word processor, microcomputer, or computer terminal.

These broader applications of keyboarding skills have increased the importance of acquiring keyboarding/typing proficiency in the middle and junior high schools, the levels for which the text is designed. Topics covered in both skill building and problem copy are geared to the needs, interests, experiences, and reading abilities of learners at this age.

OBJECTIVES

Students who complete the text should accomplish several major objectives:

- Achieve sufficient keyboarding skill to be able to operate the machines by touch.
- Acquire the habit of using their machines as a basic communication tool in the preparation of personal and school papers.
- Reach optimum keyboarding skill according to their individual abilities.
- Develop the ability to transfer thoughts from their heads directly to the keyboard.
- Review and improve basic English skills of punctuation, spelling, proofreading, and composition.

ORGANIZATION

Organized into four cycles and a total of 140 lessons and a simulation, the book may be used for a one-semester course, a two-semester course, or a short course designed primarily to cover basic key locations.

The first 70 lessons are devoted to skill development and personal writing tasks. Drill and timed writing copy is easy in the early lessons and advances in gradual stages to average difficulty. The second 70 lessons provide a thorough review and advanced work.

Keyboarding Skill. Special technique drills are included in almost every lesson. Speed and control aids are generously placed throughout the entire book. The copy appears in print, rough draft, and script in order to enable students to develop keyboarding skill under realistic con-ditions.

Keyboarding Applications. Beginning with Cycle 2, the book covers personal notes and business letters, reports, outlines, book reviews, speech and class notes, minutes, agendas, tables, and other personal papers. Students work first from model copy containing detailed reminders and later from unarranged copy.

Language Arts Development. After students have ac-quired desirable techniques, they are introduced to numerous language arts and composing activities.

Special Index. A Special Index has been compiled listing the location of:

- Language arts skills
- Timed writings (including speed ladder paragraphs)
- Problem typing
- Key location drills
- Manipulative and preapplication writings
- Technique builders
- Skill builders
- Skill comparison sentences and paragraphs.
- Guided writings
- Continuity and fluency practice
- Control builders
- Speed builders
- Rough draft sentences/paragraphs

This index provides easy reference to each activity which can be used to aid students in problem areas.

FEATURES

The introductory lessons have been reorganized so that every fourth lesson is devoted to key location reviews and technique reinforcement.

Additional color has been used to highlight information that deserves special attention.

Drill and problem copy have been rearranged on the pages to improve appearance and readability.

Language arts activities have been specially identified for easier reference.

Much of the copy in this edition is new and timely, with many topics related specifically to the Information Age.

A convenient reference section, containing frequently needed explanations and illustrations, appears in the pre-liminary pages of the book.

The final unit consists of an office simulation which gives students an opportunity to apply their keyboarding skills to the production of jobs required in a typical school office.

ACKNOWLEDGEMENTS

We sincerely appreciate the comments and suggestions received from teachers who have used previous editions. They have been most helpful in the preparation of this edition.

Berle Haggblade

S. J. Wanous

CONTENTS

CYCLE ONE — **LEARNING TO OPERATE YOUR KEYBOARD**

Unit 1 Learning to Operate the Letter Keys (Lessons 1–15) 3

2 Improving Your Keyboarding Techniques (Lessons 16–20) 27

3 Learning the Figure Keys (Lessons 21–25) 34

4 Improving Your Basic Skills (Lessons 26–30) 42

5 Learning the Basic Symbol Keys (Lessons 31–35) 49

CYCLE TWO — **BASIC PERSONAL APPLICATIONS**

Unit 6 Centering Notices and Announcements (Lessons 36–40) 59

7 Keyboarding Personal Notes and Letters (Lessons 41–50) 69

8 Keyboarding Reports and Outlines (Lessons 51–60) 90

9 Learning to Keyboard Tables (Lessons 61–70) 106

CYCLE THREE — **PREPARING PERSONAL PAPERS**

Unit 10 Learning to Format Personal/Business Papers (Lessons 71–80) 123

11 Keyboarding School Papers (Lessons 81–95) 139

12 Keyboarding for Club and Community Activities (Lessons 96–110) 162

13 Preparing a Student-Writer's Style Guide (Lessons 111–115) 183

14 Improving Your Basic Skills—Measurement (Lessons 116–120) 188

CYCLE FOUR — **INTRODUCTION TO BUSINESS COMMUNICATIONS**

Unit 15 Learning to Format Business Letters (Lessons 121–130) 197

16 Learning to Keyboard Business Forms (Lessons 131–135) 213

17 Improving Your Basic Skills—Measurement (Lessons 136–140) 220

18 Working in a School Office (Simulation) 227

MANUAL TYPEWRITER

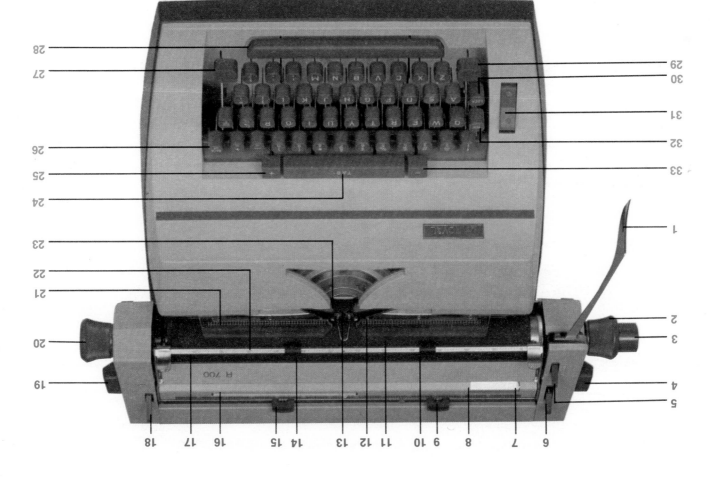

All typewriters have similar parts. These parts are identified on the photographs of the manual model shown below and on the electric model on page v. The exact location of the parts on the illustrated machines may be slightly different from the location on your machine, but the differences are, for the most part, few and slight.

To identify the parts of the typewriter, locate the numbered part on the illustration. Refer to the same number in the list below for the name of the part. The function is explained in the textbook. Learn to operate each part correctly as it is explained to you.

Extra parts peculiar to your machine can be identified by reference to the instructional booklet prepared especially for your machine.

1	Carriage return lever	12	Card and envelope holders	23	Ribbon carrier
2	Left cylinder knob	13	Printing point indicator	24	Tabulator
3	Variable line spacer	14	Paper bail roll	25	Tab set
4	Left carriage release	15	Right margin set	26	Backspace key
5	Line-space regulator	16	Paper table	27	Right shift key
6	Automatic line finder (ratchet release)	17	Cylinder (platen)	28	Space bar
7	Paper guide	18	Paper release lever	29	Left shift key
8	Paper guide scale	19	Right carriage release	30	Shift lock
9	Left margin set	20	Right cylinder knob	31	Ribbon control
10	Paper bail roll	21	Aligning scale	32	Margin release key
11	Paper bail	22	Line-of-writing scale (cylinder scale)	33	Tab clear

ELECTRIC TYPEWRITER

Electric typewriters are available with either a movable carriage as on the manual on page iv or with a rotating element which moves across the paper as the characters are keyed. The model shown above is a single-element machine.

All of the parts identified on the manual model, except the carriage return lever and the left and right carriage releases, can be found on the electric model. Some additional parts have also been identified on the electric machine.

1	Carriage return lever (not on electric—see Number 34)	13	Printing point indicator	24	Tabulator
2	Left cylinder knob	14	Paper bail roll	25	Tab set
3	Variable line spacer	15	Right margin set	26	Backspace key
4	Left carriage release	16	Paper table	27	Right shift key
5	Line-space regulator	17	Cylinder (platen)	28	Space bar
6	Automatic line finder	18	Paper release lever	29	Left shift key
7	Paper guide	19	Right carriage release	30	Shift lock
8	Paper guide scale	20	Right cylinder knob	31	Ribbon control (not shown)
9	Left margin set	21	Aligning scale	32	Margin release key
10	Paper bail roll	22	Line-of-writing scale (cylinder scale)	33	Tab clear
11	Paper bail	23	Ribbon carrier (not shown)	34	Carriage return key
12	Card and envelope holders			35	ON/OFF control

Operating a typewriter involves more than learning to stroke the keys. This page and page vii contain information regarding machine adjustments which you must know for the particular model you are using.

Pica and Elite Type

Some machines are equipped with pica type; some with elite type. Pica is larger than elite. The line-of-writing scale (22) range is from 0 to about 90 on pica type; from 0 to about 110 on elite type.

Pica:	fjfjfjfjfjfj	(10 letters per inch)
	1 inch	
Elite:	fjfjfjfjfjfjfj	(12 letters per inch)

Setting the Margin Stops

Four types of margin sets are described below. Determine which type of margin set your machine has; then follow the appropriate directions.

Push-Button Margins

1. Push down on the left margin set button, and slide it to the desired position.
2. Release the margin set button.
3. Set the right margin in the same manner, using the right margin set button.

Magic Margins

1. Pull the left magic margin lever forward; hold it while moving the carriage to the desired position.
2. Release the left magic margin lever.
3. Set the right margin in the same manner, using the right magic margin lever.

Key-Set Margins

1. Move the carriage to the left margin stop. Depress and hold the margin set key after you have reached the desired left setting.
2. Release the margin set key.
3. Set the right margin in the same manner after you move the carriage to the right margin stop.

Push-Lever Margins

1. Push in on the left margin lever set, and slide it to the desired position.
2. Release the left margin lever set.
3. Set the right margin in the same manner, using the right margin lever set.

Clearing and Setting the Tab Stops

Tab Clear Move the carriage to the extreme left of your machine (or carrier to extreme right). Depress the tab clear key (33) and hold as you return the carriage or carrier the full width of the machine.

Tab Set Move the carriage or carrier to the desired tab stop position; then press the tab set (25). Repeat this operation to set as many tabulator stops as are needed.

Paper Guide and Centering Point

There is at least one scale on every typewriter, usually the line-of-writing scale (22), that reads from 0 at the left to 85 or more at the right, depending on the width of the carriage and style of type—either pica or elite. The spaces on this scale are matched to the spacing mechanism on the machine.

To simplify directions, your instructor may ask you to insert paper into your machine so that the left edge corresponds to 0 on the line-of-writing scale. The center point of 8½" × 11" paper will then be 42 on the carriage scale for pica type and 51 for elite.

If this procedure is adopted, adjust the paper guide (7) to the left edge of your paper after it is inserted with the left edge at 0 on the scale. Note the position of the paper guide. Move it to this point at the beginning of each period.

Determining the Margin Stops

You may set the margin stops (9 and 15) for any length of line desired, such as 50-, 60-, or 70-space line. To have equal left and right margins, take these two steps.

Step 1 Subtract half the line length from the center point (42 for pica; 51 for elite). Set the left margin stop at this point.

Step 2 Add half the line length, plus 5 spaces for the end-of-line bell, to the center point. Set the right stop at this point.

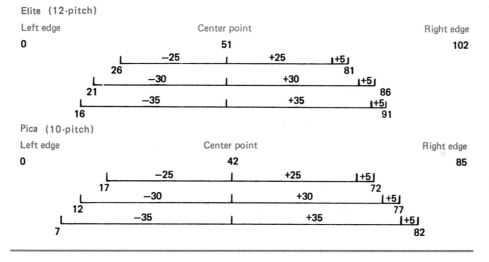

Changing the Ribbon

In general, the instructions given here apply to standard and electric typewriters. Consult the manufacturer's pamphlet accompanying your machine for special instructions.

1. Wind the used ribbon on one spool. Usually, it is best to wind it on the right side of your machine.

2. Study the route of the ribbon as you wind. Note especially how the ribbon winds and unwinds on the two spools. Note, too, how the ribbon is threaded through the ribbon-carrier mechanism (23).

3. Lift the right spool slightly off its hub to see if both sides are the same. Study both sides of the spool so you will replace it properly.

4. Remove the ribbon from the carrier, and remove both spools. Note how the ribbon is attached to the empty spool.

5. Fasten the new ribbon to the empty spool, and wind several inches of the new ribbon on it.

6. Place both spools on their hubs, and thread the ribbon through the carrier. Make sure the ribbon is straight.

Position of Hands

When keyboarding, keep your fingers deeply curved. Fingernails should be neatly trimmed.

Hold your hands directly over the keys. Turn the hands inward slightly to get straight strokes. Do not permit your hands to turn over on the little fingers.

Keep your forearms in a parallel line with the slope of the keyboard. Hold your wrists down near, but not resting on, the front frame of the machine. Do not buckle your wrists upward.

Barely touch the home keys with your fingertips. Feel the keys; do not smother them.

When a finger makes a reach from its home position to strike another key, the other fingers remain on or near their home keys. Such reaches are made by the finger without twisting the wrist or moving the arm or elbow.

Forearms parallel to slant of machine

Fingers curved

Reach with the finger

Keep arms and wrists quiet

Keyboarding Rhythm

Your goal is to strike the keys at a steady pace, without breaks or pauses. At first, you will think each letter as you key it. Later, you will think short, easy-to-type words and phrases as a whole. You will key longer, hard-to-type words by letters or syllables. Finally, you will combine whole word keyboarding with letter or syllable keyboarding into a smooth, fluent, steady rhythm.

Stroking

Center the stroking action in your fingers. Keep your elbows, arms, and wrists quiet as you keyboard. Your fingers should be deeply curved. Use quick, sharp strokes. Release the keys quickly by snapping the fingers toward the palm of the hand. Strike the keys squarely with short, quick, straight strokes.

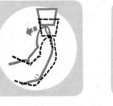

Posture

Good posture is vital in learning to keyboard well. Given below are 10 guides of good form. Study the guides care-fully. Observe them whenever you work at your machine.

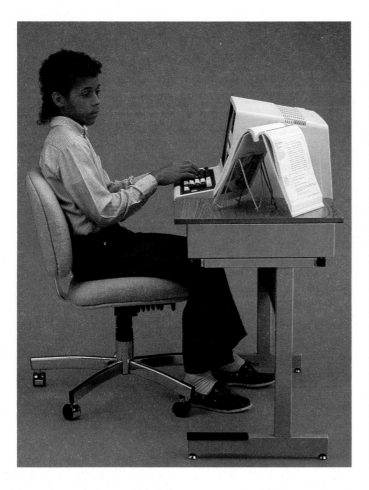

1. Book at right of machine on bookholder or with something under top for easier reading.

2. Table free of unneeded books and papers.

3. Front frame of the machine even with the edge of the desk.

4. Body centered opposite the **h** key, 6 to 8 inches from front frame of machine.

5. Body seated back in chair, shoulders erect with body leaning forward slightly from waist.

6. Elbows held near the body.

7. Wrists held low with forearms parallel to the slant of the machine. Do not rest lower hand on frame of machine.

8. Feet flat on the floor, one just ahead of the other.

9. Head turned toward book with eyes on copy.

10. Fingers curved and held over second row of keys.

Spacing Between Words

Almost one in every five strokes is made with the space bar (28). Learn to operate the space bar correctly.

1. Hold the right thumb curved under the hand just over the space bar.
2. Strike the bar with a quick down-and-in motion of the thumb.
3. Keep the wrist low and quiet as you strike the bar.
4. Keep the left thumb tucked under the hand.

Control of the space bar

Shift and Shift Lock Keys

The left shift key (29) is used when capital letters are keyboarded with the right hand. Use a one-two count as you shift.

ONE Depress the shift key with the little finger and hold it down.

TWO Strike the capital letter with the opposite hand; then quickly release the shift key and return the little finger to its home row position.

The right shift key (27) is used when capital letters are keyboarded with the left hand.

To keyboard ALL CAP items, depress the shift lock (30) with the left little finger and type. To release the shift lock, depress either the right or left shift key.

Control of left shift

Control of right shift

Daily Care of Your Machine

1. Brush the dirt and dust from the bars.
2. Keep desk free of dust, especially the area under the machine.
3. Cover the machine when it is not in use.
4. Shut off power on an electric machine after each use.

Weekly Care of Your Machine

1. Clean keys, using approved cleaner.
2. Move the carriage to extreme end positions. With cloth moistened with oil, clean the carriage rails on each side.
3. Clean cylinder (platen), feed rolls, and paper bail rolls with cloth moistened with cleaning fluid.

Returning the Carriage on a Manual Typewriter

1. Move the left hand, palm down, to the carriage return lever (1). Keep your right hand in home position and your eyes on the book.
2. Move the lever forward to take up the slack.
3. With the fingers bracing one another, return the carriage with a flick of the wrist.
4. Return your left hand at once to its home position.

Returning on an Electric Typewriter

1. Reach the little finger of your right hand to the carriage return key (34).
2. Tap the return key quickly.
3. Return the finger at once to its home-key position.

Manual return

Electric return

Carbon Copies

1. Place the carbon paper (with glossy side down) on a sheet of plain paper. The paper on which you will prepare the original is then laid on top of the carbon paper.

2. Place the sheets between the cylinder and the paper table (glossy side of carbon facing you). Roll into the typewriter. The dull surface of the carbon should be facing you.

Erasing and Correcting Carbon Copies

1. Move the carriage (carrier) to the extreme right or left so that the eraser crumbs will not fall into the machine.
2. To avoid moving the paper out of alignment, turn the cylinder forward if the erasure is to be made on the upper two thirds of the paper; backward, if on the lower third of the paper.
3. To erase on the original sheet, lift the paper bail out of the way and place a small card in back of the original copy and in front of the first carbon sheet. Use an eraser shield to protect the letters that are not being erased. Use a hard typewriter eraser. When you complete the erasure, brush the eraser crumbs away from the machine.
4. Move the card in front of the second carbon sheet if more than one copy is being made. Erase the errors on the carbon copies with a soft (or pencil) eraser first, then use the hard typewriter eraser used in erasing on the original copy.
5. When the error has been neatly erased on the original and all the carbon copies, remove the card, position the carriage to the proper point, and key the correction.

Correcting carbons

Vertical Centering

Centering material so that it will have uniform top and bottom margins is called *vertical centering*.

1. Count the lines in the copy to be centered. If your copy is to be double spaced, remember to count the spaces between the lines. There is one line space following each line of copy when material is double spaced.
2. Subtract the total lines to be used from the lines available on the paper you are using. (There are 33 lines on a half sheet, 66 on a full sheet.)
3. Divide the number of lines that remain by 2. The answer gives you the number of lines in the top and bottom margins. If the result contains a fraction, disregard the fraction.
4. Insert your paper so that the top edge is exactly even with the aligning scale (21). Bring the paper up the proper number of line spaces. Start typing one line-space below the number you calculated for your top margin.

Vertical Centering (Backspace from Center Method)

1. Insert paper to line 33 (vertical center of a piece of paper 11" long). Roll cylinder (17) back (toward you) one line space for each two lines in the copy to be keyboarded. This will place the copy in exact vertical center.
2. To keyboard a problem off-center or in *reading position*, roll cylinder back two extra line spaces.
3. Another centering method is to fold the paper from top to bottom and make a slight crease at the right edge. The crease will be at the vertical center (line 33). Insert the paper to the crease, roll the cylinder back one space for each two lines in the copy.

Horizontal Centering

Centering material so there will be equal left and right margins is called *horizontal centering*.

1. Check the placement of the paper guide (7). Turn to page vii and read the directions for adjusting the paper guide.
2. Clear tab stops (33). Set tab (25) at center point of paper (elite 51; pica 42) for paper 8½ inches wide.
3. Backspace (26) from center point once for every 2 characters or spaces in the line to be centered. If there is one character left, do not backspace for it. Begin to type at the point where the backspacing is completed.

Horizontal Placement of Tables

1. Insert paper into the machine with left edge at "0."
2. Move the left and right margin stops to the ends of the scale. Clear all tab stops.
3. Move the carriage to the center of the paper.
4. Determine number of spaces to be left between the columns (if a specific number of spaces is not given).
5. Spot the longest word or entry in each column.
6. From the center of your paper, backspace once for each 2 letters, figures, spaces, or punctuation marks in the longest word or entry in each column. If you have an extra character in any column, add that character to the first character of the next column. If one space is left over
7. Backspace once for each 2 spaces to be left between the columns. If one space is left over, disregard it.
8. Set the left margin at the point at which you stop backspacing. This is the point where the first column will start.
9. Space forward once for each letter, figure, space or punctuation mark in the longest entry in the first column and once for each space between Columns 1 and 2. Set a tab stop for the second column. Continue in this way until stops have been set for each column.

Centering Columnar Headings

1. Set the carriage at the point a column is to begin.
2. Space forward 1 space for each 2 spaces in the longest line in that column.
3. From that point, backspace once for each 2 spaces in the columnar heading.
4. Keyboard the heading. It will be centered over the column.

Finding Horizontal Center Point for Odd-Size Paper or Cards

1. Insert paper or card into the machine.
2. Add the numbers on the line-of-writing scale (22) at the left and right edges of the paper or card.
3. Divide the sum by 2. The resulting figure is the horizontal center point of the paper or card.

Keyboarding Left-Bound Reports

1. Leave a 2" top margin and a 1" bottom margin on the first page, 1" top and 1" bottom margins on all following pages.
2. Set a 1½" left margin (pica, 15 spaces; elite, 18 spaces) and a 1" right margin (pica, 10 spaces; elite, 12 spaces). Move the center point 3 spaces to the right to allow for the wider left margin.
3. Double-space the body, using 5-space paragraph indentions. Retain at least 2 lines of a paragraph at the bottom of a page and carry forward at least 2 lines of a paragraph to a new page if possible.
4. Indent long quotations of 4 lines or more 5 spaces from each margin and single space them.
5. If the first page is numbered, center the number ½" from the bottom. Place the following page numbers 4 line spaces from the top and align them with the right margin.
6. Place the heading on line 13, leaving a triple space between it and the body of the report.

leave 2" top margin

WRITING A LEFTBOUND REPORT

"The test of a book," said Ernest Hemingway, "is how much good stuff you can throw away."[1] He added that anything that does not have the ring of hard truth, that seems the least bit overdone, must go into the wastebasket. Deep feelings about something written in words that stay with the reader--this is the goal of a good writer.

1½" left margin

1" right margin

We can't all gain the fame that Hemingway knew as a writer. He worked hard and long at perfecting his skill. We can all learn how to write a short paper, however, long before we get into Hemingway's class. Almost all of us can learn to write a clear, interesting account about something we have read, heard, or seen. Let's see how you might go about this job.

Steps for Preparing a Report

Choose the right subject. To begin with, you need to select a subject you know something about. One authority says such a choice may be the most important decision you make in planning and writing your composition.[2] You can't write about

[1]T. F. James, "Hemingway at Work," Cosmopolitan, August, 1957, p. 54.

[2]John E. Warriner and Sheila Laws Graham, English Grammar and Composition, Second Course, (New York: Harcourt Brace Javanovich, Inc., 1977), p. 376.

approximately 1"

Keyboarding Superscripts and Subscripts

1. For placement of a superscript (superior number), use the automatic line finder (6) and turn the platen knob one-half space toward you.
2. Keyboard the figure or symbol, and operate the automatic line finder and platen knob to return to original position.
3. Use the same procedure for a subscript, except turn the platen knob one-half space away from you.

Keyboarding Footnotes

1. Keyboard a superior number immediately following the material in the report which will be documented by a footnote.
2. Draw a light pencil mark on your paper to mark the 1" bottom margin. Space up 2 or 3 lines from that mark for each footnote. Leave an extra line space for a DS between two or more footnotes; then space up 2 additional lines and draw a second pencil mark. This is where you will keyboard the divider line.
3. After completing the last line on the page, change to single spacing. Single space, then keyboard a 1½" divider line (15 spaces pica; 18 spaces elite) at the point where you have your second pencil mark.
4. After keyboarding the divider line, double space, indent 5 spaces and key the footnote reference. Single space each footnote; double space between footnotes.

Keyboarding Reference Citations

1. After keyboarding the quoted material, place within parentheses the author's last name, date of publication, and page number of the cited material.
2. At the end of a report, triple space and center the word "References." Triple space and keyboard in alphabetical order (by authors' last names) each complete reference.

Keyboarding a Bibliography

1. Use the same top and side margins used for the first page of your report. Center the heading over the line of writing.
2. Start the first line of each reference at the left margin. Indent other lines 5 spaces. Single space the entries; double space between entries.

---

margin →

BIBLIOGRAPHY
TS

Coon, George E., et al. American Book English. New York:
indent 5 spaces → American Book Company, 1980.
DS
Laughlin, R. M. "Fun in the Word Factory: Experiences with the Dictionary." Language Arts (March, 1978), pp. 319-21.
DS
Maxwell, John C. Ginn Elements of English. Lexington: Ginn and Company, 1974.
DS
Pollock, Thomas Clark, and Richard L. Loughlin. The Macmillan English Series. New York: Macmillan, Inc., 1973.

Keyboarding a Postal Card

1. Set margin stops 4 spaces from each edge of the card. Set a tab stop at horizontal center.

2. Begin the dateline on line 3. Use block or modified block style.

```
 1
 2              begin 3 lines from
                top edge of card
 3                              │April 13, 19--
 4    ┌─ 4 spaces                └ center point        TS
 5    │
 6    │ Dear Aunt Martha
 7                            DS
 8      The gold necklace you sent for my birthday is
 9      beautiful.  Thank you for being so thoughtful.
10                                                  DS
11      Mother said I should ask you to arrange your
12      vacation to include a visit at our house this
13      year.  Please try to come.
14                               TS
15
16              center point → Lauri
17
18
19
```

Addressing a Postal Card

1. Keyboard the return address and the address of the recipient on the opposite side of the postal card.

2. Begin the return address on the second line from the top edge of the postal card and 3 spaces from the left edge.

3. Begin the address of the recipient about 2″ from the top of the card and 2″ from the left edge.

```
    Miss Lauri Bianchi
    2487 Langston Way
    Joplin, MO  64801-4583



                Mrs. Martha Parker
                191 East Jefferson Avenue
                Denver, CO  80237-2125
```

Two-Letter ZIP Code Abbreviations

Alabama	AL	Indiana	IN	Nebraska	NE	South Carolina	SC
Alaska	AK	Iowa	IA	Nevada	NV	South Dakota	SD
Arizona	AZ	Kansas	KS	New Hampshire	NH	Tennessee	TN
Arkansas	AR	Kentucky	KY	New Jersey	NJ	Texas	TX
California	CA	Louisiana	LA	New Mexico	NM	Utah	UT
Colorado	CO	Maine	ME	New York	NY	Vermont	VT
Connecticut	CT	Maryland	MD	North Carolina	NC	Virginia	VA
Delaware	DE	Massachusetts	MA	North Dakota	ND	Washington	WA
Florida	FL	Michigan	MI	Ohio	OH	West Virginia	WV
Georgia	GA	Minnesota	MN	Oklahoma	OK	Wisconsin	WI
Hawaii	HI	Mississippi	MS	Oregon	OR	Wyoming	WY
Idaho	ID	Missouri	MO	Pennsylvania	PA		
Illinois	IL	Montana	MT	Rhode Island	RI		

Keyboarding Personal/Business Letters

1. Set your machine for single spacing.

2. Set the margins. The margins vary according to the length of the letter.

3. Space down to begin the return address. (The number of lines to space down varies with the length of the letter. The longer the letter, the fewer the number of lines.) For a modified block style letter, start the return address at the center point of the paper. For a block style letter, start the return address at the left margin.

4. Space down 4 times below the return address to the letter address.

5. Begin the salutation a double space below the letter address.

6. Begin the body of the letter a double space below the salutation. Single space the paragraphs; double space between paragraphs.

7. Begin the complimentary close a double space below the body of the letter. For a modified block style letter, start at the center point. For a block style letter, start at the left margin.

8. Keyboard the name of the writer on the 4th line space below the complimentary close. (The typewritten name of the writer is optional.)

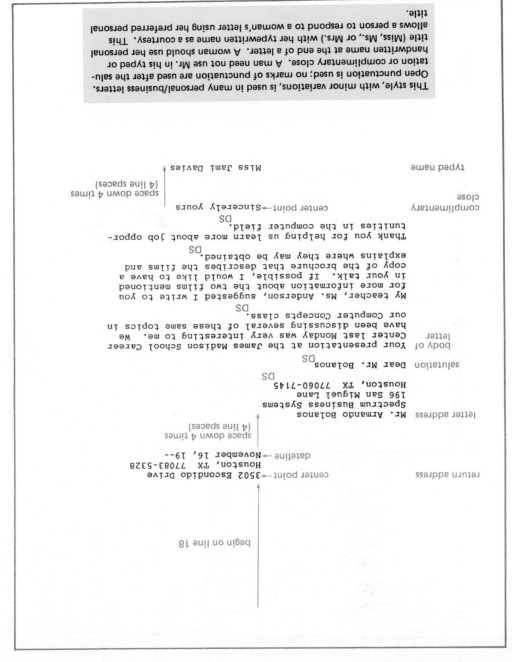

begin on line 18

return address	center point → 3502 Escondido Drive Houston, TX 77083-5328
dateline	November 16, 19--
	space down 4 times (4 line spaces)
letter address	Mr. Armando Bolanos Spectrum Business Systems 196 San Miguel Lane Houston, TX 77060-7145
	DS
salutation	Dear Mr. Bolanos
	DS
body of letter	Your presentation at the James Madison School Career Center last Monday was very interesting to me. We have been discussing several of these same topics in our Computer Concepts class. DS My teacher, Ms. Anderson, suggested I write to you for more information about the two films mentioned in your talk. If possible, I would like to have a copy of the brochure that describes the films and explains where they may be obtained. DS Thank you for helping us learn more about job opportunities in the computer field.
	DS
complimentary close	center point → Sincerely yours
	space down 4 times (4 line spaces)
typed name	Miss Jami Davies

This style, with minor variations, is used in many personal/business letters. Open punctuation is used; no marks of punctuation are used after the salutation or complimentary close. A man need not use Mr. in his typed or handwritten name at the end of a letter. A woman should use her personal title (Miss, Ms., or Mrs.) with her typewritten name as a courtesy. This allows a person to respond to a woman's letter using her preferred personal title.

Addressing a Small Envelope

1. Keyboard the writer's name and return address in the upper left corner as shown in the illustration. Begin on the second line space from the top edge and 3 spaces down from the left edge.

2. Keyboard the receiver's name about 2 inches (line 12) from the top of the envelope. Start about 2½ inches from the left edge.

3. Use block style single spacing for all addresses. City and state names and ZIP Codes (see p. xv) must be placed on one line in that order.

4. The state name may be keyboarded in full, or it may be abbreviated using the standard abbreviation or, preferably, the 2-letter state abbreviation.

Addressing a Large Envelope

1. A large envelope (9½" × 4⅛") is usually prepared for business letters or for letters of more than one page.

2. Keyboard the writer's name and return address as directed on the illustration of the small envelope.

3. Begin the name and address of the receiver 2½" from the top and 4" from the left edge of the envelope. Use block style and single spacing.

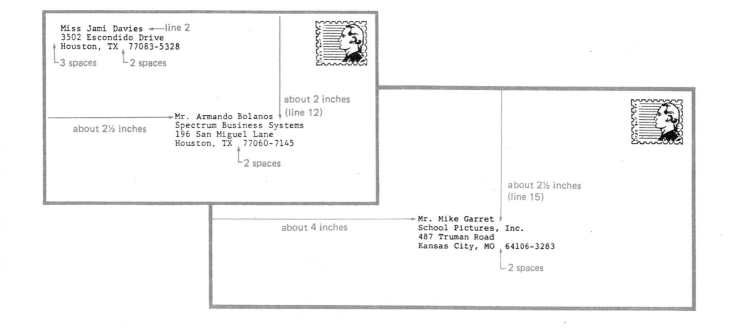

Small envelope:

Miss Jami Davies ←——line 2
3502 Escondido Drive
Houston, TX 77083-5328
└3 spaces └2 spaces

about 2 inches (line 12)

about 2½ inches →Mr. Armando Bolanos
Spectrum Business Systems
196 San Miguel Lane
Houston, TX 77060-7145
└2 spaces

Large envelope:

about 2½ inches (line 15)

about 4 inches →Mr. Mike Garret
School Pictures, Inc.
487 Truman Road
Kansas City, MO 64106-3283
└2 spaces

FOLDING LETTERS FOR SMALL ENVELOPES

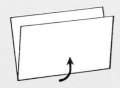

Step 1—Fold the lower edge of the letter to within half an inch of the top.

Step 2—Fold from right to left making the fold about one third the width of the sheet.

Step 3—Fold from left to right, leaving about a half-inch margin at the right in order that the letter may be opened easily.

Step 4—Insert the letter into the envelope so that the left-hand creased edge is inserted first and the last side folded is toward the backside of the envelope.

FOLDING LETTERS FOR LARGE ENVELOPES

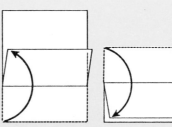

Step 1—Fold from bottom to top, making the fold slightly less than one third the length of the sheet.

Step 2—Fold the top down to within one half inch of the bottom fold.

Step 3—Insert the letter into the envelope with the last crease toward the bottom of the envelope and with the last fold up.

Formatting/Keyboarding Business Letters

General Information

Letter Styles: With slight variations, the modified block style shown on page xix is the most commonly used style for business letters. Another style that continues to grow in usage is the block style illustrated on page xx.

Punctuation Styles: Two commonly used punctuation styles are *open* and *mixed*. In *open* punctuation, no punctuation marks are used after the salutation or the complimentary close. In *mixed* punctuation, a colon is placed after the salutation and a comma after the complimentary close.

Vertical Placement of Dateline: Vertical placement of the date varies with the length of the letter. For short to average business letters, the date is placed on line 18. The address begins on the 4th line space below the date.

Margins: The line length used for business letters varies according to the number of words in the letter. A 50-space line works well for most short letters; a 60-space line works well for most average-length letters. If you prefer, set 2" side margins for short letters, 1½" side margins for average-length letters, or 1" side margins for long letters.

Attention Line

An attention line is used to direct a letter to a particular person. The attention line may appear as the second line of the letter address, or it may appear a double space below the letter address. Keyboard the attention line immediately below the company name on the envelope.

```
Edgar and Pauls, Inc.
3294 Belmont Drive
Attention Miss Alice Pauls
Cleveland, OH 44131-1037
→ DS
Ladies and Gentlemen
```

```
Edgar and Pauls, Inc.
3294 Belmont Drive
Cleveland, OH 44131-1037
→ DS
Attention Miss Alice Pauls
→ DS
Ladies and Gentlemen
```

Subject Line

When a subject line is used in a letter, it appears on the second line below the salutation. It may be centered on the line, or it may be keyboarded at the left margin.

```
Mrs. Mary Hatch
1501 East Starlight Drive
Pine Bluff, AR 71603-9371
→ DS
Dear Mrs. Hatch
→ DS
SUBJECT: Policy No. SH 34 87
```

Titles in Addresses: As a mark of courtesy to the person to whom a letter is addressed, you may use a personal or professional title on a letter, envelope, or card: *Mr. Robert Wertz, Dr. Ann Hendricks.* When a woman's preferred title is unknown, use *Ms.* as the personal title.

Abbreviations: Excessive abbreviations should be avoided. It is preferred, however, to use the two-letter state abbreviation in an address when using a ZIP Code. Leave two spaces between the state abbreviation and the ZIP Code.

Reference Initials: Reference initials of the typist should always be placed at the left margin, two line spaces below the typed name of the writer of the letter.

Stationery: Most business letters are prepared on 8½" × 11" stationery that has a letterhead which includes a name and address of the company.

Envelopes: Either large or small envelopes may be used for one-page letters. Large envelopes should be used for two-page letters and in instances where materials are enclosed with the letters.

Enclosure Notations

An enclosure notation is used when some item (or items) is sent with a letter. The notation appears at the left margin a double space below the reference initials. If two or more items are enclosed, use the plural *Enclosures.*

```
Miss Sandra Black
Sales Representative
→ DS
jp
→ DS
Enclosures
```

Postscript

A postscript is the last item in a letter. The postscript appears a double space below the enclosure notation (if used) or the reference initials if an enclosure notation is not used. The postscript need not be preceded by the letters *P.S.*

```
1g
→ DS
I'm having an examination.
```

F. J. Schauf & Company

2709 Menlo Avenue
San Diego, CA 92105-5534
Tel: (619) 284-6166

An Information
Network Center

50-space line; mixed punctuation

center point

begin on line 18 ——→ March 30, 19--

return 4 times

letter address   Mr. Gilbert Gonzalez
United Services, Inc.
3419 Marian Way
San Diego, CA 92110-1310
                                        DS
salutation   Dear Mr. Gonzalez:
                        DS
body   I am pleased to respond to your inquiry about the
services we provide at F. J. Schauf & Company.

At F. J. Schauf & Company we can locate information
on virtually any topic. Because we have a wealth
of information available in the form of statistics,
reports, forecasts, news items, and directories,
we can tailor a search to your specifications.

A search by Schauf & Company is fast and thorough,
enabling us to find in minutes what might otherwise
take hours or even days.

If you need more information, please give me a call.
                                                        DS
complimentary
close   center point ——→ Sincerely yours,

return 4 times

typed name and
official title   Ms. Karen Brooks, Manager
                                        DS
reference initials   sr

Business letter in modified block style

F. J. Schauf & Company

An Information
Network Center

2709 Menlo Avenue
San Diego, CA 92105-5534
Tel: (619) 284-6166

50-space line; open punctuation

April 5, 19-- ⟵ begin on line 18

return 4 times

letter address · Ms. Tricia Hoffman
H & S Distributors
908 Tamarindo Way
Chula Vista, CA 92011-5097

DS

salutation · Dear Ms. Hoffman

DS

body · Thank you for inquiring about the charges for an
information search at F. J. Schauf & Company.

A search at F. J. Schauf & Company can be surpris-
ingly inexpensive. Simple topics can be searched
for as little as $30. More complex searches may
cost as much as $100 or more. Charges are based
on actual computer costs, plus our service fee.
Our job is to help you shape your questions so you
can be assured the best results at a minimum cost.

Please call if I may be of further assistance.

DS

complimentary
close · Very truly yours

DS

company name in
closing lines · F. J. SCHAUF & COMPANY

return 4 times

typed name · William E. Rice
official title · Assistant Manager

DS

reference initials · sr

Business letter in block style

Capitalization Guides (pp. 80, 99, 114, 220)

Capitalize:

1. The first word of a complete sentence.

2. The first word of a quoted sentence. (Do not capitalize fragments of a quotation resumed within a sentence.)

3. Languages and numbered school courses, but not the names of other school subjects.

4. The pronoun *I*, both alone and in contractions.

5. Titles of organizations, institutions, and buildings.

6. Days of the week, months of the year, and holidays, but not seasons.

7. Names of rivers, oceans, and mountains.

8. *North*, *South*, *etc.*, when they name particular parts of the country, but not when they refer to directions.

9. Names of religious groups, political parties, nations, nationalities, and races.

10. All proper names and the adjectives made from them.

11. The names of stars, planets, and constellations. except the sun, moon, and earth, unless these are used with other astronomical names.

12. A title when used with a person's name.

13. First words and all other words in titles of books, articles, periodicals, headings, and plays, except words which are articles, conjunctions, and prepositions.

14. The first and last words, all titles, and all proper names used in the salutation of a business letter.

15. Only the first word of a complimentary close.

16. All titles appearing in the address of a letter.

17. The title following the names of the dictator in the closing lines of a business letter.

Spacing Guides (pp. 5, 13, 14, 18, 25, 26, 49, 51, 52, 54, 57, 125, and 132)

1. Space twice after a period that ends a sentence, except when the period comes at the end of the line. When it does, return the carriage without spacing.

2. Space once after a question mark within a sentence; twice after a question mark at the end of a sentence.

3. Space twice after an exclamation point at the end of a sentence.

4. Space twice after a colon except when stating time.

5. Space once after a semicolon or comma.

6. Space once after a period that ends an abbreviation; twice if that period ends a sentence. (Do not space after a period within an abbreviation.)

7. Space once between a whole number and a "made" fraction.

8. Do not space between the $ and the number which follows it.

9. Do not space before or after a diagonal.

10. Do not space between a number and a following % sign.

11. Do not space between parentheses and the material they enclose.

12. Do not space before or after the apostrophe unless the apostrophe is at the end of a word.

13. Do not space between quotation marks and the material they enclose.

14. Do not space before or after a dash.

15. Do not space before or after the hyphen in a hyphenated word.

Number Expression Guides (pp. 128, 149, 155, 194, and 204)

1. Keyboard even sums of money without decimals or zeros.

2. Keyboard distances in figures.

3. Use figures to keyboard dates. When the day comes before the month, use a figure and follow it with *th*, *st*, or *d*.

4. Spell a number beginning a sentence even though figures may be used later in the sentence.

5. Use figures with *a.m.* and *p.m.* Use words with *o'clock*.

6. Keyboard amounts of money, either dollars or cents, in figures.

7. Keyboard policy numbers without commas.

Word-Division Guides

Divide:

1. Words only between syllables.

2. Hyphenated compounds at the point of the hyphen; for example, *self-control*.

3. Words so that *cial*, *tial*, *cion*, *sion*, or *tion* are retained as a unit.

4. A word that ends in double letters after the double letters when a suffix is added, such as *fill-ing*.

5. A word in which the final consonant is doubled when a suffix is added between the double letters, such as *control-ling*.

Do not:

1. Divide words of one syllable, such as *thought*.

2. Separate a syllable of one letter at the beginning of a word, such as *across*.

3. Separate a syllable of one or two letters at the end of a word, such as *ready* or *greatly*.

4. Divide words of five or fewer letters.

5. Divide the last word on a page.

Punctuation Guides

Apostrophe (p. 193)

1. Use an apostrophe in writing contractions.
2. *It's* means *it is*. *Its*, the possessive pronoun, does not take an apostrophe.
3. Use the contraction of *o'clock* (of the clock) in writing time.
4. Add 's to plural nouns that do not end in *s*.
5. If a plural noun does end in s, add only an apostrophe after the *s*.
6. The apostrophe denotes possession. Do not use it merely to form the plural of a noun.
7. Use 's to form the plural of figures, letters, signs, and words referred to as words.

Colon (p. 169)

1. Use a colon to introduce a list of items or expressions.
2. Use a colon to separate the hours and minutes when they are expressed in figures.
3. Use a colon to introduce a question or long quotation.

Comma (pp. 136 and 160)

1. Use a comma after each item in a series, except the last.
2. Use a comma to separate consecutive adjectives when the *and* has seemingly been omitted. Do not use the comma when the adjectives do not apply equally to the noun they modify.
3. Use a comma to separate a dependent clause that precedes the main clause.
4. Use a comma to separate the independent parts of a compound sentence joined by *and, but, for, or, neither, nor.*
5. Use a comma to prevent misreading or confusion.
6. Use a comma to set off a direct quotation from the rest of the sentence.
7. Do not set off an indirect quotation from the rest of the sentence.
8. Use commas to set off parenthetic expressions that break the flow of a sentence. If the parenthetic expression begins or ends a sentence, use one comma.
9. Use a comma to set off *yes, no, well, now.*
10. Use commas to set off appositives that give additional information about the same person or object and that can be omitted without changing the meaning of the sentence.
11. Use commas to set off the name of the person addressed.
12. Do not use a comma to separate two nouns, one of which identifies the other.

Dash and Parentheses (p. 174)

1. Use a dash to show a sudden break in thought.
2. Use a dash before the name of an author when it follows a direct quotation.
3. Use parentheses to enclose an explanation.

Period, Question Mark, Exclamation Point (p. 132)

1. Use a period after a sentence making a statement or giving a command.
2. Use a period after each initial.
3. Use a period after most abbreviations. (Nicknames are not followed by periods.)
4. Use a question mark after a question.
5. After requests and indirect questions, use a period.
6. Use an exclamation point to express strong or sudden feelings.

Quotation Marks (p. 178)

1. Place quotation marks around the exact words of a speaker.
2. When the quotation is broken to identify the speaker, put quotation marks around each part. If the second part of the quotation is a new sentence, use a capital letter.
3. Use no quotation marks with an indirect quotation.
4. Use quotation marks around the titles of articles, songs, poems, themes, short stories, and the like.
5. Always place the period or comma inside the quotation mark.

Semicolon (p. 162)

1. Use a semicolon between the clauses of a compound sentence when no conjunction is used. (If a conjunction is used to join the clauses, use a comma between them.)
2. Use a semicolon between the clauses of a compound sentence that are joined by such words as *also, however, therefore,* and *consequently.*
3. Use a semicolon between a series of phrases or clauses that are dependent upon a main clause.

Alphabetic sentences

An alphabetic sentence is included in each Keyboard Review, beginning on page 34.

Easy sentences

An easy sentence is included in each Keyboard Review, beginning on page 34.

Figure sentences

A figure sentence is included in many Keyboard Reviews, beginning on page 47.

Figure/Symbol Sentences

A figure/symbol sentence is included in most Keyboard Reviews, beginning on page 50.

Continuity practice
28, 29, 31, 32, 33, 35, 36, 40, 45, 53, 54, 65, 81, 163, 170

Control practice
91, 107, 115, 125, 128, 141, 149, 156, 164, 167, 169, 213, 220, 221, 226

Fluency practice
6, 8, 9, 11, 12, 106

Guided writings
Paragraphs: 38, 43, 44, 46, 60, 63, 70, 75, 83, 85, 90, 93, 98, 101, 107, 115, 117, 188, 193, 208

Sentences: 30, 31, 37, 41, 42, 60, 108, 111, 114, 116, 117, 120

Key location drills
a, 4, 5, 8, 10; b, 20, 21, 24; c, 13, 14, 16; d, 4, 5, 8, 10; e, 6, 7, 8; f, 4, 5, 8, 10; g, 16, 17, 21; h, 6, 7, 8, i, 10, 11, 14; j, 4, 5, 8, 10; k, 4, 5, 8, 10; l, 4, 5, 8, 10; m, 20, 21, 24; n, 12, 14, 29; o, 7, 8, 10; p, 23, 24, 32; q, 24, 31; r, 12, 14; s, 4, 5, 8, 10; t, 7, 8, 10, 29; u, 16, 17, 21; v, 18, 19, 21; w, 10, 11, 14; x, 23, 24, 32; y, 18, 19, 21, 31; z, 26, 27; an, 24; at, 42; b/m, 24; br, 129; c/i, 134, 141; ei, 130, 169; er, 29; eve, 159; exa, 162; ha, 43; he, 25, 47; is, 45; it, 46; nd, 31; ou, 27; re, 30; to, 11, 32; u/i, 167; vu, 22; xp, 25; ampersand, 51; apostrophe, 54; asterisk, 56, 57; colon, 38, 39; comma, 24; dash, 51; diagonal, 49; dollar sign, 49; exclamation point, 54; hyphen, 51, 106; number sign, 49; parentheses, 52; percent sign, 51; period, 13, 14, 16; question mark, 26, 27; quotation marks, 56; semicolon, 4, 5, 8, 10; underline, 56, 57; Made signs: division, 194; equal, 162; plus, 194; times, 162; Numbers: one, 35, 36, 41; two, 39, 40, 46; three, 35, 36, 37, 42; four, 38, 39, 45; five, 36, 37, 43; six, 41; seven, 35, 36, 37, 42; eight, 38, 39, 45; nine, 36, 37, 43; zero, 29, 40, 46

Language arts skills
capitalization guides: 80, 99, 114, 220
composing at the typewriter: 61, 70, 99, 118, 157, 177, 198, 207, 209, 220, 226
creative typing: 221
dictation: 61, 71, 81, 91, 103, 111, 117
number expression guides: 128, 149, 155, 194, 204
proofreading: 28, 60, 69, 79, 90, 95, 100, 110, 116, 117
punctuation guides: 132, 136, 160, 162, 169, 174, 178, 193
spacing guides: 5, 13, 14, 18, 25, 26, 49, 51, 52, 54, 57, 125, 132
spelling: 60, 69, 71, 79, 81, 90, 91, 95, 100, 103, 110, 111, 116, 117
titles of published works: 114, 218

Manipulative and preapplication activities
Addressing envelopes, 84, 87
Attention line, 206
Backspacer, 45
Bell, 47, 48
Bibliography, 147
Carbon copies, 95
Carriage return, 4
Centering, column headings, 117; horizontal, 63, 67, 108; reading position, 92; vertical, 61, 92
Centering on odd-size paper or postal cards, 67
Class notes, 102
Correcting errors, 65, 139, 148, 156
Enclosure notation, 205
Footnotes, 143
Horizontal center point, 67
Indented items, 142
Margin release, 47
Margin stop, vii, 2
Outline, 100
Postscript, 208
Proofreader's marks, 66
Reference citations, 145
Spread headings, 139
Subject line in letters, 206
Superscripts/subscripts, 143
Tabulation, 20, 22, 43, 48
Title page, 147
Typing outside the margins, 45
Word division, 124

Problem measurement: 190, 192, 195, 222, 224, 225, 226

Problem typing: 65, 71, 73, 75, 81, 85, 88, 95, 96, 104, 108, 111, 113, 117, 121, 125, 128, 129, 133, 135, 136, 138, 141, 147, 150, 152, 153, 154, 157, 159, 161, 164, 166, 167, 168, 173, 174, 176, 178, 180, 181, 182, 183, 185, 186, 187, 199, 202, 205, 210, 211, 215, 217, 218, 219
Rough draft: 66, 68, 78, 81, 92, 100, 103, 104, 110, 174, 176, 181, 204, 211

Script: 31, 37, 39, 44, 47, 48, 65, 69, 72, 80, 100, 103, 110, 171

Skill builders
Paragraphs: 22, 25, 51, 92, 132, 150, 157, 171, 174, 199, 204, 210

Sentences: 15, 17, 27, 69, 72, 222, 225

Skill comparison
47, 50, 100, 106, 110, 117, 176, 193, 214

Speed Builders
126, 151, 159, 160, 165, 172, 179, 191, 194, 202, 209, 216, 223

Speed ladder writings
Paragraphs:
1': 50, 55, 124, 131, 140, 149, 156, 163, 170, 177, 189, 198, 207, 214, 221
3': 50, 55
Sentences:
64, 130, 153, 197, 213

Straight-copy timed writings
1': 20, 23, 48, 53, 129, 138, 147, 155, 161, 185, 187, 199, 209, 212, 219
2': 91, 96, 98, 183, 226
3': 45, 47, 48, 52, 53, 57, 67, 71, 77, 79, 89, 91, 96, 98, 104, 112, 120
5': 126, 129, 138, 147, 155, 159, 161, 168, 172, 175, 179, 182, 183, 185, 187, 199, 209, 212, 219, 226

Sustained skill building
29, 31, 32, 33, 37, 41

Technique builders
Keystroking:
adjacent keys, 123, 155, 160, 178, 185, 190
balanced-hand, 90, 106, 176
bottom row, 60
combination, 106, 204, 142, 185, 204
direct reaches, 60, 90, 103, 106, 132, 150, 161, 179, 183, 199, 213, 220
double letters, 93, 106, 112, 208, 209
fingers, 1st, 112, 188; 2d, 112, 188; 3d, 112, 188, 224; 4th, 172, 183, 188, 210, 216
home keys, 4, 5, 8, 10, 112, 174, 206
left hand, 181, 193, 206
long reaches, 153, 175, 199
one-hand, 47, 90, 93, 100, 106, 176
phrases, 30, 35, 37, 40, 46, 57, 69
review, 9, 11, 12, 14, 21
stroking, 4, 6, 8, 9, 11, 12, 14, 17, 21, 25, 44, 52, 131, 215
top row, 60
words, 27, 29, 33, 52, 136, 164, 223

Machine parts:
backspacer, 45
carriage and carrier return, 4, 15
margin release, 47
shift keys, 13, 14, 15, 16, 18, 19, 21, 26, 50, 139, 151, 157, 165, 176
shift lock, 44
space bar, 3, 23
tabulator, 20, 22, 23, 43, 48

A location of, 3
Abbreviations, use in business letters, xviii, 199; ZIP Code, xv, xviii, 116, 199
Acceptance, informal, 127
Address, *See* Envelopes, Postal cards
Admission tickets, 167
Agenda of meeting, 164, 165, 167
Alignment of paper *See* Paper, alignment of
Amounts, in figures and spelled out, xxi, 204
Ampersand (&), location of, 51; spacing, 51
Announcements, 125, 126; centered, 63, 64; on odd-size paper, 67, 68; postal card, 128, 190
Apostrophe ('), location of, 54; punctuation guides, xxii, 193; spacing before and after, xxi; uses of, xxii, 193
Asterisk, location of, 56
Attention line, xviii, 206
Automatic line finder, location of iv, v, xiii, 143

B location of, 19
Backspace key, location of, 45; typing outside the right and left margins, 45
Bar graph, horizontal, 171, 172
Basic techniques, viii-xi; *See also* specific technique
Bell, listening for the, 47, 48
Bibliographical cards, 153, 154
Bibliography, xiv, 147, 148
Block style, business letters, xx, 202, 203; personal notes, 71, 72, 76; personal/business letters, 88, 135, 185; *See also* Business letters
Book review, 104, 105; outline of directions for, 104
Books, titles of, 59, 114
Budget, school organization, 173
Bulletin board notices, *See* Notices, bulletin board
Business letters, address in, 200, 203; attention line in, xviii, 206; **block style**, xx, 202, 203; capitalization in, xviii, 220; dateline in, xviii, xx, 199; enclosure notation, xviii; enumerated items, 211; envelopes, 199; general information, xviii, 199; letterhead, xviii; margins, xviii, 199; mixed punctuation, xviii, xix, 200; **modified block style**, xix, 199, 200; open punctuation, xviii, xx, 203; postscript, xviii, 208; reference initials, xviii, 199, 201; stationery size, xviii, 199; subject line, xviii, 206; table in, 210; titles in addresses and closing lines, xviii, 199

C location of, 13
Capitalization guides, xxi, 80, 99, 114, 220; business application of, 103; business letter parts, 220; publications, 220
Carbon copies, xi, 95; erasing and correcting on, xi
Card and envelope holders, location of, iv, v; adjusting, 77
Carriage return, key xi, 4; lever xi, 4
Center point, for elite type, vii; for pica type, vii; of leftbound manuscripts, 145; of odd-size paper or cards, xii, 67
Centering, *See* Horizontal centering, Vertical centering
Citations, *See* Reference citations
Class notes, formatting 102; with side headings, 102

Club schedule, *See* Tables, club schedule
Colon (:), location of, 38; punctuation guides, xxii, 57, 169; spacing after, 57, 125; uses of, xxii, 169
Columnar headings, centering, xiii, 117
Comma (,), location of, 24; punctuation guides, xxii, 136, 160; uses of, xxii, 136, 160
Contents, *See* Table of Contents
Correcting errors, *See* Errors, correcting
Cylinder, iv, v

D location of, 2
Dash (--), location of, 51; how to type, 51; punctuation guides, xxii, 57, 174; spacing before or after, 51; uses of, xxii, 174
Dateline, vertical placement in, business letters, xviii; personal/business letters, xvi; postal cards, xv
Diagonal (/), location of, 49; spacing before and after, 49
Dividing words, *See* Word-Division Guides
Division sign (÷), how to type, 194
Dollar sign ($), location of, 49; in columns, 173; spacing between a number and, 49; total amount, 173

E location of, 5
Eight (8), location of, 38
Elite type, vi, vii, 96
Enclosure notation, xviii, 137, 205
Envelopes, addressing large, xvii, 87; addressing small, xvii, 84; folding letters for large, xviii, 87; folding letters for small, xvii, 84; sizes to use, xvii, 199; two-letter ZIP Code abbreviations, xv, 199
Equal sign (=), how to type, 162
Errors, correcting, 65; carbons, xi; spreading letters, 156; squeezing letters, 148
Exclamation point (!), location of, 54; punctuation guides, xxii, 132; spacing after xxi, 125; at the end of a sentence, 54; uses of, 132

F location of, 3
Five (5), location of, 36
Folding letters, *See* Letters, folding
Footnotes, directions for typing, xiv, formatting in reports, 143
Forms, *See* specific form
Four (4), location of, 38
Fractions, how to make, 155

G location of, 16
Gwam (gross words a minute), 15; how to figure on paragraph copy, 20

H location of, 5
Headings, spread, 139; *See also* center point
Home keys, location of, 3
Horizontal bar graph, *See* Bar graph, horizontal
Horizontal centering, xii, 63; on odd-size paper or cards, 67
Horizontal placement of tables, xii, 108
Hyphen (-), location of, 51; punctuation guides, 57; spacing before and after, 51, 125

I location of, 10

Indenting for paragraphs, vi, 20
Insertion of paper, 2
Internal citations, *See* Citations
Interoffice memorandum, *See* Memorandums, interoffice
Invitations, 125; informal, 127
Invoices, 217; with table, 217, 218

J location of, 3

K location of, 3
Keystroking (illustrated), 3

L location of, 3
Leaders, 173
Leftbound reports, centering headings in, 145; contents page, 184; spacing for, 94; title page for, 147; *See also* reports.
Letters, folding, for large envelopes, xvii, 87; for small envelopes, xvii, 84; *See* Business letters, Personal/business letters
Line length, *See* Margin stops, setting for a 50-, 60-, or 70-space line
Line-space regulator, location of, iv, v
Line-of-writing scale, location of, iv, v; vi

M location of, 19
Machine adjustments, vi-vii, 2; *See* specific adjustment
Machine parts (illustrated), *See* Typewriter, operating parts of
Manuscripts, *See* Reports
Margin release key, location of, iv, v
Margin stops, determining, vii, xviii; flush with right margin, 164; setting for a 50-, 60-, or 70-space line, vii
Margins, justified right margin, 182; types of: key-set, vi; magic margin, vi; push button, vi; push-lever, vi; typing outside of, 45, 47
Membership cards, 167
Memorandum, interoffice, 215, 216, 218; with table, 219
Minutes of meetings, 166, 187
Mixed punctuation, xviii, 85, 199
Modified block style, business letters, xix, 200, 210; personal/business letters, xvi, 81, 82, 85; postal cards, 77; *See also* Business letters

N location of, 11
New keys, plan for learning, 5
Newspaper copy, article with justified right margin, 182; preparing, 180, 181
Nine (9), location of, 36
Note cards, 154, 155
Notices, 164, 187; bulletin board, 178
Number expression guides, xxi; *See* individual categories
Number sign (#), location of, 49; spacing, 49
Numbers at beginning of sentence, 149

O location of, 7
Odd-size paper or cards, finding the horizontal center point of, 67
On/Off control, location of, v
One (1), location of, 41; lower case 1 as, 34
Open punctuation, xviii, 199
Operating parts of the typewriter (illustrated), *See* Typewriter, operating parts of

Order form, 137
Order letter, 137
Outline, final, for leftbound report, 152; preliminary, for leftbound report, 152; sentence, 100, 151; topic, 101, 150

P location of, 22
Page numbering, reports, 145
Paper, alignment of, 2, 139; removal of, 4
Paperbail, location of, iv, v
Paper guide, location of, vi; adjusting the, vi
Paper release lever, location of, iv, v
Parentheses [( )], location of 52, punctuation guides, xxii; spacing between them and words enclosed, 52; uses of, xxii, 132
Percent (%), location of, 51; spacing between a figure and, 51
Period (.), location of, 13; punctuation guides, xxii, 57, 132; spacing guides, 13, 18, 125; within an abbreviation, 57, 132; uses of, xxii, 132
Periodicals, *See* Titles of published works
Personal/business letters, directions for formatting, xvi, 81; from unarranged copy, 86; in block style, xvi, 135; in modified block style, xvi, 81, 82, 133
Personal letter, in semibusiness form, 129, 130
Personal note, in block style, 71; in modified block style, 73, 74
Personal titles, in address of letter, *See* Titles, in addresses
Pica type, vi, vii, 96
Position, at typewriter, 2; of hands, viii, 3; of wrists, vii, 7
Postal cards, addressing, xv, 77; announcements, 128, 190; in modified block style, 78
Postscript (P.S.), xviii, 208
Posture at typewriter, ix, 2
Printing point indicator, location of, iv, v
Program, luncheon and menu, 176; of meeting, 174
Proofreader's marks, 66
Proofreading your work, 28
Punctuation, *See* Mixed punctuation; Open punctuation
Punctuation guides, xxii, 132, 136, 160, 162, 169, 174, 178; *See also* Names of individual marks

Q location of, 24
Question mark (?), location of, 26; punctuation guides, xxii, 178; spacing guides, 26, 125; uses of, 132
Quotation marks (''), location of, 56; punctuation guides, xxii, 178; spacing between them and words enclosed, 56; uses of, xxii, 178
Quotations, long/short within reports, 143

R location of, 11
Reading position, 92
Reference citations, xi, 145
Reference guide, xii-xix; *See* individual entries
Reference initials, in letters, xviii, 199, 201
Reports, bibliography, xiv, 147, 148, 161; contents page, 184; enumerated items in, 142; footnotes xiv, 143; general guides for, 94; headings, 94, 102; **leftbound,** *See* Leftbound reports; margins and spacing, 94; page numbering, 96; partially filled page with footnotes, 143; quoted copy within, 143, 158; tables within, 121; reference citations, xiv, 145; title page, 147; **topbound,** *See* Topbound reports; **unbound,** *See* unbound reports
Return address, on envelopes, 84, 87; on postal cards, xv, 77
Ribbon, changing the, vii
Ribbon control lever, location of, 28; adjusting the, 28
Ruled lines, typing on, 136

S location of, 3
Semicolon (;), location of, 3; punctuation guides, xxii, 162; spacing guides, 5, 125; uses of, xxii, 162
Sentence outline, *See* Outline, sentence
Seven (7), location of, 34
Shift keys, location of, left, x, 13; right, x, 18; operating the, x
Shift lock, location of, x, 44; operating the, x, 44
Simulation, working in a school office, 221-231
Six (6), location of, 41
Space-bar, location of, iv, v
Space-bar control, x, 3
Spaces, vertical, in half sheet, 62; in full sheet, 62; per inch, 67
Spacing, double (DS), 6; single (SS), 6; triple (TS), 6
Spacing guides, xxi, 5, 13, 14, 18, 25, 26, 49, 51, 52, 54, 57, 125, 132; *See also* names of punctuation marks, symbols, etc.
Special drills, index to, xxiii
Spread headings, *See* Headings, spread
Spreading letters and squeezing letters, *See* Errors, correcting
Stroking, viii, 3, 8

Style guide, student-writer's, 183
Subject line, xviii, 206
Syllable intensity (si), 28

T location of, 7
Table of contents, iii; style guide, 184
Tables, four column, 116, club schedule, 138; formatting, 117; horizontal placement, xii, 108; three-column, 113, 119; two-column, 108, 109; vertical placement, 108; with columnar headings, xiii, 118; with subheading, 111, 113; within business letter, 210; within interoffice memorandum, 219; within report, 121
Tabulator bar (key), location of, 20
Tabulator control, 43, 48
Tabulator stops, clearing and setting, vi, 20
Thank you letters, 127, 135
Three (3), location of, 34
Time of day, expressing, 128
Times sign (X), 162; spacing before and after, 162
Titles of published works, 114, 218
Topbound report, spacing, 94; *See also* Reports.
Topic outline, *See* Outlines, topic
Two (2), location of, 39
Typewriter, care of, x; operating parts (illustrated), electric, v, manual, iv

U location of, 16
Unbound reports, illustration of, 94; spacing for; *See also* Reports
Underline (__), location of, 56; broken/continuous, 57; double lines for total, 173

V location of, 18
Variable line spacer, location of, iv, v
Vertical centering, xii, 61; backspace from center method, 92; exact vertical centering, 92; reading position, xii, 92; shortcut, xii, 92

W location of 10
Word division, 124; guides for, xxi
Writing a report, 152

X location of, 22

Y location of, 18

Z location of, 26
Zero (0), location of, 39
ZIP Code, *See* abbreviations

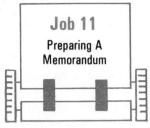

Job 11
Preparing A Memorandum

1. Keyboard this memorandum.
2. Use a 60-space line.

TO: Eric Quesada, Columbia Student Council | FROM: Coach Eric Johnson | DATE: Current date | SUBJECT: Student Council Support for Sports Program

(¶) On behalf of all our players and coaches, I want to thank you for your fine support this year. Your many efforts and ideas assured us a successful season. I know the students, faculty, and staff here at Columbia are proud of the leadership you have provided.

(¶) Congratulations for an outstanding job.

Job 12
Preparing An Announcement

1. Center this announcement on a full sheet of paper.
2. Space as directed on the illustration.

EVERYONE'S INVITED TO . . . .

SADIE HAWKINS DAY, MAY 6

Jazz Band *Concert*	Strolling Mimie Troupe
Spaghetti Eating Contest	Baloon Pop Booth
Hee-Haw talent contest	Live Juke box
Funny Photos Booth	Paper Flower Sale
Tank Dunk	Ring Toss Booth
Teacher Auction	Assembly: "Any thing Goes"
Sponge Throw Booth	Dance: 8-11 p.m.

ENTERTAINMENT ↑ GOOD FOOD ↑ CONTESTS ↑ FUN ↑ PRIZES

Job 13
Preparing A Postal Card

1. Keyboard this postal card message.
2. Refer to p. 77.

Mr. Paul Bozzo | P. O. Box 2530 | Clovis, CA 93703-3811 | Dear Paul

(¶) Thank you for your continued support of our Columbia Boosters Club.

(¶) We are looking forward to seeing you at the annual Boosters Barbecue in the school cafeteria on May 16 at 6:00 p.m.
Greg Pelton | Director of Student Activities

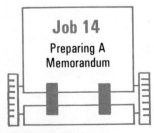

Job 14
Preparing A Memorandum

1. Keyboard this memorandum.
2. Use a 60-space line.

TO: All Faculty | FROM: Greg Pelton, Director of Student Activities | DATE: Current date | SUBJECT: Scholastic Awards Program

(¶) Last Monday I sent each of you a list of all students who have been nominated for awards this semester.

(¶) This recognition means a great deal to our students, and we do not want to miss anyone. Therefore, will you please check the list carefully and let me know of any omissions. Also, please inform the students that those who have not picked up their tickets for the dinner must do so today at the Student Activities Office.

(¶) I would like to remind you, too, that students do appreciate your attendance at this important event. Please try to attend if at all possible.

CYCLE ONE

Learning to Operate Your Keyboard

Job 9

Preparing Minutes

1. Keyboard these student council minutes in the form illustrated on p. 166.

2. Set your machine for a 1½" left margin and a 1" right margin.

COLUMBIA STUDENT COUNCIL MEETING

Minutes of Meeting

Date: Current date
Time: 10:05 a.m.
Place: Room 14, C Building
Present: L. Bishop, J. Brandon, C. Brown, M. Bruno, C. Brower, P. Emi, M. Folcarelli, Mr. Pelton, E. Quesada, R. Robles, J. Savala

1. The meeting was called to order by Eric Quesada, President.

2. John Savala presented a proposed policy to ban the use of all radios on campus. It was moved by Cynthia Brower that the policy be approved. The motion was seconded by Mark Bruno. It passed unanimously.

3. The Drama Club Constitution was submitted for Student Council approval. After a brief discussion, Mr. Pelton suggested that the petition be sent back for some minor adjustments.

4. Pat Emi reported on the CASC meeting held April 5 in Santa Clara.

5. The meeting was adjourned at 11:40 a.m.

Marty Folcarelli, Secretary

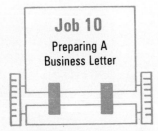

Job 10

Preparing A Business Letter

1. Keyboard this letter using a 50-space line.

2. Use modified block style, mixed punctuation.

Mr. Wayne Chapin | Chapin's Computer Center | 1392 North Sierra Vista | Fresno, CA 93703-5566 | Dear Mr. Chapin:

(¶) Please add my name to the list of those who will attend your seminar on Wednesday, June 6. I am looking forward to learning how we might utilize the microcomputer in the Student Activities Office here at Columbia Middle School.

(¶) As you requested, I made several copies of your letter and distributed them to various members of our staff. A number of our teachers have indicated an interest in evaluating the latest educational software in reading, spelling, and mathematics.

Very truly yours, | Greg Pelton | Director of Student Activities

GET READY TO TYPE

Adjust Your Machine

The numbers in parentheses following names of machine parts are those assigned to machine parts on pages iv and v.

1. Paper guide (No. 7): Adjust the paper guide so that the left edge of your paper is on "0" on the line-of-writing scale (No. 22).

2. Line-space regulator (No. 5): Set the line-space regulator at "2" for double spacing.

3. Margin stops (Nos. 9 and 15): Set the margin stops for a 50-space line (center-25; center + 25 + 5). When a standard sheet of paper (8½ × 11 inches) is inserted into a machine with the paper guide set at 0, the center point for pica type is 42 on the line-of-writing scale. The center point for elite type is 51.

Insert Paper into Your Machine

1. Place typing paper to the left of the machine.

2. Pull the paper bail (No. 11) away from the cylinder (No. 17).

3. Grasp the paper in the left hand.

4. Place the paper behind the cylinder (No. 17) and against the paper guide (No. 7). At the same time, bring the right hand to the right cylinder knob (No. 20) and twirl it with a quick movement of the fingers and the thumb.

5. Adjust the paper bail (No. 11) so that it holds the paper against the cylinder. If necessary, adjust the paper-bail rolls (No. 14). The paper-bail rolls should be about 2 inches from the left and right edges of the paper.

6. If the paper needs straightening after it is inserted, release it long enough to straighten it. Use the paper-release lever (No. 18).

Check Your Position at Your Machine

See page ix for a larger posture illustration.

1. Place this book to the right of your machine on a bookholder, or put something under the top of the book to raise it for easier reading.

2. Have the front of the keyboard even with the edge of the desk. Your body should be centered opposite the h key.

3. Your body should be 6 to 8 inches from the frame of the machine.

4. Don't slump; sit erect. Hold your elbows near your body.

5. Place your feet on the floor, one just ahead of the other in order to give you good balance.

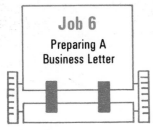

Job 6

Preparing A
Business Letter

1. Keyboard this letter on a 50-space line.
2. Use modified block style, mixed punctuation.

Ms. Sandra Harris| Student Activities Director| Sherwood Middle School| 849 Rexford Road| Modesto, CA 95356-8754| Dear Sandra:

(¶) I have enclosed a copy of the new form we now use for requesting a school car.

(¶) You will notice several changes that should make the forms more efficient for everyone. If the car is used locally, only the building assistant's signature is required. For trips outside the district, the principal must also sign.

(¶) Please call me if you have any questions.

Cordially yours,| Greg Pelton| Director of Student Activities

---

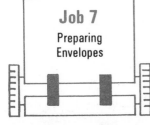

Job 7

Preparing
Envelopes

1. Address a large envelope to each Boosters Club member shown on this list.
2. Refer to p. 87 for assistance in correct placement of envelope address

Ms. Ronda Karriem
2930 Keil Avenue
Fresno, CA 93726-3685

Mr. Paul Bozzo
P.O. Box 2530
Clovis, CA 93703-3811

Mr. Wade Mendonca
903 North Tyson Street
Fresno, CA 93701-3544

Mrs. Nadine Dworian
33 San Roman Boulevard
Fresno, CA 93741-3202

Dr. Reynaldo Monreal
2047 East Hamilton
Fresno, CA 93712-3600

Ms. Tina Facchini
1108 Pierce Way
Fresno, CA 93712-3628

Job 8

Preparing A
Memorandum

1. Keyboard this memorandum using a 60-space line.
2. Refer to p. 215 for proper format.

TO: All Activity Advisors| FROM: Greg Pelton, Director of Student Activities| DATE: Current date| SUBJECT: Student Council and Class Officer Elections

(¶) Our Activities Handbook states that elections for student council and class officers must take place no later than the third Thursday in May preceding the school year in which they are to serve. We have therefore designated May 16 as election day.

(¶) Please remind your advisory group that anyone wishing to be a candidate for any office must present a petition to the student council vice-president no later than May 2. The petition must be signed by ten members of the candidate's class. No person may sign more than one petition for the same student council or class office.

Unit 1 ■ Learning to Operate the Letter Keys (Lessons 1–15)

LESSON 1

1a ● Find the Home Keys and Space Bar

4 \ 3 \ 2 \ 1   1 \ 2 \ 3 \ 4
left fingers   right fingers

1. Place the fingers of your left hand on **a s d f**.

2. Place the fingers of your right hand on **j k l ;**.

3. Take your fingers off the home keys. Replace them. Say the keys of each hand as you touch them. Repeat several times to get the "feel" of these keys.

4. Hold your right thumb over the middle of the space bar. Strike it with a quick, inward motion of your right thumb. Keep the left thumb out of the way.

5. Curve your fingers. Hold them very lightly over the home keys. Type the line below. Say and think each letter as you strike it.

```
ff jj dd kk ss ll aa ;; fj dk sl a; fj dk sl a; fj
```

hands upright over keys

1b ● Use Proper Techniques

Hand Position

Hold your hands directly over the keys, keeping your fingers deeply curved.

Do not permit your hands to turn over on the little fingers. Turn the hands inward slightly to get straight strokes.

Hold your wrists down near, but not resting on, the front frame of the typewriter. Keep your forearms in a parallel line with the slope of the keyboard.

Barely touch home keys with the fingers.

fingers deeply curved

Stroking

Center the stroking action in your fingers. Keep elbows, arms, and wrists quiet as you type. Your fingers should be deeply curved. Use quick, sharp strokes.

Release the keys quickly by snapping the fingers toward the palm of the hand. Hit the keys squarely with short, quick, straight strokes.

quick finger stroke

Spacing Between Words

Hold the right thumb curved under the hand just over the space bar. Strike the bar with a quick down-and-in motion

of the thumb. Keep wrist low and quiet as you strike the bar.

space with right thumb

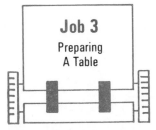

Job 3
Preparing A Table

1. Center this list of Student Council officers on a half sheet of paper.
2. TS after the heading; DS between items.
3. Leave 10 spaces between columns.

STUDENT COUNCIL OFFICERS

President	Eric Quesada
Vice-President	Robin Allen
Secretary	Marty Folcarelli
Treasurer	Marlene Miyaki
Speaker	Terry Schultz
Assemblies	Ron Robles
Communications	Sue Lizardo
Organizations	Cynthia Brower

Job 4
Preparing a Business Letter

1. Keyboard this letter for the Student Council president on a 50-space line.
2. Use block style, open punctuation.

Miss Susan Espuda | JSC President | Jefferson Middle School | 1800 North Cedar Avenue | Fresno, CA 93703-6611 | Dear Susan

(¶) On behalf of the Columbia Middle School Student Council, I want to express my appreciation to all of you at Jefferson for your help in co-sponsoring the Sharp Show with us last Tuesday evening.

(¶) The program was certainly of mutual benefit to both our student bodies. The great entertainment the Sharps provided was thoroughly enjoyed by our students who attended the performance.

(¶) We are pleased to cooperate with you and look forward to similar joint programs in the future.
Sincerely yours, | Eric Quesada | CSC President

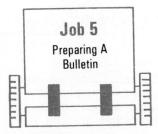

Job 5
Preparing A Bulletin

1. Keyboard these items for tomorrow's *Daily Bulletin* on a 60-space line.
2. Center the heading on line 13.
3. SS the numbered items; DS between them.

DAILY BULLETIN

1. All participants in the Charlie Brown play having 4th or 5th period lunch are to meet in K building during the morning break.
2. The seventh grade soccer team plays Kerman today at 3 p.m. The bus will leave from the gym parking lot at 1:30 p.m.
3. Members of the decorations committee should report to Ms. Jasutis in the cafeteria immediately after school today.
4. Our District Choral Sing will be held this evening in Clark Auditorium. The Program will begin at 7:30 p.m.
5. Mrs. Chavez would like to see any members of the student library staff who have not been assigned working hours for this month.
6. Students who plan to participate in the Carnation sale will meet during 5th period in Mr. Pelton's Office.
7. The C.S.F. meeting scheduled for tonight has been canceled. Our meeting will be held during the regular time next week.

Manual return

Electric return

think and
say each
letter

Returning the Carriage (Manual)

1. Move the left hand, palm down, to the carriage return lever (No. 1).

2. Move the lever forward to take up the slack.

3. With the fingers bracing one another, return the carriage with a flick of the wrist.

4. Return your left hand at once to its home position.

Returning the Carriage or Carrier (Electric)

1. Reach the little finger of your right hand to the carriage return key (No. 34).

2. Tap the return key quickly.

3. Return the finger at once to its home-key position.

1c ● Home-Key Practice

Directions: Keyboard each line with your teacher at least once.

Technique Goal: Think and say each letter as you strike it.

home
keys

1 ff jj ff jj ff jj ff jj ff jj fj fj fj fj fj fj fj

2 dd kk dd kk dd kk dd kk dd kk dk dk dk dk dk dk dk

3 ss ll ss ll ss ll ss ll ss ll sl sl sl sl sl sl sl

4 aa ;; aa ;; aa ;; aa ;; aa ;; a; a; a; a; a; a; a;

5 fj dk sl a; fj dk sl a; fj dk sl a; fj dk sl a; fj

6 fj dk sl a; fjdk sla; fjdk sla; fjdk sla; fj dk sl

1d ● Technique Builder: Stroking

Directions: Keyboard each line once with your teacher. Repeat the lines a second time by yourself.

Technique Goal: Curve your fingers. Use quick, sharp strokes.

use quick,
sharp strokes

home
keys

1 as ask as ask as ask all all lass lass as all lass

2 all fall all fall all all fall fall all fall falls

3 ad lad ad lad ad lad all a lad all a lad all a lad

4 a lad; a lad asks; a lass; a lass asks; ask a lass

5 a lass; as a lass; as a lass falls; as a lad falls

6 a lad asks; a lass asks; ask a lass; ask all lads;

1e ● Remove the Paper

1. Pull the paper bail (No. 11) out from the cylinder (No. 17).

2. Pull the paper release lever forward (No. 18).

3. Remove paper with your free hand.

4. Return the paper bail and paper release lever to original positions.

5. If using a movable carriage, depress carriage release (No. 4 or 19); hold cylinder knob (20) firmly and center the carriage.

Unit 18 ▪ Working in a School Office (Simulation)

General Directions

Unit 18 is designed to give you an opportunity to apply your basic skills and knowledge in a simulated office situation. You will be performing the types of jobs often found in offices. General instructions are given in the "Guide for Office Employees" in Job 1 below. Specific instructions are included with each job.

You will be working as a typist for one period each day in the office of Mr. Greg Pelton, Director of Student Activities at Columbia Middle School, 5590 North Millbrook, Fresno, CA 93710-2626. In addition, you may be asked to type for other faculty members and students on school related matters.

Accuracy is a trait that is valued highly in an office worker. Proofread your work carefully and correct all errors. Make certain you understand the instructions for each job before you begin; then work as efficiently as you can to produce quality work.

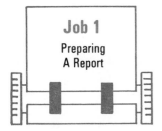

Job 1
Preparing A Report

1. Keyboard this report on a 60-space line.

2. Center the heading on line 13.

3. SS the numbered items; DS between them.

GUIDE FOR OFFICE EMPLOYEES

1. Report for work at the time that you have been assigned. Please sign the attendance sheets each day.

2. If you are going to be absent, telephone the activities office between 7:30 and 8:00 a.m.

3. Specific instructions will be included with each job requiring formatting of letters. Keyboard the current date on line 18. Prepare a carbon copy and address an envelope for each letter.

4. Refer to your textbook whenever you need help in placing material attractively on the page.

5. Proofread each job and correct all errors before you remove the paper from your machine.

6. Leave all completed jobs on my assistant's desk. You will be told whether you are to keep unfinished jobs for the next day or to leave them for someone else.

Job 2
Preparing A Business Letter

1. On a 60-space line, keyboard this letter for Mr. Pelton's signature.

2. Use modified block style, mixed punctuation.

Ms. Susan Knapp| Marketing Representative| Assemblies Incorporated| 127 Beverly Drive| Palo Alto, CA 91104-6755| Dear Ms. Knapp:

(¶ Thank you for sending me a listing of the assembly programs available through your organization. You have a varied and interesting selection from which to choose.

(¶) As I mentioned to you on the telephone, we have two open dates that we need to fill for next fall. They are Thursday, October 18, and Tuesday, November 27. Because our final budget has not yet been determined, however, I can commit us only for the October 18 program.

(¶) If you will please send the contract to me, we shall go ahead and schedule "Computers in Society" for that date.

Sincerely yours,| Greg Pelton| Director of Student Activities

LESSON 2

2a ● Keyboard Review

Review the Get Ready to Type Procedure explained on page 2.

Directions: Keyboard each line once with your teacher.

Posture Goal: Place your feet flat on the floor for balance.

home keys

think each key as you strike it

```
1  ff jj dd kk ss ll aa ;; ff jj dd kk ss ll aa ;; fj

2  fj dk sl a; fj dk sl a; fj dk sl a; fj dk sl a; fj

3  as as; ask a; ask a lass; ask a lad; ask all lads;

4  lad lad lads ask ask lass lass all all fall fall a

5  all lads fall; ask a lass; as a lass falls; a lass
```

2b ● Location of E and H

Plan for Learning New Keys

1. Find new key on keyboard chart.

2. Locate key on your type-writer.

3. Place fingers over home keys.

4. Know what finger strikes each key.

5. Watch your finger as you make the reach to the new key.

6. Type each short drill twice on the same line. Be sure to use the correct finger.

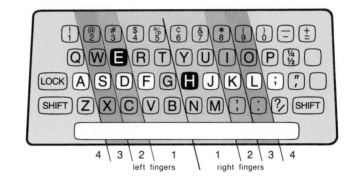

4 3 2 1   1 2 3 4
left fingers   right fingers

Reach to E

1. Find e on the chart.
2. Find it on your keyboard.
3. Place your fingers over the home keys.
4. Reach to e with the d finger.

5. Touch ed lightly without moving the other fingers from their typing position.
6. Type the drill below twice on the same line.

```
ded ded ed ed ed led led
```

Reach to H

1. Find h on the chart.
2. Find it on your keyboard.
3. Place your fingers over the home keys.
4. Reach to h with the j finger.

5. Touch hj lightly without moving the other fingers from their typing position.
6. Type the drill below twice on the same line.

```
jhj jhj hj hj ha had had
```

LESSON 140

140a ● Keyboard Review

5 minutes

Directions: Keyboard each sentence three times SS. DS between 3-line groups.

alphabet   Howard ate five big pretzels and drank exactly two quarts of my juice.

figure   Going 90 miles an hour, a skier jumped 281 feet on February 26, 1933.

shift   Last August, Yvette went to Atlanta to see the Braves play the Giants.

easy   Do not tell others of their faults until you have no more of your own.

| 1 | 2 | 3 | 4 | 5 | 6 | 7 | 8 | 9 | 10 | 11 | 12 | 13 | 14 |

140b ● Timed Writings

12 minutes

Directions: **1.** Take a 1' control writing on each ¶ in 136d, page 221. Circle errors. Figure *gwam*.

2. Take a 5' control writing on all five ¶s combined. Circle errors and figure *gwam*.

140c ● Problem Measurement

28 minutes

Directions: Problem 1 Interoffice Memorandum

Keyboard the following memorandum on a 60-space line. Space twice after the colon in the heading in the first line and set the left margin. Set the right margin 60 spaces to the right of the left margin.

do not pause between words

TO: Shirley Schramm | FROM: Robert J. Pierson | DATE: April 14, 19-- | SUBJECT: Additional Copies of Ellis Report

(¶) Please run off 35 additional copies of the Ellis Report. They are to be attached to the staff meeting minutes of April 3. Please return the original copy to me.

(¶) If you do not have time to distribute this material, give Jack a call and he will get someone to help you. It would probably be a good idea to remind him that all engineers are to receive these copies, even if they were not in attendance at the last meeting. Thanks very much for your help. | xx

Directions: Problem 2 Invoice

Keyboard the invoice below. Set left margin and tab stops for each column. Refer to 133c, page 217, if necessary. Figure total and enter under amount.

SOLD TO Stevenson's Stereo Shop | 239 Caldwell Place | Buffalo, NY 14218-7645 | DATE July 8, 19-- | OUR ORDER NO. 3206 | CUST. ORDER NO. 2204 | SHIPPED VIA Tim's Transit | SALESPERSON Sam Washington | TERMS 2/10, n/30

Quantity	Description	Unit Price	Amount
1	AA RI-6 AM/FM Stereo Receiver	319.95	319.95
6	BF 220 Cordless Telephone	49.50	297.00
12	L-750 Video Cassette Tape	5.99	71.88

140d ● Extra Credit Typing: Composing a Business Letter

Directions: Compose a letter to Mr. M. E. Minich, 35 Marine Drive, Tempe, AZ 85823-7623. Your purpose is to let him know his schedule for the Management Development Program. Include in the body of your letter the table given in 138c, Problem 2, page 224. Use modified block style with mixed punctuation.

2c ● Location Drills: E and H

Directions: Keyboard each line once with your teacher. Repeat the lines a second time by yourself.

Technique Goal: Think and say each letter as you strike it.

```
      ded ded ded ded ed ed ed ed led led fled fled fled

  e   fee fee feed feeds feels feels less less else else

      sell sell sale sales deal deal desk desk jade jade


      jhj jhj jhj hj hj hj hj ha ha has has had had half

  h   has ash ash lash flash flash hall hall shall shall

      had a half; had a half; has a half; has had a half
```

2d ● Technique Builder: Eyes on Copy

Directions: Set the line-space regulator at "1" to single-space the drill. Keyboard each line twice as shown.

Technique Goal: Keep your eyes on the book. Think each letter as you keyboard it.

To double-space (DS), operate the carriage return lever or key twice.
To triple-space (TS), operate the carriage return lever or key three times.

single-space (SS) repeated lines

double-space (DS) when you start a new line

triple-space (TS) between parts of a lesson

```
  1  fjdk sla; fjdk sla; ed hj ed hj ed hj he he she he
     fjdk sla; fjdk sla; ed hj ed hj ed hj he he she he
                                                         DS
  2  she she held held lad lad lass lass she head heads
     she she held held lad lad lass lass she head heads
                                                         DS
  3  as as has has lash lash; flash flash; flask flasks
     as as has has lash lash; flash flash; flask flasks
                                                         DS
  4  sale sale; a sale a sale; lake lake; a lake a lake
     sale sale; a sale a sale; lake lake; a lake a lake
```

2e ● Fluency Practice

Directions: Keyboard each line twice SS. DS after each 2-line group.

Technique Goal: Use quick, sharp strokes. Release the keys instantly.

```
  1  a lad; a lass; as a lad; as a lass; sell sell else

  2  he he held held he held; he held; she has; as she;

  3  all fall; all fall; a deal; a deal; a half; a half

  4  fee fee feel feel asked asked; he asked; she asked

  5  as a; as a lad; as a lad falls; a lass; as a lass;
```

Remove paper—Center carriage.

139b ● Building Skill

Directions: Keyboard each sentence three times SS. DS between 3-line groups.

I believe the booklet entitled <u>Your Career</u> is on the desk in Room 239.

Disney's <u>Wonderful World of Color</u> should be shown tonight at 7:30 p.m.

Pam Beck (who attended Fort Miller last year) will run the 220 for us.

The old Abbott and Costello films can be rented for approximately $15.

Only 15% of those who invested will receive more than 9 cents a share.

| 1 | 2 | 3 | 4 | 5 | 6 | 7 | 8 | 9 | 10 | 11 | 12 | 13 | 14 |

139c ● Problem Measurement

Directions: Problem 1 Business Letter from Script

1. Keyboard the letter shown below in block style with open punctuation. Set margins for a 50-space line; place today's date on line 18.

2. Make one carbon copy.

3. Address a large envelope.

Mrs. Ruth Lee / 21 Arden Way / Napa, CA 94558-2316 / Dear Mrs. Lee
(¶) Enclosed is our refund check for $18.50 covering the purchase price of the blender you recently returned.
(¶) We hope this method of handling your order meets with your approval. Please think of us again when you need kitchen appliances. / Yours truly / John Schmidt / Customer Services / xx / Enclosure

Directions: Problem 2 Interoffice Memorandum

Keyboard the following memorandum on a 60-space line. Space twice after the colon in the heading in the first line and set the left margin. Set the right margin 60 spaces to the right of the left margin.

TO: All employees | FROM: Wayne Brooks, Manager | DATE: March 23, 19-- | SUBJECT: Excessive Employee Absence

(¶) During the last two weeks, several supervisors have brought to my attention the fact that excessive absences among staff members have been causing some work load problems in our various departments.

(¶) I realize that the majority of you are most conscientious about using your sick leave only for its intended purpose. You know that each employee was hired to do a job because that particular job has to be done. If you are not here, some others must attempt to do your work in addition to their own. Naturally, when we are considering people for promotions, we have to give a good deal of weight to past attendance records.

(¶) Again, I do want to stress that the sick leave program is to be used when needed; but I want you to be aware of the problems continued absences cause your fellow employees and the management. I know I can count on your cooperation. | xx

Directions: Problem 3 Business Letter from Script

Retype the letter in Problem 1 above. Make the following changes: **1.** Address the letter to Ms. C. E. Nelson, 41 Andover Road, Erie, PA 18018-5887. **2.** Change the amount of the check to $23.75.

LESSON 3

3a ● Keyboard Review

Spacing: Double
Margin: 50-space line
(Refer to page vi)

Directions: Keyboard each line once with your teacher. Repeat the lines a second time by yourself.

Posture Goal: Sit erect. Hold elbows near the body. Keep wrists low and quiet and eyes on copy.

```
e   ded ded ed ed see feel less see sale else desk see

h   jhj jhj hj hj he held had has hall half dash shall

    add add ask ask less less head head fall fall feel
all letters
taught   jell jell; she shall see; has a desk; held a sale;
```

3b ● Location of T and O

Reach to T

1. Find t on the chart.
2. Find it on your keyboard.
3. Place your fingers over the home keys.
4. Reach to t with the f finger.
5. Touch tf lightly without moving other fingers from their typing position.

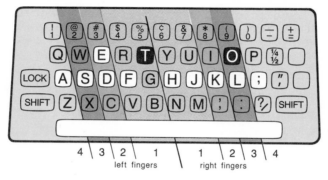

left fingers   right fingers

Reach to O

1. Find o on the chart.
2. Find it on your keyboard.
3. Place your fingers over the home keys.
4. Reach to o with the l finger.
5. Touch ol lightly without moving other fingers from their typing position.

```
ftf ftf tf tf tf the the        Type twice on same line        lol lol ol ol ol old old
```

3c ● Location Drills: T and O

Reach to t

Reach to o

Directions: Keyboard each line once with your teacher. Repeat a second time by yourself.

Technique Goal: Snap the finger toward the palm of the hand after each stroke.

```
     ftf ftf ftf ftf tf tf tf tf the the that that that
t    the that the that last let last let late late last
     late take talk tell take talk tell these these set

     lol lol ol ol ol old old told told hold hold holds
o    of of of to to to those those too too took took of
     do do does does so so; do so; do so; does so; does
```

138c ● Problem Measurement

Directions: Problem 1 Block Style Letter in Rough Draft

1. Keyboard/format the letter shown below in block style with open punctuation. Set margins for a 50-space line; begin the dateline on line 18.

2. Make one carbon copy.

3. Address a small envelope.

June 20, 19--

~~Miss~~ *Mrs.* Donna Hudson
47 Park ~~Drive~~ *Avenue*
Bowie, MD 20616-4312

Dear Mrs. Hudson

We have recieved a copy of ~~your~~ *the* letter which you wrote to Mr. Cords at our home office concerning problems you are having with your blender. (new Speedy)

As I explained to you in our conversation lastweek, we want to assist our customers through the local dealerships whenever possible. Since we had not heard anything further from you, we had assumed that ~~everything was fine~~ *the matter had been settled.*

I have informed our service representative for your area, Miss Diana Semrau, of the problem. She will be in touch with you shortly so that the two of you may get together ~~at that time~~ *to discuss the matter.*

Sincerely *yours*

Mrs. Georgette ~~Simms~~ *Simis*
Manager, Consumer Relations

xx

Directions: Problem 2 Table

Keyboard the table below on a half sheet of paper in exact vertical center. Leave 6 spaces between columns; DS items.

MANAGEMENT DEVELOPMENT PROGRAM

Topic	Date	Leader
What Is Management	September 12	Mr. Minich
Management Decision Making	October 10	Miss Cutler
Management Communication	November 7	Mrs. Lewis
Management Policy	December 12	Mrs. Hendry

LESSON 139

70-space line

5 minutes **139a ● Keyboard Review**

Directions: Keyboard each sentence three times SS. DS between 3-line groups.

alphabet John and William quickly packed the five dozen very big express boxes.

figure Ancient card packs contained 56 ordinary cards, 21 tarots, and a fool.

3d finger Millions of colorful followers all over the world tolled solemn bells.

easy One of the big problems she had was to think of a title for her theme.

| 1 | 2 | 3 | 4 | 5 | 6 | 7 | 8 | 9 | 10 | 11 | 12 | 13 | 14 |

3d ● Technique Builder: Finger Action Stroking

Directions: Set line-space regulator at "1" to single space. Keyboard each line twice.

Technique Goal: Move your fingers, not your arms or wrists.

double-space (DS) after second typing of line

triple-space (TS) between lesson parts

```
1 fjdk sla; fjdk sla; ed hj tf tf ol ol late late at
2 to to of of too too took took hold hold holds does
3 at at late late look look food food off off let to
4 lot lot left left loss loss felt felt sold sold so
5 foot foot lost lost take take too too set set take
6 the the that that these these those those that the
```

3e ● Fluency Practice

Directions: Keyboard each line three times SS. DS between 3-line groups.

Technique Goal: Keyboard without pauses.

type each line three times

type without pauses

```
1 she looks; she looks at; he took; he took the desk
2 she does; he does; she has; he has; she has a half
3 a joke; that jet; that lot; the shoe; the old shoe
4 he has a half; had a talk; had a loss; held a sale
5 to the; to that; to do; do so; at the; at the sale
```

LESSON 4 REVIEW LESSON

Spacing: Double
Margins: 50-space line

4a ● Keyboard Review

Directions: Keyboard each line once with your teacher. Repeat the lines again by yourself.

Posture Goal: Sit back in your chair with body centered opposite h key. Keep your eyes on the copy.

Finger-Action Stroking

When one of your fingers reaches from its home position to strike another key, keep the other fingers curved on the home keys. Make the reach without raising the wrist or moving your arm or elbow.

```
home  fj dk sl a; fj dk sl a; all all fall as ask ad add
row
   e  ded ded ed ed fed feed deed deal desk else see led
   h  jhj jhj hj hj he had has she shall held half heads
   t  ftf ftf tf tf at that late date let tell the these
   o  lol lol ol ol of off old told holds look took food
```

LESSON 138

138a ● Keyboard Review

5 minutes   **Directions:** Keyboard each sentence three times SS. DS between 3-line groups.

keep arms and
wrists quiet

alphabet	Dixieland jazz and also quaint folk music are being played everywhere.
figure	The first electric vacuum cleaner (made about 1905) weighed 92 pounds.
long words	Periodically, specimens of fish never before identified are recovered.
easy	She said she did her civic duty when she drove down there for a visit.

| 1 | 2 | 3 | 4 | 5 | 6 | 7 | 8 | 9 | 10 | 11 | 12 | 13 | 14 |

---

10 minutes **138b ● Speed Builder**

Directions: Take two 1' writings on each ¶; try to increase speed on the second writing. Figure *gwam*.

Alternate Procedure: Work for speed as you take one 5' writing on all four ¶s combined. Figure *gwam*.

all letters used 1.4 si 5.3 awl 85% hfw

	gwam 1'	5'
A recent survey of our nation's public libraries showed that a lot	13	2 | 51
of things checked out today won't fit on your bookshelves. What they	27	5 | 54
stock, in addition to the usual books and magazines, reflects the tastes	42	8 | 57
and needs of those who use their materials and services. Just take a	56	11 | 59
look at some of the items you can find there.	65	13 | 61
At the time this particular study was being made, for example,	13	16 | 64
one library had a waiting list for some of the gardening and yard tools	27	18 | 67
that could be checked out. No matter whether one needed to turn over	41	21 | 69
soil in the garden, cut some bushes, or dig a hole, the proper piece of	55	24 | 72
equipment could be obtained.	61	25 | 73
People who enjoy taking care of their own automobile repairs can	13	28 | 76
find help in the library too. In addition to books on this subject,	27	31 | 79
of course, one library lends a special kind of meter and light used to	41	33 | 82
time an auto engine. It also has available a creeper, the low platform	55	36 | 85
on wheels that lets you get under your car.	64	38 | 86
You can be sure that their regular job, that of helping us with	13	41 | 89
books and information, is still being done. In fact, the task of find-	27	43 | 92
ing answers to our questions has been speeded up a great deal by the	41	46 | 94
use of modern aids such as computers and television.	51	48 | 96

gwam 1' | 1 | 2 | 3 | 4 | 5 | 6 | 7 | 8 | 9 | 10 | 11 | 12 | 13 | 14 |
     5' | 1 | 2 | 3 |

4b ● Basic Techniques Review

Directions: Keyboard each line twice. Strive to achieve the specific goal provided for each set of five lines.

Posture Goal: Keep head turned toward book; wrists held low; elbows near body; fingers curved.

keep eyes on copy

```
1 adds adds fall falls dad dads fad fads asks flasks
2 sales shell asked fled deal sell deed jade lake he
3 had has she he shall held half dash head hall lash
4 take these test last date left fast tell felt talk
5 those look to told took hold loss looked food shoe
```

Technique Goal: Keep fingers deeply curved; use quick, sharp strokes.

use quick, sharp keystrokes

```
1 lass lass lads lads asks flask falls fads jak jaks
2 sales deals lease desks keel flake fled flesh safe
3 she shell shells shall flash flesh head heads half
4 state feet late staff health test sheet east steel
5 holds fold joke soft stood sold food told too took
```

Technique Goal: Strike space bar with quick down-and-in motion of thumb.

use quick down-and-in motion of thumb

```
1 a a as as as ask ask ad ad ads ads all all jak jak
2 see eke fee feel less she head he fell fed led she
3 ha had has half he she heads ah ash dash lash sash
4 the at let set jet that at let set jet the at that
5 of old off so do to too hold loss lot toe does oak
```

4c ● Fluency Practice

Directions: Keyboard each line three times.

Technique Goal: Try to achieve fluency by cutting out pauses and wasted movements in your arms, elbows, and wrists.

```
1 she sold; she sold those; she sold those old shoes

2 eat the food; look at that desk; take these tests;

3 he asked; he asked to see the jet; she told a joke

4 he talks to; she talks to; she talks to the staff;
```

LESSON 137

137a ● Keyboard Review

5 minutes **Directions:** Keyboard each sentence three times SS. DS between 3-line groups.

alphabet	We made only the best quality kegs for all our expensive frozen juice.
figure	Jan lives at 5767 North Bond Street; her telephone number is 432-1980.
weak fingers	Pamela was plainly opposed to Opal's plan to attend the Atlanta opera.
easy	Now is the time for more of them to make a few plans for their future.

| 1 | 2 | 3 | 4 | 5 | 6 | 7 | 8 | 9 | 10 | 11 | 12 | 13 | 14 |

137b ● Building Skill: Figures and Symbols

10 minutes

Directions: Keyboard each sentence once SS. Take two 1' writings on each sentence.   Work at your control level.

1 On July 2, 1971, Robert F. May threw a frisbee a distance of 285 feet.

2 Lynn Cox (at only 15) swam the English Channel in 9 hours, 57 minutes.

3 Your Invoice #89 for $74.50 was marked "Paid" on 6/2/86 by Check #341.

| 1 | 2 | 3 | 4 | 5 | 6 | 7 | 8 | 9 | 10 | 11 | 12 | 13 | 14 |

137c ● Problem Measurement: Business Letters

30 minutes

Directions: Problem 1 Modified Block Style Letter

1. Keyboard/format the letter shown below in modified block style with mixed punctuation. Set margins for a 60-space line; begin the dateline on line 18.

2. Address a small envelope.

> The opening and closing lines of this letter are in problem form. Capitalize and punctuate them correctly.

january 5, 19-- | mr harold e lane | 1428 chestnut drive | atlanta ga 30360-3425 | dear mr lane

(¶) We appreciate very much your attendance at the recent preview showing of our latest office equipment. We were glad that such a large number of people were able to come on rather short notice.

(¶) It was a real pleasure for us to explain the new 110 Series family of computers. Although it was our intention to make this first session as complete as possible, we realize there may be areas of special interest to you in which you would like more information. Should you have questions about any aspect of this system, I hope you will stop in to see us at our main supply room. We will be happy to help you.

(¶) Thank you again, Mr. Lane, for being with us.

sincerely yours | terry ray | sales representative | xx

Directions: Problem 2 Business Letter with Subject Line

Keyboard the letter above as you did in Problem 1. Add this subject line: SUBJECT: Preview Showing of 110 Series

Directions: Problem 3 Business Letter with Attention Line

Keyboard the letter above as you did in Problem 1. Address the letter to: G & L Office Supply | Attention Mrs. Betty   Goertzen | 12 Laurie Lane | Marietta, GA 30060-9966 | Ladies and Gentlemen

LESSON 5

5a ● Keyboard Review

Spacing: Double
Margin: 50-space line

Directions: Keyboard once; repeat.

Technique Goal: Use quick, sharp strokes. Release the keys instantly.

```
home
 row   fjdk sla; fjdk sla; fj as ask all fall ad had jade

   t   ftf ftf tf tf to too took the these that take tell

   o   lol lol ol ol old of off do does hold look do food

all letters   least staff jet dot test stood foot steel date oak
   taught
       she sold all the old shoes; he looked at the food;
```

5b ● Location of W and I

Reach to W

1. Find **w** on the chart.
2. Find it on your keyboard.
3. Place your fingers over the home keys.
4. Reach to **w** with the **s** finger.
5. Touch **ws** lightly without moving other fingers from their typing position.

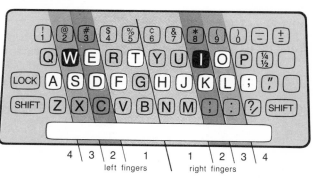

left fingers   right fingers

Reach to I

1. Find **i** on the chart.
2. Find it on your keyboard.
3. Place your fingers over the home keys.
4. Reach to **i** with the **k** finger.
5. Touch **ik** lightly without moving other fingers from their typing position.

```
sws ws ws wish wish wish      Type twice on same line      kik kik ik ik id did did
```

5c ● Location Drills: W and I

Reach to w

Reach to i

Directions: Keyboard each line once with your teacher. Repeat a second time by yourself.

Technique Goal: Reach to w and i without moving your hands forward. Hold the wrists low and quiet.

```
     sws sws sws sws ws ws ws ws we week week who whose
  w  wall wall walk walk well well how how law law laws
     west west show show few few week weeks was was low


     kik kik kik kik ik ik ik ik did did slid slid dike
  i  dike is is this this dish dish fish fish fill fill
     its its like likes list list still still life life
```

136d ● **Speed Ladder Paragraphs**

Directions: Take a 1' writing on ¶1 DS. Repeat procedure on succeeding ¶s. Take three 1' writings on any ¶ you do not finish in the time given.

> **Alternate Procedure:** Work on control as you take a 1' writing on ¶1. Move to succeeding ¶s when you complete each one within the error limit specified by your teacher. If time allows, repeat any ¶s in which you exceeded the error limit.

all letters used   1.4 si

	gwam 5'	
Although there has been talk for years about moving people via	3	55
fast trains, monorails, or tubes, the automobile continues to reign	5	57
supreme. Auto makers say there may soon be as many cars in the land	8	60
as there are adults.	9	61
No one knows, of course, just what cars of tomorrow will be like.	11	64
The consumer might be able to buy a tiny shopping car for use around	14	66
town, a large cruiser to drive out on the highway, and a specialized	17	69
vehicle for any recreational needs.	18	70
Safety will be the aim of many changes in cars of the future. One	21	73
official predicts that warning lights to alert drivers to dangers such	24	76
as tires that are low on air will be common. Engineers are working on	27	79
rear-view devices that will be better than mirrors.	29	81
If the trend to more and more cars continues, there is no doubt	31	83
that some kind of traffic control systems will be required. Some now	34	86
in limited use are connected to computers that change traffic light	37	89
timing of the direction of traffic in freeway lanes to speed the flow	40	92
of cars.	40	92
Disposing of old cars as they wear out will also pose a massive	43	95
problem. About six million cars are junked every year in the United	45	97
States alone. Laid end to end they would stretch nearly around the	48	100
earth at the equator or fill an eight-lane highway bumper-to-bumper	51	103
from New York to San Francisco.	52	104

gwam 5' | 1 | 2 | 3 |

136e ● **Language Arts Skills: Creative Typing**

Directions: Keyboard a short unbound report on ways you plan to use your typing skills. Refer to page 94, if necessary.

5d ● Technique Builder

Directions: Keyboard each line twice.   **Technique Goal:** Quick, sharp keystrokes.

double-space (DS) when you start a new line

release the keys instantly

```
1 jfdk sla; ik ik ik ws ws ws did did dike dike wide
2 will will with with wait wait like likes it it its
3 we we well well side sides still was was wash wash
4 if if wife wife wide wide field fields while while
5 who who what what two two said said life life list
```

5e ● Fluency Practice

Directions: Keyboard each line three times.   **Technique Goal:** Keep arms and wrists still.

type steadily

```
1 it was; it will; it will last; it will last a week
2 he was; she was; he said; she said; she saw a show
3 this file; these files; these weeks; all this week
4 at the side; at the west side; is at the east side
```

LESSON 6

Spacing: Double
Margins: 50-space line

6a ● Keyboard Review

Directions: Keyboard once; repeat.   **Posture Goal:** Sit erect; eyes on copy.

```
w sws sws ws ws wish wise with was wall walk who how
i kik kik ik ik did did slid slid dike dike hid hide
t o of to the that let these so do those take last too
  weeks date fast steel aid jail whole test fit like
  she held a safe lead; he looked at the white dish;
```

all letters taught

6b ● Location of R and N

Reach to R
1. Find r on the chart.
2. Find it on your keyboard.
3. Place your fingers over the home keys.
4. Reach to r with the f finger.
5. Touch rf lightly without moving other fingers from their typing position.

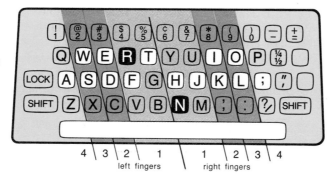

Reach to N
1. Find n on the chart.
2. Find it on your keyboard.
3. Place your fingers over the home keys.
4. Reach to n with the j finger.
5. Touch nj lightly without moving other fingers from their typing position.

```
frf frf rf rf fo for for        Type twice on same line        jnj jnj nj nj an and and
```

Unit 17 ■ Improving Your Basic Skills—Measurement

General Directions

As your teacher directs, prepare the problems on special forms provided in the workbook or on plain paper.

Use a 70-space line (center − 35; center + 35 + 5) unless otherwise directed. SS sentences and drill lines. DS paragraphs.

This unit includes measurement of straight-copy and problem typing skills. You will be expected to format/keyboard the lessons with less directional material by applying what you have learned in previous lessons.

LESSON 136

5 minutes **136a ● Keyboard Review**

Directions: Keyboard each sentence three times SS. DS between 3-line groups.

alphabet Benjamin expects to have twelve dozen big prints made from it quickly.

figure Their personal computer, introduced in 1985, has 512K bytes of memory.

direct reaches Irv brought the brand new gun he received at my annual charity brunch.

easy There is going to be a good market for their product in foreign lands.

| 1 | 2 | 3 | 4 | 5 | 6 | 7 | 8 | 9 | 10 | 11 | 12 | 13 | 14 |

5 minutes **136b ● Control Builder**

Directions: Take four 1' writings on the ¶ below at the control level.

Goal: 2 or fewer errors per writing.

1.4 si

When our western states were young, travel across their arid lands posed a problem. In seeking an answer, someone proposed the camel. It could carry heavy loads, move quickly across deserts, go without water, and live on prickly pears and scrub brush. Although the beasts did well, the railroads soon took their jobs away.

5 minutes **136c ● Language Arts Skills: Capitalization Guides**

Directions: The following are capitalization guides for *business letter parts* followed by lines to illustrate those guides. Study each guide; then keyboard the line that illustrates the guide. Keyboard each line three times SS; DS between 3-line groups.

Capitalize the first word, titles, and proper names used in the salutation.
Dear Sir: My dear Tom: Dear Mr. Smith: Dear Dr. Johnson: Dear Fran:

Capitalize only the first word of the complimentary close.
Yours truly, Sincerely yours, Yours very truly, Cordially yours, Yours

Capitalize all titles appearing in the address.
Ms. Doris Ewy, Manager; Miss Ellen Day, Secretary; Mr. Ben Blue, Chief

If a title follows the name of the writer in the closing line, it must be capitalized.
Lori Brown, President; Rita Hill, Attorney; John Stone, Vice-President

6c ● Location Drills: R and N

Directions: Keyboard each line once with your teacher. Repeat a second time by yourself.

Technique Goal: Strike each key with a quick, sharp stroke; release quickly.

r
```
frf frf frf frf rf rf rf rf for for her here there
are are here here their their real real work works
```

n
```
jnj jnj jnj jnj nj nj nj nj an an and and sand end
land land ran ran end end lend lend than than then
```

6d ● Technique Builder

Directions: Keyboard each line twice SS. DS between each 2-line group.

Technique Goal: Use quick, sharp keystrokes.

```
1 nj nj rf rf an and and hand hands than than thanks

2 in in kind kind one one done done far far her hers

3 here here there there first first air air red read

4 no no not not note notes think thinks thank thanks

5 near near own own down down front front word words
```

6e ● Fluency Practice

Directions: Keyboard each line three times SS. DS between each 3-line group.

Technique Goal: Keyboard steadily without pauses between strokes.

```
1 if he is; if he is here; if she is; if she is here

2 we went; we went to the store; it was; it was fine

3 on the land; on the road; in the air; in the world

4 two or three; two or three lines; one or two words
```

LESSON 7

7a ● Keyboard Review

Directions: Keyboard once; then repeat.

Posture Goal: Curve fingers over keys.

r
```
frf frf rf rf for far nor nor hear hard fire start
```

n
```
jnj jnj nj nj an an and land need need new new now
```

all letters
taught
```
when know send want line free join sent rate shown

needs a loan; wrote his friend; sent her the news;
```

10 minutes   **135b ● Timed Writings**

Directions: **1.** Take a 1' controlled writing on each paragraph in 131d, page 214. Circle errors. Figure *gwam*.

2. Take one 5' controlled writing on all five ¶s combined. Circle errors and figure *gwam*.

30 minutes   **135c ● Problem Typing**

Directions: **Problem 1 Memorandum with Table**

Keyboard the interoffice memorandum below in the form shown in 132c, page 215. Use a 60-space line. Leave 6 spaces between columns in the table. DS above and below the table. Prepare one carbon copy.

keep your feet
flat on the floor

TO: Terry Wetmore FROM: Pat Murphy DATE: June 4, 19-- SUBJECT: Open Enrollment Period

(¶) The open enrollment period for term life insurance, written by Northern National Life Insurance Company, has been extended through June 30. This period affords our employees the rare opportunity to obtain life insurance at a reasonable rate regardless of their physical condition.

(¶) I have listed below the names and social security numbers of the people in your section who enrolled in the program last year:

Lanny E. McBride	539 29 4374
Stephanie Petrucci	592 03 5748
Richard E. Tellier	487 33 2893

Please notify all of your other employees of this extended enrollment period.

Directions: **Problem 2 Table**

Keyboard the following table centered vertically on a full sheet. TS between the heading and the first item; DS the items. Leave 6 spaces between columns. Prepare one carbon copy.

WESTERN REGION ADDRESS LIST

Mrs. Lupe Rodriguez	15 Carroll Drive	Logan, UT 84321-5632
Miss Rebecca Falk	539 Otis Avenue	Baker, CA 33612-3210
Mr. T. Hillman Wills	14 Chickadee Lane	Redding, CA 96001-8817
Dr. Laurie Groth	86 Gearheart	Butte, MT 59701-9845
Mr. John Highfill	12 Viola Drive	Boise, ID 83705-1212
Ms. Caroline Rameriz	5221 Griffith Way	Spokane, WA 99216-6792
Mr. Jerry Kilbert	14 Grove Circle	Phoenix, AZ 86001-4545
Ms. Marilyn Martino	282 Cedar Street	Seattle, WA 98118-7456
Dr. D. L. Pierson	29 Main Street	Chico, CA 95926-3453

135d ● Extra Credit

Directions: **Problem 1**

Keyboard the memorandum in 132c, Problem 1, page 215. Fill in the heading as follows: TO: T. A. Young FROM: Earle J. Moore DATE: May 15, 19-- SUBJECT: (Same)
Prepare a carbon copy.

Directions: **Problem 2**

Keyboard the table in 135c, page 219 on a full sheet of paper. Center in reading position. TS after the heading; SS the items. Leave 4 spaces between columns. Prepare a carbon copy.

7b ● Location of C and . (period)

Reach to C

1. Find **c** on the chart.
2. Find it on your keyboard.
3. Place your fingers over the home keys.
4. Reach to **c** with the **d** finger.
5. Touch **cd** lightly without moving other fingers from their typing position.

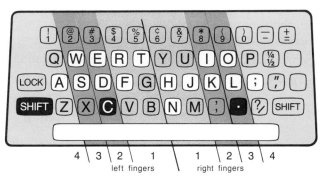

4 \ 3 \ 2 \ 1 \ 1 \ 2 \ 3 \ 4
left fingers · right fingers

Reach to . (period)

1. Find **.** on the chart.
2. Find it on your keyboard.
3. Place your fingers over the home keys.
4. Reach to **.** with the **l** finger.
5. Touch **.l** lightly without moving other fingers from their typing position.

```
dcd dcd cd cd ca car car        Type twice on same line        l.l .l .l .l fell. fell.
```

Reach to c

Reach to . (period)

7c ● Location Drills: C and . (period)

Directions: Keyboard each line once with your teacher. Repeat the lines a second time by yourself.

Technique Goal: Reach to the new keys without moving your hands out of position.

```
      dcd dcd dcd dcd cd cd cd cd car car cars call call
  c   can can care care cards cards call calls cost cost
      each each class class act acts force force car car

        l.l l.l l.l .l .l .l fill. fell. sell. call. hall.
(period) . ill. ail. all. wall. well. hail. fail. real. seal.
```

Spacing Guide
Space twice after a period that ends a sentence. When the period comes at the end of a line, return without spacing. Space only once after a period following an initial or abbreviation.

7d ● Shifting for Capitals: Left Shift Key

1. The left shift key (No. 29) is used to keyboard capital letters with the right hand.
2. Use a one-two count.

One Depress the shift key with the a finger. Hold it down.
Two Strike the capital letter; then quickly release the shift key and return the a finger to its typing position.

Reach to left shift key

Directions: Change to single spacing. Keyboard each line two times. DS between each set of two lines.

Posture Goal: Hold shoulders erect with body leaning slightly forward.

```
1  Ha Ha Hal Hall La La Lane Ja Ja Jan Jan Ka Ka Karl
2  Lee ran.  Lee ran here.  I see it.  I can see Kit.
3  H. J. Hill had a hat.  Jo will write ft. for feet.
```

134b ● Language Arts Skills: Titles of Published Works

Directions: 1. The first sentence gives the rule for the sentences following.   2. Keyboard each sentence three times.   3. Take a 1' writing on each sentence.

return carriage
quickly

1 The title of a short poem, article, or song is set in quotation marks.
2 Today, each English class will read Longfellow's "Paul Revere's Ride."
3 We saw it in Leigh White's article, "Chicago's Airport of the Future."
4 Sue Smith went to the symphony to hear Bach's "Well Tempered Clavier."

| 1 | 2 | 3 | 4 | 5 | 6 | 7 | 8 | 9 | 10 | 11 | 12 | 13 | 14 |

5 minutes   **134c ● Problem Typing**

Directions: Problem 1 Interoffice Memorandum

Format/keyboard the memorandum below on a 60-space line. Refer to 132c, page 215 if necessary.

TO: All Staff FROM: E. R. Mead, Manager DATE: November 12, 19-- SUBJECT: Wrist Calendars

(¶) Many of you have commented about the excellent response you received from customers regarding the wrist calendars we provided as gifts last year. We are, therefore, planning to give these handy calendars to our regular customers and friends again this year.

(¶) Please pick up your supply from Mark Johnson in Room 119. If you think you will need more than he has set aside for you, you can request extras after all employees have received their original supply.

(¶) You will note they are printed on each side for use with either a yellow or white gold watch band. | xx

Directions: Problem 2 Invoice

Keyboard the invoice below. Set left margin and tab stops. Figure total and enter under amount. Refer to 133c, page 217, if necessary.

SOLD TO Russell and Coe, 538 Indian Hills Drive, Fort Wayne, IN 46809-6723
DATE December 12, 19-- OUR ORDER NO. 98736 CUSTOMER ORDER NO. 3749
SHIPPED VIA Union Freight SALESPERSON D. L. Bastady TERMS 2/10, n/30

Quantity	Description	Unit Price	Amount
2	M53 C-2594 Hand Mixers	15.95 ea	31.90
10 pr	FM-79Z Wire Cutters	4.45 pr	44.50
8 gal	23-60 White House Paint	8.95 gal	71.60

LESSON 135

70-space line

30 minutes   **135a ● Keyboard Review**

Directions: Keyboard each sentence three times SS. DS between 3-line groups.

alphabet Mark will need seven jars of equal size for this next biology project.
figure On December 17, 1903, Orville Wright made the very first plane flight.
4th finger All the people we saw appeared happy with the apparatus at the bazaar.
easy You have to use the right touch if you want to do good work in typing.

| 1 | 2 | 3 | 4 | 5 | 6 | 7 | 8 | 9 | 10 | 11 | 12 | 13 | 14 |

7e ● Technique Builder: Shift Key Control

Directions: Keyboard each line two times SS. DS between 2-line groups.

Technique Goal: Hold the shift key down until you strike the capital letter; then release it quickly.

space twice after period at end of a sentence

1 It is here. Nan hit it. Jeff can see it. I ran.

2 He can sell it. I can take it. Jo will tell her.

3 I ran fast. I ran to school. Lane ran to school.

4 Joan went there. Joe called. Nan called for her.

5 Jake has a friend. He is her friend. He is late.

6 I like to work. Jo works hard. He needs to work.

LESSON 8

Spacing: Double
Margin: 50-space line

8a ● Keyboard Review

Directions: Keyboard once, then repeat.

Posture Goal: Wrists held low; elbows near body.

hold wrists low

keep elbows near body

w sws sws ws ws who whose how laws week was what few

i kik kik ik ik it its with this side file fill life

r frf frf rf rf for are were there three works world

n jnj jnj nj nj in fine fan one soon known when than

c dcd dcd cd cd costs close clean chief child chance

. l.l l.l .l .l .l ill. fill. will. all. call. fall.

Shift Hi Hi Hill Lil Lil; Lil Kine; Kate Kate; Kate Kane

8b ● Basic Techniques Review

Directions: Keyboard each line twice; concentrate on the technique goal.

Technique Goal: Keep fingers curved; make quick, sharp strokes.

quick, sharp strokes

1 we week well west who what was how few two law low

2 is this it with will his if its like life said did

3 for are were here there where their her first work

4 and in on one not an than thank then when own need

5 can call case card cost check which each since act

133c ● Problem Typing: Invoices

Directions: Problem 1

Keyboard the invoice as shown below. Clear all tabs stops; set your margin and tab stops as indicated. Use the tab key or bar to type across each line. After you keyboard the last amount, underline and DS to keyboard total. Make a carbon copy.

If a form is not available, type the copy as shown without the heading or lines.

An invoice is a bill. It is a printed form on which are typed the quantities and items delivered, the unit prices, the extensions, and the total. Some invoices have ruled columns; some do not.

Technical Services, Inc.

1385 Bellview, Green Bay, WI 54301-7896 (715) 291-0804

Invoice

Date	February 10, 19--
Our Order No.	3892
Cust. Order No.	2160-70
Shipped Via	Speedy Freight
Salesperson	Tom Shields

Custom Data Service
144 East Sinclair Street
Lowell, MA 01649-8923

Terms 2/10, n/30

Quantity	Description	Unit Price	Total
1	8230-X Ergonomic Workstation DS	259.95	259.95
3	FE-LF 727 Disk Drive Shelf SS	16.50	49.50
8	1538-C Floppy Carrier	1.40	11.20
			320.65
left margin	1st tab	2d tab	3d tab

Directions: Problem 2

Keyboard the invoice below as directed in Problem 1.

SOLD TO Village Systems | 297 Bellevue Drive | Worcester, MA 01610-2367
DATE March 2, 19-- OUR ORDER NO. 4016 CUST. ORDER NO. 2398-70 SHIPPED
VIA Northeast SALESPERSON G. Acosta TERMS 2/10, n/30

Quantity	Description	Unit Price	Amount
1	7213-X Mobile Terminal Stand	165.95	165.95
4	2979-C Fluorescent Keyboard Light	24.50	98.00
2	FE-FC 607 Glare Guard	99.40	198.80
			462.75

LESSON 134

5 minutes **134a ● Keyboard Review**

Directions: Keyboard each sentence three times SS. DS between 3-line groups.

alphabet Rex must have delivered the wrong size pack to Fuji quite by accident.

figure We could buy $28,750 worth of protection for $14.96 a month at age 32.

e,i Their niece received a prize when she hiked over here in nine minutes.

easy Rains which fell in the city during the night helped to clean the air.

| 1 | 2 | 3 | 4 | 5 | 6 | 7 | 8 | 9 | 10 | 11 | 12 | 13 | 14 |

8b Continued

Reach to left shift key

Directions: Keyboard each line twice. Concentrate on the technique goal.

Technique Goal: Depress shift key with the a finger. Strike the capital letter; quickly release shift key.

1 Jane Noakes and Karl Hicks; Lane Katt and Nan Hale

2 Jill North and Keith Halls; Jo Lind and Kent Hart;

3 John called Lil Nolan. He called Joan Noakes too.

4 Jon wrote to Joan Lands. Jeff wrote to Kate Haak.

Manual return

Technique Goal: Flick wrist to return manual carriage. Tap electric return key quickly with ; finger.

1 I said she
2 ran there.

3 Jan took a ride
4 in the new jet.

Electric return

5 He went to the lakes
6 in her fine old car.

7 I will walk to that store
8 if I need dark red shoes.

9 Kent starts to work there as a
10 clerk at the end of this week.

8c ● Sentence Skill Builder

Directions: Keyboard a 1-minute writing on each line below. Compute your gross words a minute (*gwam*).

Technique Goal: Use quick, crisp, short strokes.

Computing Gross Words a Minute (*gwam*)

Five characters/spaces are counted as one typewritten word. Each line in 8c has 50 strokes, or 10 words. For each full line typed, give yourself 10 *gwam*. For a partially typed line, note the scale under the sentences. Add the figure below the last character or space typed to your complete sentence score. This is your gross words a minute (*gwam*).

1 I was asked to look at the north side of the door.

2 Jan wants to trade her old car for a nice new one.

3 One word in the line was too hard for her to read.

4 He saw lots of fine artwork at the fair this week.

5 Lil said that she was not late to her first class.

| 1 | 2 | 3 | 4 | 5 | 6 | 7 | 8 | 9 | 10 |

Lesson 8

15

Directions: Problem 2
Keyboard the following memorandum using the directions given in Problem 1.

TO: Richard Rogers, Office Manager FROM: J. B. Ross, General Manager DATE: July 25, 19-- SUBJECT: Staff Meeting
(¶) Our next staff meeting will be held on Wednesday afternoon at 3:15. We shall have to meet in the committee room on the third floor because our regular committee room is being used for a sales conference. Please notify all the members in your department of the time and place.
(¶) Your report will be the first item we have to consider. If you can have copies made for everyone, I think we can save quite a bit of time. Since we have a full agenda, it looks as though the meeting will probably last until 5:00. xx

LESSON 133

70-space line

5 minutes **133a ● Keyboard Review**

Directions: Keyboard each sentence three times SS. DS between 3-line groups.

alphabet	All six kids are crazy about having peanut butter with jam frequently.
figure	On April 11, 1965, tornadoes struck the Middle West at least 37 times.
4th finger	Zelda passed the science quiz and got an extra quill for her desk set.
easy	The problem they have right now is caused by the slant of their hands.

| 1 | 2 | 3 | 4 | 5 | 6 | 7 | 8 | 9 | 10 | 11 | 12 | 13 | 14 |

10 minutes **133b ● Speed Builder**

Directions: Take a 1' writing on each ¶; try to increase speed on the second writing. Figure *gwam*.   Work for speed as you take one 5' writing on all three ¶s combined. Figure *gwam*.

all letters used 1.4 si 5.3 awl 85% hfw   *gwam* 1' | 5'

	1'	5'
Every summer many thousands of teenagers search for jobs in which	13	3	41
they can earn some money for a trip, a new fishing rod, or simply to	27	5	44
help out with the family budget. Getting a paycheck of your very own	41	8	47
can be fun, but there are several points that should be kept in mind	55	11	50
in obtaining summer employment.	61	12	51
Try to get employment that is in line with your career plans. In	13	15	54
that way you can gather first-hand information about your chosen career.	28	18	57
You will be able to decide whether or not you and your career make a	42	21	59
good team. It's quite important that you learn this about yourself.	56	23	62
This is not the only principle to keep in mind, however.	67	26	64
A summer job gives you a chance to learn how to work. Capitalize	13	28	67
on the opportunity to interact with other people, to take directions,	27	31	70
and to put what you presently know to an acid test. This is the payoff	42	34	73
for summer work--a golden opportunity to learn just what is expected,	55	37	75
plus a chance to see how well you can fill the bill.	66	39	78

gwam 1' | 1 | 2 | 3 | 4 | 5 | 6 | 7 | 8 | 9 | 10 | 11 | 12 | 13 | 14 |
       5' | 1 | 2 | 3 |

LESSON 9

9a ● Keyboard Review

Directions: Keyboard once, then repeat.

Posture Goal: Sit erect; eyes on copy.

keep eyes
on copy

c cd cd check checks card cards face face cost costs

. 1.1 1.1 .1 .1 .1 .1. ill. ital. kil. dal. Lt. Ill.

shift Lance Jones and Jane Keel; Jack Halls and Nan Ides

all letters
taught

It took one whole week for her to find the stores.

Jane and he were asked to stand close to the door.

| 1 | 2 | 3 | 4 | 5 | 6 | 7 | 8 | 9 | 10 |

9b ● Location of G and U

Reach to G
1. Find g on the chart.
2. Find it on your keyboard.
3. Place your fingers over the home keys.
4. Reach to g with the f finger.
5. Touch gf lightly without moving other fingers from their typing position.

Reach to U
1. Find u on the chart.
2. Find it on your keyboard.
3. Place your fingers over the home keys.
4. Reach to u with the j finger.
5. Touch uj lightly without moving other fingers from their typing position.

fgf fgf gf gf go got got   Type twice on same line   juj juj uj uj us use use

9c ● Location Drills: G and U

Reach to g

Reach to u

Directions: Keyboard once with your teacher; a second time by yourself.

Technique Goal: Reach your fingers, not your hands, to the new keys.

fgf fgf fgf fgf gf gf gf gf go good good gone gone

g got got sign sign light light right right get gets

eight eight age age girl girls green green gas gas

juj juj juj juj uj uj uj uj us use used hour hours

u out out our our could could should should due dues

just just such such full full four four hour hours

LESSON 132

132a ● Keyboard Review

5 minutes

Directions: Keyboard each sentence three times SS. DS between 3-line groups.

alphabet The explosive magazine articles were rejected only by a quirk of fate.

figure The 1,256 scouts marched 38 blocks before more than 24,970 spectators.

weak fingers Pablo and Paul Perez acquainted us with techniques of raising azaleas.

easy The biggest mistake we can make is to believe that we cannot make one.

| 1 | 2 | 3 | 4 | 5 | 6 | 7 | 8 | 9 | 10 | 11 | 12 | 13 | 14 |

132b ● Technique Builder: Stroking

10 minutes

Directions: Take two 1' writings on each line SS. DS between 2-line groups.

keep your eyes
on the copy

1 quiz azure police apply taxes flaw hazy axe zero soap war palm was set

2 upon square zone plow lamp play flax cases quick zipper zeal possesses

3 They politely applauded the players although the acting was very poor.

4 The lazy pupils did not apply themselves and promptly failed the quiz.

| 1 | 2 | 3 | 4 | 5 | 6 | 7 | 8 | 9 | 10 | 11 | 12 | 13 | 14 |

132c ● Problem Typing: Interoffice Memorandums

30 minutes

Interoffice Memorandums are used for correspondence within a company.

If a form is not available, set the left margin approximately 1½" from the left edge of the paper. Beginning on line 12, backspace into the left margin to keyboard the TO:, FROM:, DATE:, and SUBJECT: in ALL CAPS. Set the right margin 60 spaces to the right of the left margin.

Directions: Problem 1

Keyboard the memorandum below on a 60-space line. Space twice after the colon in the heading in the first line (TO:) and set the left margin. Set the right margin 60 spaces to the right of the left margin.

TO: Members, Planning Commission
DS
FROM: R. G. Chung, Director
DS
DATE: August 1, 19--
DS
SUBJECT: Notice of Hearing, Blackhawk Regional Plan
TS

The Board of Supervisors voted on July 28 to schedule public hearings to consider adoption of the Blackhawk Regional Plan. The hearings will begin at 2:00 p.m. on Tuesday, September 4, in Room 102, Hall of Records, Lansing and Kingston Streets, Spokane, Washington.
DS
The Plan area consists of lands lying west of Highway 34 and south of the Squaw River. Excluded from the Plan are lands within the Deer Valley Regional Plan area. The Environmental Impact Report is available for review in my office.
DS
xx

(continued on next page)

9d ● Technique Builder: Wrists Low and Steady

Directions: Keyboard each line two times SS. DS between 2-line groups.

Technique Goal: Curve your fingers. Hold your wrists low and steady.

curve your fingers

keep wrists and elbows still

```
1 uj gf uj gf such such glad glad long long run runs
2 four four though though thought thought turn turns
3 just just would would sound sounds through through
4 to do; to do the; to go; to go to the; to go there
5 if he; if she; if he can; if she can; if we do the
6 I can go.  He will go there.  He can go there too.
7 He will need four hours.  He will go in two hours.
  | 1 | 2 | 3 | 4 | 5 | 6 | 7 | 8 | 9 | 10 |
```

Keep wrists low

Position of Wrists

Keep your wrists low, but do not allow them to touch the typewriter. Keep forearms parallel to the slant of the typewriter.

Forearms parallel to slant of machine

9e ● Sentence Skill Builder

Directions: Keyboard two 1' writings on each sentence. Figure your *gwam*.

Posture Goal: Keep the wrists low.

```
1 I can do the work if I find the tools that I need.

2 He will learn the rules that she has on the cards.

3 I know that he and she can gain a good high skill.
  | 1 | 2 | 3 | 4 | 5 | 6 | 7 | 8 | 9 | 10 |
```

LESSON 10

10a ● Keyboard Review

Spacing: Double
Margin: 50-space line

use quick, sharp strokes

Directions: Keyboard once; repeat.

Posture Goal: Keep eyes on copy.

```
g great great light lights large large charge charge
u would would south south course course thing things
  I know I did well.  Kate did well on the test too.
  Karl and Joan each ran a good race for our school.
  | 1 | 2 | 3 | 4 | 5 | 6 | 7 | 8 | 9 | 10 |
```

all letters taught

131d ● Speed Ladder Paragraphs

Directions: 1. Take 1' writings on ¶1 DS until you complete the ¶ in 1'.
2. When you complete ¶1 in 1', continue on to ¶2. Repeat this procedure as you try to complete each of the five ¶s in the time given.
3. Take three 1' writings on any ¶ you cannot finish in the given time.

all letters used   1.4 si   *gwam* 5'

reach with your fingers; keep hands and wrists quiet

Just about the time you think no one could possibly come up with	3	55
a new kind of electronic device, a gadget more exotic than ever appears	5	57
on the scene. The number of them invented each year is enough to boggle	8	60
your mind.	9	61
Those products that amaze most of us one year seem to become slow,	11	63
clunky, and just plain obsolete the next. Not only do they perform a	14	66
wider variety of tasks, but they also manage to get smaller, faster,	17	69
and much cheaper at the same time.	18	70
Items range from electronic flea collars that aid your dog to video	21	73
games that people control by means of electric impulses from their	24	76
heads. There is a color television set so small it will fit in the	27	79
palm of your hand and a stereo the size of a credit card.	29	81
It's in the world of telephones that some of the greatest changes	31	83
are being made. Not very long ago many people were trying to decide	34	86
whether to purchase a push button model or one that didn't require a	37	89
cord. Such decisions were simple compared to those you'll have to make.	40	92
Telephones used to look alike, but that's not the case any more.	43	95
One model closes so you can lock it with a key; it also includes room	45	97
for photographs of several people whose numbers the phone is programmed	48	100
to dial. If you want, however, you can get one that resembles your	51	103
favorite soft drink can.	52	104

gwam 5' | 1 | 2 | 3 |

5 minutes **131e ● Skill Comparison**

Directions: Take four 1' writings on the ¶ in 131b, page 213. Compare rates.

10b ● Location of V and Y

Reach to V

1. Find v on the chart.
2. Find it on your keyboard.
3. Place your fingers over the home keys.
4. Reach to v with the f finger.
5. Touch vf lightly without moving other fingers from their typing position.

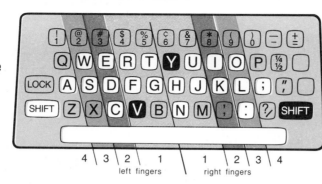

4 3 2 1 | 1 2 3 4
left fingers | right fingers

Reach to Y

1. Find y on the chart.
2. Find it on your keyboard.
3. Place your fingers over the home keys.
4. Reach to y with the j finger.
5. Touch yj lightly without moving other fingers from their typing position.

```
fvf fvf vf fiv five five          Type twice on same line          jyj jyj yj yj ja jay jay
```

10c ● Location Drills: V and Y

Reach to v

Reach to y

Directions: Keyboard each line once with your teacher. Repeat by yourself.

Technique Goal: Think the letters as you type. Use quick, sharp strokes.

```
      fvf fvf fvf fvf vf vf vf vf five fives lives lives
  v have have five five give give dive dive hive hives
      save saves gave gave wave waved raves leave leaves


      jyj jyj jyj jyj yj yj yj yj jay jays lay lays slay
  y sly sly fly fly try try jay jay ray ray stay stays
      the they eye eyes try tray fry fray lay lays yells
```

10d ● Shifting for Capitals: Right Shift Key

Spacing Guide
Remember to space twice after a period that ends a sentence (except at the end of a line).

1. The right shift key (No. 27) is used to keyboard capital letters with the left hand.
2. Use a one-two count.

One Depress the shift key with the ; finger. Hold it down.

Two Strike the capital letter; then quickly release the shift key and return the ; finger to its typing position.

Reach to right shift key

Directions: Keyboard each line twice. Use single spacing.

Posture Goal: Use a quick, firm reach to the shift key.

```
1 Ted Ted Fran Fran; Ted and Fran; Fran and I; Frank
2 Ted is here.  Fran can see Ted.  She can see Fran.
3 Frank is ill.  I need Art here.  She and I see it.
```

Unit 16 ■ Learning to Keyboard Business Forms (Lessons 131–135)

General Directions Use a 70-space line (center − 35; center + 35 + 5) for drills and timed writings in this unit. SS sentences and drill lines. DS paragraph copy. As your teacher directs, prepare the problems on special forms provided in the workbook or on plain paper.

LESSON 131

5 minutes **131a ● Keyboard Review**

Directions: Keyboard each sentence three times SS. DS between 3-line groups.

alphabet Five or six quarters, won as prize money, jingled in the boy's pocket.

figure Nearly 102.3 million Americans swim, but only 72.2 million ride bikes.

direct reach Marvin brought the necessary linoleum and lumber to replace our floor.

easy Neither of the two had enough chairs to handle such a tough situation.

| 1 | 2 | 3 | 4 | 5 | 6 | 7 | 8 | 9 | 10 | 11 | 12 | 13 | 14 |

5 minutes **131b ● Control Builder**

Directions: Take four 1' writings on the ¶ below at the control level. **Goal:** 2 or fewer errors per writing.

all letters used 1.4 si

One computer expert has been quoted as saying that some people have actually tried to kill their computers. The machines have been shot at, stabbed, and bombed by owners who were crazed by frustration. They have been electrically shorted out with a metal key and in at least one case jammed with the heel of a woman's shoe.

10 minutes **131c ● Speed Ladder Sentences**

Directions: Keyboard each sentence for 1'. Your teacher will call the guide at 15", 12", or 10" intervals. As time permits, repeat sentences on which you were not able to complete a line with the call of the guide.

		guide 15"	12"	10"
1	Be sure your feet are flat on the floor.	32	40	48
2	One foot should be placed ahead of the other.	36	45	54
3	Proper position of the feet will aid your balance.	40	50	60
4	Remember to keep the elbows in close to your body, too.	44	55	66
5	Hold your wrists down low, just above your typewriter frame.	48	60	72
6	Keep the hands quiet and space quickly with a down - and - in motion.	52	65	78
7	Make quick, sharp strokes with your fingers well curved over the keys.	56	70	84

| 1 | 2 | 3 | 4 | 5 | 6 | 7 | 8 | 9 | 10 | 11 | 12 | 13 | 14 |

10e ● Technique Builder: Shift Key Control

Directions: Keyboard each line three times SS. DS after the third line.

Technique Goal: Hold the shift key down until you strike the capital letter; then release quickly.

return without spacing after . at end of line

1 vf yj vf yj day day dry dry say say stay stay days
2 yes yet hear the they ray gray tray sly slay style
3 She can. She can have her turn. I can give five.
4 Jan and I can stay. Jan can stay there five days.
5 Ann and Karl are here. Jan left her friend there.
6 I can learn. She can get all the funds she needs.

LESSON 11

Spacing: Double
Margin: 50-space line

11a ● Keyboard Review

Directions: Keyboard once; repeat.

Posture Goal: Sit back in chair. Eyes on copy.

return carriage quickly

v give give live live gave gave view views save save
y you you years years way way ways says says why why
shift Fred Sills and Ann Shields; Rick Weld and Sue Todd
all letters taught Fran went to class at two. Juan said we could go.
Vera asked us if we had heard the news last night.

| 1 | 2 | 3 | 4 | 5 | 6 | 7 | 8 | 9 | 10 |

11b ● Location of B and M

Reach to B
1. Find b on the chart.
2. Find it on your keyboard.
3. Place your fingers over the home keys.
4. Reach to b with the f finger.
5. Touch bf lightly without moving other fingers from their typing position.

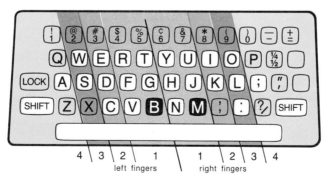

Reach to M
1. Find m on the chart.
2. Find it on your keyboard.
3. Place your fingers over the home keys.
4. Reach to m with the j finger.
5. Touch mj lightly without moving other fingers from their typing position.

fbf fbf bf bf ib fib fib   Type twice on same line   jmj jmj mj mj ja jam jam

130b ● Timed Writings

Directions: Take a 1' writing on each paragraph of 126c, page 207, *or* take a 5' writing on all paragraphs combined. Circle errors; figure *gwam*.

130c ● Problem Typing: Business Letters

Directions: Problem 1

1. Keyboard in modified block style, mixed punctuation. Set 60-space line; begin dateline on line 18.

2. Use today's date; make one carbon copy; address a large envelope.

Miss Monica Johnson | 3978 North Fifth Street | Baltimore, MD 21225-4590 | Dear Miss Johnson:

(¶) I am returning to you the charge slip from Weinstock's Automotive Service for the recent towing of your car. Since claims of this type are always handled on a reimbursement basis, I will need a receipted bill before your claim can be processed. When you pay the bill, please ask for a receipt which you can submit to us. We shall then reimburse you up to the amount stipulated in your contract.

(¶) I have also enclosed an Information Request Form which you will need to complete and return with your receipt. It will assist the Service Department in promptly considering your claim.

(¶) Thank you for your cooperation, Miss Johnson. I hope to hear from you soon.

Cordially yours, | James R. Castenada | Claims Manager | xx | Enclosures

Directions: Problem 2

1. Keyboard in block style, open punctuation. Set 60-space line; begin on line 18.

2. Make one carbon copy; address a large envelope.

October 12, 19-- | Ms. Margaret Anderson | 2109 Coles Road | Columbia, SC 29203-7175 | Dear Ms. Anderson

(¶) As of December 1, Allied Legal Systems, Inc, will be taking over the administration of your legal service plan from Atlantic General Corporation. We are therefore enclosing a new membership card and certificate of coverage to replace those you now hold.

(¶) This change affects only the administration of your plan. Our system of providing prompt and reliable legal advice will operate just as in the past. The services provided are the same, and the same law firm will continue to provide them.

(¶) Should you have any questions about this change, please write us or call the attorney hot-line number and ask to be connected with our membership department. We look forward to being of service to you.

Very truly yours | ALLIED LEGAL SERVICES, INC. | Ms. Christine Ortega | President | xx | Enclosures

---

130d ● Extra Credit

Directions: Problem 1

Compose an answer to the letter in Problem 1 of 130c. Tell Mr. Castenada you have paid the bill and are sending him the receipt and completed Information Request Form. Use the letter style you prefer and your own return address.

Directions: Problem 2

Prepare Problem 1, 124d, page 205 in block style with open punctuation.

Directions: Problem 3

Prepare Problem 2, 129c, page 211 in modified block style with mixed punctuation. Add a subject line.

Manual tabulation

Electric tabulation

11c ● Location Drills: B and M

Directions: Keyboard each line once with your teacher. Repeat a second time by yourself.

Technique Goal: Use finger, not hand, motions as you reach for these keys.

```
      fbf  fbf  fbf  fbf  bf  bf  bf  bf  buff  buff  job  job  jobs
   b  big  big  both  both  boy  boy  boys  blue  blue  ball  ball
      bus  bus  by  by  buy  buy  but  but  hub  hub  lab  lab  burn


      jmj  jmj  jmj  jmj  mj  mj  mj  mj  jam  jam  make  make  made
   m  men  men  mean  mean  them  them  come  come  much  much  am
      same  same  game  games  more  more  most  most  from  from
```

11d ● Indenting for Paragraphs

1. Clear all tab stops Move the carriage (or carrier) so that the point of typing is at the right margin of your paper. Depress the tab clear key (No. 33) and hold it down as you return the carriage (carrier) so that the point of typing is at the left margin of your paper. You have cleared all tab stops.

2. Set a tab stop Space in 5 spaces from the left margin. Depress the tab set key (No. 25). You have set a tab stop at paragraph point.

3. Tab to paragraph point Return the carriage (carrier) so that the point of typing is at the left margin. Find the tab key or bar (No. 24) on your machine. Touch lightly the tab key using the closest little finger, or use the index finger to hold down the tabulator bar until the carriage stops. You are now at paragraph point.

11e ● Paragraph Typing

Directions: Clear all tab stops. Set your machine for a 5-space paragraph indention. Keyboard the paragraphs twice DS. Repeat if time permits.

Technique Goal: Reach to the tab key or bar with your finger; release and quickly return finger to home-key position.

Computing Gross Words a Minute (*gwam*).

To figure *gwam* on paragraph copy, note the figure at the end of the last complete line typed in the column at the right. For a partially typed line, note (in the scale at the bottom of the paragraphs) the last stroke typed. Add this figure to the figure at the end of the last complete line typed. The total is your *gwam*.

gwam 1'

```
tab——→The girls have a tent near the lake.  They     9

      stay at the lake all day in the fall.  Kay says   18

      I can use her raft if I like.                     24

tab——→Nancy can drive there in a day in her car.      33

      Ken and I can ride in it.  She says that she is   42

      sure there is gas in the car.                     48
```

| 1 | 2 | 3 | 4 | 5 | 6 | 7 | 8 | 9 | 10 |

129c ● Problem Typing: Business Letters with Special Features

Directions: Problem 1 Business Letter with Enumerated Items

1. Keyboard in modified block style, mixed punctuation. Set 60-space line; begin on line 18.

2. Use today's date; make one carbon copy; address a large envelope.

Miss Mary Miller| 3197 Conifer Street| Flint, MI 48108-5004| Dear Miss Miller: (¶) As one of our best customers, you are eligible for the enclosed Superior Chargecard. Here are a few of the card's many advantages:

1. It is honored by over 50,000 merchants in Michigan.

2. It identifies you as a person of good credit standing.

3. There are no dues and no interest charges when you pay within 30 days.

(¶) If you wish, Miss Miller, you may extend your payments by paying as little as 5 percent of your outstanding balance or $10 each month, whichever is greater. Need we say more?

Cordially yours,| Robert Pengilly| Sales Representative| xx| Enclosure

Directions: Problem 2 Business Letter in Rough-Draft Form

1. Keyboard in block style, open punctuation. Set 50-space line; begin on line 18.

2. Make one carbon copy; address a large envelope.

April 14, 19- -

Mr. Jeffrey L. Dakkedahl
287 Laurel Ave. *spell out*
Casper, WY 82604-8463 *Dear Mr. Dakkedahl*

Enclosed with this letter is a new set of cards for you use when
making your monthly mortgage payments. Please destroy any old
cards you may habe and use the new ones *beginning July 1.*
have
We made this change because our recordkeeping *has been converted* from
a ser vice bureau to in-house computer. *an*

Sincerely yours
Mrs. Leslie Delara Controller
xx
Enclosure

LESSON 130

5 minutes **130a ● Keyboard Review**

Directions: Keyboard each sentence 3 times SS. DS between 3-line groups.

stroke smoothly, without pauses

alphabet The Zeta Psi award was given to a very excited Mr. Jacques F. Barkals.

figure The Great Pyramid, 755 feet across and 481 feet high, covers 13 acres.

e, i Neither of their neighbors knew of vacancies in the secretarial field.

easy Very few are too busy to take the time to tell just how busy they are.

| 1 | 2 | 3 | 4 | 5 | 6 | 7 | 8 | 9 | 10 | 11 | 12 | 13 | 14 |

LESSON 12

12a ● Keyboard Review

Spacing: Double
Margin: 50-space line

Directions: Keyboard once; repeat.

Posture Goal: Elbows in; wrists low.

```
g  fgf fgf gf gf get great glad gone long light right
u  juj juj uj uj out our hour four would should could
v  fvf fvf vf vf five give have save gave leave drive
y  jyj jyj yj yj yes yet you yours years days way say
b  fbf fbf bf bf be been back best bill both board by
m  jmj jmj mj mj more most much means mind some homes
```

12b ● Basic Technique Review

Directions: Keyboard each line twice.
Concentrate on the technique goal.

Posture Goal: Shoulders erect with body
leaning slightly forward.

Technique Goal: Keep the fingers deeply curved; make quick, sharp strokes.

```
1  sign large length charge change eight wrong strong
2  source just due such thus thought runs found house
3  view voice have gives five serve gave leave drives
4  style young years yet eyes stays try why ways gray
5  brought bank book club blue big doubt job base buy
6  farm whom make made film from times them same name
```

Technique Goal: Depress right shift key with the ; finger. Strike the capital letter; quickly release the shift key.

```
1  Dee Smith and Ray Brown; Deb Green and Frank Sands
2  Sue Thoms and Bob Arndt; Barb Vance and Thane Eads
3  Ana saw Don Reese.  Rosa Ramos rode with Sam Weld.
```

Technique Goal: Flick wrist to return the manual carriage. Tap electric return key quickly with ; finger.

```
 1  Both girls
 2  came late.
 3  Their class met
 4  once each week.
 5  Each girl will bring
 6  a gift for her date.
 7  We thought our team would
 8  lose the game that night.
 9  They can all stay at school so
10  no one will have to walk home.
```

128c ● Problem Typing: Business Letters with Tables

Directions: Problem 1

1. Keyboard/format the letter below in modified block style with mixed punctuation. Set margins for a 60-space line; begin dateline on line 18.

2. Center the table horizontally, leaving 6 spaces between columns. SS tabular material; DS before and after the table.

3. Make 1 carbon copy; address a small envelope.

April 23, 19-- | Ms. Georgia Hansen, President | Kokomo World Affairs Club | 826 Murray Lane | Kokomo, IN 46902-7153 | Dear Ms. Hansen:
(¶) We are happy to announce that Wayne R. Chapin, Field Services Representative for Indiana, will be in your area during June. His schedule is as follows:

Kokomo	June 10-14
Muncie	June 17-21
Anderson	June 24-28

(¶) Mr. Chapin would like to speak to the entire membership at your Wednesday luncheon meeting. We also hope you can schedule a special evening meeting during the week so he may spend additional time with your executive board.
(¶) If some of your people would find it more convenient to attend Mr. Chapin's presentation in one of the other cities, please encourage them to do so.
Sincerely, | WORLD AFFAIRS CLUB | Mrs. Andrea Davidson | Director | xx

Directions: Problem 2

Keyboard/format the letter in Problem 1 in block style with open punctuation. Margin and date placement remain the same. Address the letter to:

Dr. A. L. Karr, President
Muncie World Affairs Club
2038 University Avenue
Muncie, IN 47303-5170

LESSON 129

5 minutes **129a ● Keyboard Review**

Directions: Keyboard each sentence 3 times SS. DS between 3-line groups.

keep your feet flat on the floor

alphabet Frank soon realized how very much Peg enjoyed excellent Baroque music.

figure Their bill came to $465.70, but it was not due until December 3, 1986.

4th finger Pamela saw that Pat wasn't able to adapt adequately to that apparatus.

easy Fine typists have learned to keep their eyes on the copy as they type.

| 1 | 2 | 3 | 4 | 5 | 6 | 7 | 8 | 9 | 10 | 11 | 12 | 13 | 14 |

10 minutes **129b ● Skill Builder**

Directions: **1.** Take a 1' writing on the ¶ in 127b, page 208. The last word typed will be your goal word.
2. Take a 5' writing with the return called after each minute. When the return is called, start the paragraph over again. Try to reach your goal each minute as the return is called.

12c ● Paragraph Skill Builder

Directions: Five-space paragraph indention DS. Keyboard the paragraph (¶) once for practice; then take three 1' writings on it. Figure your *gwam* on the best writing.

gwam 1'

tab——▶Set your goals if you want to make the best 9

use of your time. This is true for your work at 19

home as well as what you do at your school. You 29

will get more work done when you know what it is 39

you want to do. 42

| 1 | 2 | 3 | 4 | 5 | 6 | 7 | 8 | 9 | 10 |

LESSON 13

13a ● Keyboard Review

Directions: Keyboard once; repeat.

Posture Goal: Keep feet flat on the floor, one ahead of the other.

use quick, sharp strokes

b fbf fbf bf bf board board doubt doubts bring bring

m jmj jmj mj mj him him room room my my month months

v y yj vf yj vf voice voice leave leave you your young

in in fine find kind line mine thin think thing since

all letters taught

I think all the girls did a good job at the games.

A few of you will soon have to take the cars back.

| 1 | 2 | 3 | 4 | 5 | 6 | 7 | 8 | 9 | 10 |

13b ● Location of X and P

Reach to X
1. Find x on the chart.
2. Find it on your keyboard.
3. Place your fingers over the home keys.
4. Reach to x with the s finger.
5. Touch xs lightly without moving other fingers from their typing position.

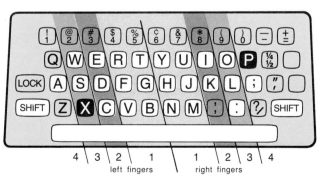

4 3 2 1 / 1 2 3 4
left fingers   right fingers

Reach to P
1. Find p on the chart.
2. Find it on your keyboard.
3. Place your fingers over the home keys.
4. Reach to p with the ; finger.
5. Touch p; lightly without moving other fingers from their typing position.

sxs sxs xs xs ix six six   Type twice on same line   ;p; ;p; p; p; pa par par

Directions: Problem 2 Compose a Business Letter

1. Compose a letter in reply to the letter in Problem 1 in modified block style with mixed punctuation. Use today's date; address the letter to: Mr. Douglas Simpson, Sales Manager| Jan Publishing Company| 2398 York Street| Kansas City, MO 64129-2687| Ms. Watchel will be the signer of the letter.

2. In the letter, thank Mr. Simpson for his prompt attention to the damaged shipment and for the complimentary book. Also, extend him a personal invitation to visit the new store.

3. Address a small envelope.

LESSON 128

70-space line

128a ● Keyboard Review

5 minutes

Directions: Keyboard each sentence three times SS. DS between 3-line groups.

strike keys with quick, sharp strokes

alphabet	Judge Roby was quick to penalize all sixteen for moving the green car.
figure	Track and field events attracted 427,171 persons at the 1932 Olympics.
double letters	All smaller book committees will still meet three weeks in succession.
easy	Four of their friends had to pay more than usual for items they found.

| 1 | 2 | 3 | 4 | 5 | 6 | 7 | 8 | 9 | 10 | 11 | 12 | 13 | 14 |

128b ● Speed Builder

10 minutes

Directions: Take two 1' writings on each ¶; try to increase speed on the second writing. Figure *gwam*.

Alternative Procedure: Work for speed as you take one 5' writing on all four ¶s combined. Figure *gwam*.

all letters used 1.4 si 5.3 awl 85% hfw

	gwam 1'	5'
One topic that has long been given a good deal of attention at the	13	3	50
junior high school level is career education. Students at this age	27	5	53
soon realize that making plans for the future requires a lot of advance	41	8	56
thought if one is to have a happy and rewarding life.	52	10	58
Today more and more women think in terms of an actual career rather	14	13	61
than think only about a job that enables them to earn extra spending	27	16	64
money or to help pay the bills. They want to be doctors, lawyers, and	42	19	67
business leaders instead of working at menial tasks or staying at home	56	22	69
all day with the children.	61	23	71
Having two wage earners in a family is not exactly the same thing	13	25	73
as having two career people in one family. In the former instance it	27	28	76
is likely that the wife's position is lower, both in status and pay.	41	31	79
If both have careers, the chances of their two incomes being more nearly	56	34	82
equal are much greater.	60	35	83
The trend toward marriages in which there are two careers is re-	13	37	85
garded by some to be one of the major social changes of our time. It	27	40	88
has the potential to alter the division of labor in the home as well	41	43	91
as the way children are raised. It makes careful career planning more	55	46	94
important than ever for those in school today.	64	48	96

gwam 1' | 1 | 2 | 3 | 4 | 5 | 6 | 7 | 8 | 9 | 10 | 11 | 12 | 13 | 14 |
5' | 1 | 2 | 3 |

13c ● Location Drills: X and P

Directions: Keyboard each line once with your teacher. Repeat a second time by yourself.

Technique Goal: Reach to the new keys with your fingers. Keep your wrists low.

```
   sxs sxs sxs sxs xs xs xs xs six six fix fix ox box
 x lax lax flax flax flex flex next next fox fox hoax
   excel excel flux flux hex hex relax relax axe axes

   ;p; ;p; ;p; ;p; p; p; p; p; par par part pass pass
 p past past page page pay pay put put trip trip kept
   flip flip slip slip pile pile play play spar spare
```

13d ● Technique Builder: Down-and-in Motion of Right Thumb

Directions: Keyboard each line twice SS. DS between 2-line groups.

Technique Goal: Strike space bar with quick down-and-in motion.

curve right thumb over space bar

use quick down-and-in motion of thumb

```
1 xs p; sx p; sx p; flax flax help help cap caps six
2 fox tax fox lax six jinx box hex coax hoax vex axe
3 top stop lot lay play plan plus post nap hope ship
4 fix the step; keep the box; pay the tax; six steps
5 I can pay it.  He can pay for it.  She can pay it.
6 I paid six of the girls for the good job they did.
  |  1  |  2  |  3  |  4  |  5  |  6  |  7  |  8  |  9  |  10  |
```

13e ● Paragraph Typing

Directions: Set machine for a 5-space paragraph indention. Keyboard the ¶ twice DS. Repeat if time permits.

Technique Goal: (Manual) Hold the tab bar or key down until the carriage stops. (Electric and some manuals) Strike the tab key; release it and return the finger to home key at once.

keep wrists and elbows still

gwam 1'

```
tab──────▶You can type at a high rate if you hold your   9

        hands still as you reach for the keys.  Just keep   19

        your eyes on this page.  These are the things you   29

        need to do as you type.  Try these hints and see.   39
        |  1  |  2  |  3  |  4  |  5  |  6  |  7  |  8  |  9  |  10  |
```

LESSON 127

5 minutes

127a ● Keyboard Review

Directions: Keyboard each sentence three times SS. DS between 3-line groups.

reach to keys
with fingers

alphabet	Very few sixth graders in the math class ever joked about pop quizzes.
figure	Grange, retired in 1935, carried the ball 32,820 yards in 4,000 tries.
double letters	All room committees agreed that baggage accommodations were very good.
easy	The right mind set will help you make the typewriter do its work well.

| 1 | 2 | 3 | 4 | 5 | 6 | 7 | 8 | 9 | 10 | 11 | 12 | 13 | 14 |

10 minutes

127b ● Paragraph Guided Writings

Directions: **1.** Set goals of 40, 50, and 60 words a minute. Take two 1' writings at each rate. Try to reach your goal word as time is called.

2. Your teacher may call the quarter or half minutes to guide you.

3. Keyboard additional writings at the 50- and 60-word rates as time permits.

1.4 si

Very few foods are more American than the hot dog. The billions
eaten each year prove it. Still, there are two other sandwiches that
rank ahead of the famous weiner and bun. Would you believe that peanut
butter and jelly is first and the hamburger second? Because of this,
those who sell hot dogs will have to try harder.

30 minutes

127c ● Problem Typing: Business Letters with Special Features

Directions: Problem 1 Business Letter with Postscript

1. Keyboard/format the letter below in modified block style with mixed punctuation. Set margins for a 50-space line; begin dateline on line 18.

2. Make 1 carbon copy; address a small envelope.

A postscript is the last item in a letter. The postscript appears a DS below the enclosure notation (if used) or the reference initials if an enclosure notation is not used. The postscript need not be preceded by the letters *P.S.*

```
1g
   ←DS
I'm having an examination
```

December 10, 19--| Ms. Susan Wachtel, Manager| The Campus Bookstore| 395 Lugo Avenue | Miami, FL 33152-7032 | Dear Ms. Wachtel: | SUBJECT: Damaged Shipment

(¶) Please accept our apology for the damaged shipment of books you received on December 4. If you find it necessary to return any of these books, we shall issue credit on Invoice No. 5976G. Just refer to this letter when returning the books to us.

(¶) Our new representative in your area, Terry Munoz, tells me you will be leaving your present position soon to open your own store. I want to wish you the best of luck in this new venture and to let you know we want to continue to serve you in the future.

Very truly yours, | Doug Simpson | Sales Manager | xx | I'm having an examination copy of Agnew's Reference Manual mailed to you today.

(continued on next page)

LESSON 14

14a ● Keyboard Review

Spacing: Double
Margin: 50-space line

Directions: Keyboard once; repeat.

Posture Goal: Keep fingers deeply curved.

```
  x    sxs sxs xs xs six six lax flax next next flex flex
  p    ;p; ;p; p; p; par part pal pail plan pain tip trip
 b m   bf mj bf mj mail mail best best name names bad bad
  an   an and can man change chance plan plant stand want
all letters   Type with a fixed goal in mind; use sharp strokes.
taught   A job will give you the chance to test your skill.
       |  1  |  2  |  3  |  4  |  5  |  6  |  7  |  8  |  9  | 10  |
```

14b ● Location of Q and , (comma)

Reach to Q
1. Find q on the chart.
2. Find it on your keyboard.
3. Place your fingers over the home keys.
4. Reach to q with the a finger.
5. Touch qa lightly without moving other fingers from their typing position.

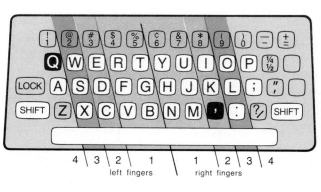

left fingers   right fingers

Reach to , (comma)
1. Find , on the chart.
2. Find it on your keyboard.
3. Place your fingers over the home keys.
4. Reach to , with the k finger.
5. Touch ,k lightly without moving other fingers from their typing position.

```
aqa qa qa quit quit quit        Type twice on same line        k,k k,k ,k rk, irk, irk,
```

Reach to q

Reach to , (comma)

14c ● Location Drills: Q and , (comma)

Directions: Keyboard each line once with your teacher. Repeat the lines again by yourself.

Spacing Guide: Space once after a comma within a sentence.

```
       aqa aqa aqa qa quit quite quiet quills quips equip
  q    pique quilt square quench queen quart quote quotes
       quaint quake quick queue squid squeak equal plaque


       k,k k,k k,k ,k ,k work, rock, broke, trick, truck,
, (comma)   fork, forks, sock, socks, dock, dike, lock, clock,
       kick, choke, steak, rake, kale, king, chock, soak,
```

126c ● Speed Ladder Paragraphs

Directions: 1. Take 1' writings on ¶1 DS until you complete the ¶ in 1'.
2. When you complete ¶1 in 1', continue on to ¶2. Repeat this procedure as you try to complete each of the five ¶s in the given time.

all letters used   1.4 si

	gwam 5'

A wise person once cautioned young people to choose their careers   3 | 55
carefully by explaining to them that going to work will really break up   6 | 58
their day. Although the remark was made in jest, the advice is worth   8 | 61
considering.   9 | 61

Recent studies show that more than two-thirds of all people who   11 | 64
work today are unhappy with what they do. Furthermore, it has been   14 | 67
estimated that the average person can expect to change jobs at least   17 | 69
eight times within his or her lifetime.   19 | 71

Facts such as those above should help you realize the importance   21 | 74
of discovering all that you can about your aptitudes and interests.   24 | 76
One good way to find out more about yourself is through the courses   27 | 79
you take, knowing in which areas you do and don't do well.   29 | 81

Various types of career guidance are being offered at more and more   32 | 84
schools all over the country. Career guidance can help youths a great   35 | 87
deal when it comes to narrowing down their interests. You can even get   37 | 90
help from computers that ask questions about your skills and talents.   40 | 93

What you are interested in and what you are good at are not always   43 | 95
the same thing. Your interests may change; what you are interested in   46 | 98
today may not predict what you will want to do in the future. You may   49 | 101
have an incorrect opinion of your own abilities, too; it can be either   52 | 104
too high or too low.   53 | 105

gwam 5' | 1 | 2 | 3 |

126d ● Language Arts Skills: Composing at Your Machine

Directions: Compose a paragraph, telling what the following quotation means to you.

"There are no elevators in the house of success."

14d ● Technique Builder

Directions: Keyboard each line twice SS; then keyboard 1-minute writings on the last three lines.

Technique Goal: Do not look from the copy to the typewriter and back again. Keep eyes on copy at all times.

space once after a comma within a sentence

1 qa ,k qa ,k qa ,k quit, qualm, quip, quite, squeal
2 quick, quill, queen, quotes, qualms, quilt, quench
3 to quote, to quit, the quick, the queen, the quilt
4 I was quick to quote the girls with the red quilt.
5 Drive right, as the life you save may be your own.
6 As you type, use quick, short, firm, sure strokes.
7 We can gain the high skills we need for this work.

| 1 | 2 | 3 | 4 | 5 | 6 | 7 | 8 | 9 | 10 |

14e ● Paragraph Skill Builder

Directions: Set tab for a 5-space indention. Keyboard the ¶ DS once for practice; then take three 1-minute writings on it. Figure *gwam* on the best writing.

gwam 1'

tab———▶It is said that they who sling mud must give   9
ground. There is much truth in these words. You   19
will lose more than you gain when you give way to   29
the use of words and thoughts that are too harsh.   39

| 1 | 2 | 3 | 4 | 5 | 6 | 7 | 8 | 9 | 10 |

LESSON 15

Spacing: Double
Margin: 50-space line

15a ● Keyboard Review

Directions: Keyboard once; repeat.

Technique Goal: Wrists low and still.

q | aqa aqa qa qa quit quits quote quotes quart quarts
, (comma) | k,k k,k ,k ,k work, all, fork, fill, dark, squall,
x p | xs p; xs p; tax tax box box up up group group keep
he | he he she she held held the them these their there
all letters taught | Jan was told to quickly mark a box with a red pen.
 | I will have to buy two new math guides for school.

| 1 | 2 | 3 | 4 | 5 | 6 | 7 | 8 | 9 | 10 |

125c ● Problem Typing: Business Letters with Special Features

An attention line is used to direct a letter to a particular person. The attention line may appear as the second line of the letter address, or it may appear a DS below the letter address. Type the attention line immediately below the company name on the envelope.

```
Edgar and Pauls, Inc.
Attention Miss Alice Pauls
3294 Belmont Drive
Cleveland, OH  44131-1037
                        ←DS
Ladies and Gentlemen
```

```
Edgar and Pauls, Inc.
3294 Belmont Drive
Cleveland, OH  44131-1037
                        ←DS
Attention Miss Alice Pauls
                        ←DS
Ladies and Gentlemen
```

When a subject line is used in a letter, it appears on the second line below the salutation. It may be centered on the line, or it may be typed at the left margin as shown.

```
Mrs. Mary Hatch
1501 East Starlight Drive
Pine Bluff, AR  71603-9371
                     ←DS
Dear Mrs. Hatch
                     ←DS
SUBJECT:  Policy No. SH 34 87
```

Directions: Problem 1 Business Letter with Attention Line

1. Keyboard/format the letter below in block style with mixed punctuation. Set margins for a 60-space line; begin the dateline on line 18.

2. Address a large envelope.

June 12, 19-- | Edgar and Pauls, Inc. | Attention Miss Alice Pauls | 3294 Belmont Drive | Cleveland, OH 44131-1037 | Ladies and Gentlemen:

(¶) In order for me to take appropriate action in handling the accident claim of Mr. George Blackburn, I must receive a complete accident report from you by June 20. A complete copy of the accident file is enclosed.

(¶) I recommend that you get in touch with the Blackburn family, as well as any other passengers in the Blackburn car at the time of the accident. Please determine from them the extent of any injuries they may have sustained as a result of the accident.

(¶) With the assistance of your thorough service, I should be able to reach a final decision in early July.

Very truly yours, | George A. Eckenrod | Claims Department | xx | Enclosure

Directions: Problem 2 Business Letter with Subject Line

1. Keyboard/format the letter below in modified block style with open punctuation. Set margins for a 50-space line; begin the dateline on line 18.

2. Address a small envelope.

May 15, 19-- | Mrs. Mary Hatch | 1501 East Starlight Drive | Pine Bluff, AR 71603-9371 | Dear Mrs. Hatch | SUBJECT: Policy No. SH 34 87

(¶) Your homeowner's policy listed above is due to expire on July 1.

(¶) According to your present contract, your principal dwelling at 1501 East Starlight Drive is insured for $135,000. You also have $50,000 additional coverage on your farm property located at 2343 Sybil Road. This optional coverage secures your farm equipment as well as the two frame buildings on the premises.

(¶) All these amounts appear to be adequate, based on the current information in our files. If you have made any changes in the past year that you think should alter these figures, pleae let me know so we can provide for them in the renewal contract.

Sincerely | WARREN INSURANCE COMPANY | Wilfred S. Mallios | Agent | xx

LESSON 126

70-space line

126a ● Keyboard Review

Directions: Keyboard each sentence three times SS. DS between 3-line groups.

alphabet	Dozens of bombs exploded high over the quaint city just as dawn broke.
figure	The Japanese constructed 31,900 operating robot installations by 1983.
left hand	Sweet tastes were decreased as excess treats were served as a dessert.
easy	If you get some bumps, it is a sign you are traveling out of your rut.

| 1 | 2 | 3 | 4 | 5 | 6 | 7 | 8 | 9 | 10 | 11 | 12 | 13 | 14 |

126b ● Skill Comparison

Directions: Take three 1' writings each on 102b, page 171, and 124c, page 204. Figure *gwam*; compare your script and rough-draft copy rates.

15b ● Location of Z and ? (question mark)

Reach to Z

1. Find z on the chart.
2. Find it on your keyboard.
3. Place your fingers over the home keys.
4. Reach to z with the a finger.
5. Touch za lightly without moving other fingers from their typing position.

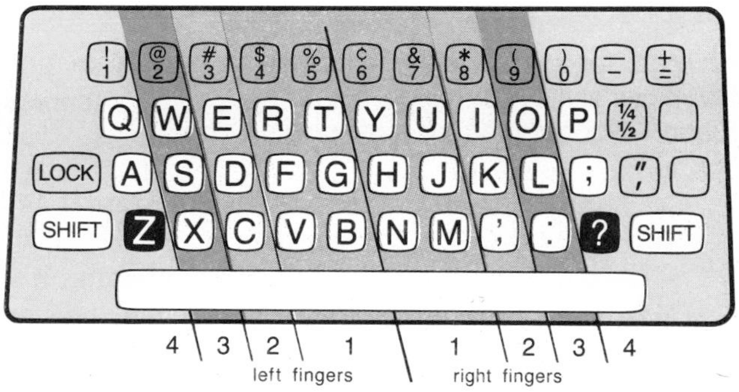

Reach to ? (question mark)

1. Find ? on the chart.
2. Find it on your keyboard.
3. Place your fingers over the home keys.
4. Reach to ? with the ; finger.
5. Hold down left shift key as you reach your right little finger to the question mark.

```
aza za za zone zone zone          ;?; ?; ;?; ?;? Why? Why?
```

Type twice on same line

15c ● Location Drills: Z and ? (question mark)

Reach to z

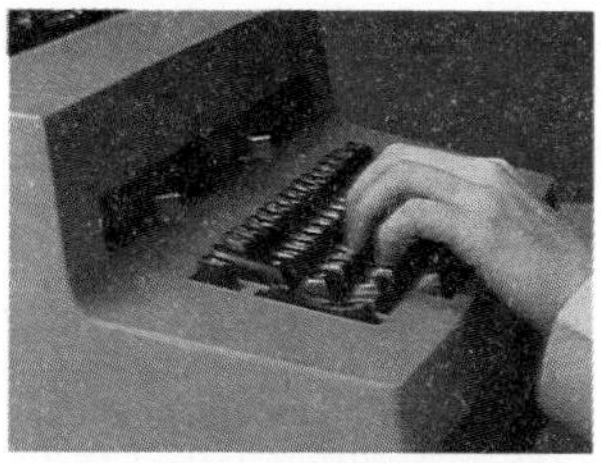

Reach to ? (question mark)

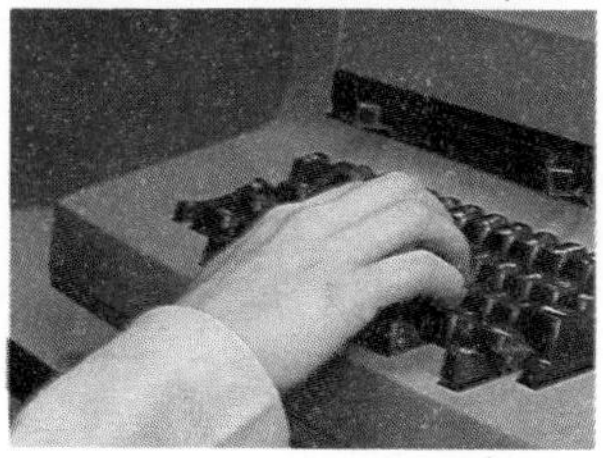

Directions: Keyboard once with your teacher. Repeat again by yourself.

Technique Goal: Reach to the shift key without moving your arms or wrists.

```
  aza aza aza za za za zone zones zero zip zeal zinc
z zoo size maze maze gaze graze doze quiz quiz froze
  haze haze lazy prize prize raze raze razing dozing

  ;?; ;?; ;?; ?; ?; ?; Is it?  Can they go?  Why go?
? Can he tell them how? or why?  Whom will she take?
```

space once — space twice

15d ● Technique Builder

Spacing Guide
Space twice after a question mark at the end of a sentence; space once after a question mark within a sentence.

Directions: Keyboard each line two times. Take three 1′ writings on the ¶ below.

Technique Goal: Hold shift key down; release it quickly. Try to keep a steady, even pace.

```
1 za ?; za ?; What zinc?  Who froze it?  Whose zone?
2 Does Jorge know?  When can Pam come?  Is Zak sure?
3 Can we go?  Is this the zone?  Was the prize here?
4 Do you want Steve to get the prize in May or June?
  | 1 | 2 | 3 | 4 | 5 | 6 | 7 | 8 | 9 | 10 |
```

gwam 1′

```
     Now that you know where to find each of the     9
keys, your job is to work hard and learn to type    18
well.  This is a goal that all of you can reach.    28
| 1 | 2 | 3 | 4 | 5 | 6 | 7 | 8 | 9 | 10 |
```

124d ● Problem Typing: Business Letters with Enclosure Notations

Directions: Problem 1

1. Keyboard/format the letter below in modified block style with mixed punctuation. Set margins for a 50-space

line; begin dateline on line 18.

2. Address a large envelope.

```
Miss Sandra Black
Sales Representative
    ←DS
jp←DS
Enclosures
```

An enclosure notation is used when some item (or items) is sent with a letter. The notation appears at the left margin a DS below the reference initials. If two or more items are enclosed, use the plural **Enclosures**.

November 10, 19--| Dr. Joel Bluestein | 146 Tulip Road | Nashville, TN 38109-2740| Dear Dr. Bluestein:

(¶) Thank you for your generous contribution to the Big Brothers/Big Sisters of Nashville. Your continued support will help us greatly in our efforts to maintain a quality program with reduced public funds.

(¶) In the Nashville area, approximately 20 percent of one-parent youths are urgently in need of adult guidance. A Big Brother or a Big Sister can help these young people over some of the rough spots encountered in growing up without mothers or fathers.

(¶) Please accept the enclosed membership certificate as a token of our appreciation for your assistance.

Very truly yours,| James M. Wong| Executive Director| xx| Enclosure

Directions: Problem 2

1. Keyboard/format the letter below in block style with open punctuation. Set margins for a 50-space line; begin dateline

on line 18.

2. Address a large envelope.

If necessary, see directions for addressing large envelopes on page 87.

October 14, 19--| Mr. Mario Silvio | 117 Delta Drive | Charleston, WV | 25312-6974| Dear Mr. Silvio

(¶) It was good to see you at the automation conference last weekend. I hope the enclosed materials will answer some of the questions you asked at the conference.

(¶) Our SR-20 letter quality printer will do an excellent job for you. In addition to printing in six different colors, this model allows you to choose from many styles of daisy wheels and ribbons. It is also extremely quiet, a feature often difficult to find in daisy wheel printers.

(¶) I'll plan to stop by next Tuesday afternoon, after you have a chance to study the complete description of the printer more thoroughly.

Very truly yours| Miss Sandra Black| Sales Representative| xx| Enclosures

LESSON 125

70-space line

5 minutes

125a ● Keyboard Review

Directions: Keyboard each line three times SS. DS between 3-line groups.

return carriage quickly

alphabet	Few know Blanca Munoz has very little equity in that adjoining duplex.
figure	The 985A jet can cruise at 620 miles per hour for the 7,143 mile trip.
adjacent key	We were quite sure that we saw several more lions there near the pool.
easy	He should use the turn signal when moving over to the right hand lane.

| 1 | 2 | 3 | 4 | 5 | 6 | 7 | 8 | 9 | 10 | 11 | 12 | 13 | 14 |

10 minutes

125b ● Timed Writings

Directions: 1. Take a 1' writing on each paragraph of 121c, page 198, *or* take a 5'

writing on all paragraphs combined. Circle errors; figure *gwam*.

Unit 2 ■ Improving Your Keyboarding Techniques (Lessons 16–20)

General Directions

Use a 50-space line for all lessons in this unit (center − 25; center + 25 + 5). SS sentences and drill lines. DS between repeated groups of lines. DS paragraph copy. Set tabulator for a 5-space paragraph indention.

Practice time is given for each section of a lesson in this unit. If it seems best to vary the schedule, do so with the approval of your teacher.

LESSON 16

7 minutes   **16a ● Keyboard Review**

Directions: Keyboard each line twice SS. DS between 2-line groups.

sit erect; feet flat on floor

```
z   aza aza za za zeal zones doze quiz maze graze zest
?   ;?; ;?; ?; ?; Who?  When?  How many?  Is she here?
ou  our four found house south though course out doubt
    Jack expects to take the very hard quiz in August.
    Only some boys and girls will take it before then.
```
alphabet

```
|  1  |  2  |  3  |  4  |  5  |  6  |  7  |  8  |  9  | 10  |
```

---

5 minutes   **16b ● Technique Builder: Typing Whole Words**

Directions: Keyboard each line as your teacher dictates SS. DS between 2-line groups.

think and type whole words

```
1  to to do do to do to do if if he he if he if he is
2  it it is is it is it is if it is if it is if it is
3  go go to go to go if it is to go if it is to go to
4  he the she to the if she if it is she if it is the
```

---

13 minutes   **16c ● Sentence Skill Builder**

Directions: Keyboard each sentence two times; then take a 1′ timed writing on each sentence. Figure your *gwam*.

type short easy words as a whole

```
1  If he is to do this job for us, he must do it now.
2  I say that any job she and I do will be done well.
3  If they are to go there, they can do all the work.
4  To type right, she must think each word she types.
5  He can do the drill right if he types whole words.
```

```
|  1  |  2  |  3  |  4  |  5  |  6  |  7  |  8  |  9  | 10  |
```

Directions: Problem 3

1. Keyboard/format the letter shown below in block style with open punctuation. Set margins for a 50-space line; begin the

dateline on line 18.

2. Address a small envelope.

January 10, 19--| Mrs. Janice Arrants| 2190 North Princeton Street| Portland, OR 97203-7055| Dear Mrs. Arrants

(¶) Thank you for your check. It pays your loan in full. I want to compliment you on the prompt manner in which you handled this account.

(¶) Now that we are well acquainted, the First Citizens Bank is the logical place to come whenever you may again be in need of extra cash. We hope, too, that you will consider opening a savings account with us in the near future. An account can be started with as little as five dollars or as much as you desire.

(¶) Please stop in soon. We shall be happy to serve you.

Yours very truly| FIRST CITIZENS BANK| Lloyd Johnson| Manager| xx

LESSON 124

70-space line

124a ● Keyboard Review

5 minutes

Directions: Keyboard each line 3 times SS. DS between 3-line groups.

keep wrists and arms quiet

alphabet	Julie knew by the quizzical expression on my face that I had given up.
figure	A plane speed record of 266.59 miles an hour was set November 4, 1923.
combination	if they see, if they look, if they wear, if they jump, if they address
easy	People should realize there is nothing much busier than an idle rumor.

| 1 | 2 | 3 | 4 | 5 | 6 | 7 | 8 | 9 | 10 | 11 | 12 | 13 | 14 |

124b ● Language Arts Skills: Number Expression Guides

5 minutes

Directions: Keyboard each sentence 3 times. The first sentence gives the rule; the remaining sentences apply the rule.

1 Amounts of money, either dollars or cents, should by typed in figures.

2 If you want the books, too, the cost of the set is $17.50, not $14.39.

3 Please buy four $4.50 tickets, four $5.50 tickets, and two $6 tickets.

124c ● Skill Builder from Rough Draft Copy

5 minutes

Directions: Take four 1' writings on the paragraph; keyboard for control.

1.3 si

words

If you are looking for an unusual hoby, you might consider try keeping bees. Bee keeping maybe thought of as an academic hobby. It is easy to think of bees as people, since they have a habit of storing far more honey than they ever use. Like people, they work hard gathering wealth they don't have a need for.

15
29
42
55
66

16d ● Proofreading Your Work

Directions: Some common typing errors are listed below to help you locate and mark each of your own errors.

As you read each error description, note circled examples to the right.

1. Circle the whole word containing an error. Count one error to a word.
2. A cut-off capital letter is an error.
3. Failure to space between words is an error.
4. A missing stroke is an error.
5. A wrong letter or a strikeover is an error.
6. An omitted or added word is an error.
7. An incorrect or omitted punctuation mark is an error.

(Hole) your (rist) low and stil
(Do) not arch or move them up and
(thekeys). (Youcan) learn to type r
Keep (y ur) eyes on this book
drills. Do (mot) look at the (keys)
                    @
be able to gain˄high rate if (if)
you (peck,)

The syllable intensity (si) is given for the ¶s below. It is a guide to the difficulty of the material. Copy of average difficulty has an si of 1.5. The material in these ¶s is rated easy.

16e ● Continuity Practice

Directions: Keyboard the copy below one time DS; circle your errors. Take a 1'

writing on each ¶. Try to make fewer errors.

type without pauses

	gwam 1'	total words
1.0 si		
Hold your wrists low and still as you type.	9	9
Do not arch or move them up and down as you strike	19	19
the keys. You can learn to type right.	27	27
Keep your eyes on this book as you type the	9	36
drills. Do not look at the keys, as you will not	19	46
be able to gain a high rate if you must peek as	28	55
you peck.	30	57

| 1 | 2 | 3 | 4 | 5 | 6 | 7 | 8 | 9 | 10 |

Set the ribbon control lever.

16f ● Adjusting the Ribbon-Control Lever   3 minutes

Directions: 1. Look to see if your typewriter has a ribbon-control lever (No. 31).
2. If it does, set the ribbon-control lever to type on the upper portion of the ribbon.

3. Note the position of the ribbon-control lever.
4. If you are using a machine with a ribbon-control lever, check at the beginning of a lesson to see that it is in the proper position.

F. J. Schauf & Company

2709 Menlo Avenue
San Diego, CA   92105-5534
Tel: (619) 284-6166

An Information
Network Center

50-space line; open punctuation

words

April 5, 19-- ←——begin on line 18   3
                  return 4 times

letter address   Ms. Tricia Hoffman   7
                  H & S Distributors   10
                  908 Tamarindo Way   14
                  Chula Vista, CA   92011-5097   20
                                      DS

salutation   Dear Ms. Hoffman   23
                                      DS
body   Thank you for inquiring about the charges for an   33
                  information search at F. J. Schauf & Company.   42

                  A search at F. J. Schauf & Company can be surpris-   52
                  ingly inexpensive. Simple topics can be searched   62
                  for as little as $30. More complex searches may   72
                  cost as much as $100 or more. Charges are based   82
                  on actual computer costs, plus our service fee.   92

                  Our job is to help you shape your questions so you   102
                  can be assured the best results at a minimum cost.   112

                  Please call if I may be of further assistance.   122
                                                              DS
complimentary   Very truly yours   125
close   DS
company name in   F. J. SCHAUF & COMPANY   130
closing lines   return 4 times

typed name   William E. Rice   133
official title   Assistant Manager   137
                                  DS
reference initials   sr   137

Business letter in block style

LESSON 17

17a ● Keyboard Review

7 minutes

Directions: Keyboard each line twice SS. DS between 2-line groups.

keep eyes on copy; sit erect

```
n   jnj jnj nj nj no not note need test text knew know
t   ftf ftf tf tf to tone tune tack take ton torn this
er  here other were where serve order there ever every
    Axel made a very quick trip to the Azores in July.
alphabet  We saw a large fleet of boats in the small harbor.
    | 1 | 2 | 3 | 4 | 5 | 6 | 7 | 8 | 9 | 10 |
```

17b ● Technique Builder: Typing Whole Words

14 minutes

Directions: Keyboard each line three times SS. DS between 3-line groups.

type short words as a whole

```
1  I am to work as fast as I can to get the job done.
2  Your form has a big part in how well you can type.
3  She can go to the lake to see me work on the dock.
4  Can we take a train to the game if our team plays?
   | 1 | 2 | 3 | 4 | 5 | 6 | 7 | 8 | 9 | 10 |
```

17c ● Continuity Practice

10 minutes

Directions: Keyboard the copy below DS; circle all errors. Repeat.

Use the 1' column at right and the 1' scale underneath the ¶s to figure your 1' rate. Use the 2' column and scale to figure your 2' rate.

```
all letters used  1.0 si                          gwam 1'   2'

    A small car may not have quite as much zip        9   4

as you would like, and you know that it will not     18   9

have room for six or eight of your friends.          27  14

    It will do some good things, though.  It will     9  18

use just half as much gas as a great big car, and    19  23

you will not need to look so far to find a spot to   29  28

park it.                                             31  29

gwam 1' | 1 | 2 | 3 | 4 | 5 | 6 | 7 | 8 | 9 | 10 |
     2' |   1   |   2   |   3   |   4   |   5   |
```

17d ● Sustained Skill Building

14 minutes

Directions: **1.** Keyboard two 1' writings on each ¶ in 17c DS. Circle errors. Figure *gwam*.

2. Take two 2' writings on both ¶s combined. Circle errors. Figure *gwam*. Compare rates on 1' and 2' writings.

123b ● Speed Builder

Directions: Take two 1' writings on each ¶; try to increase speed on the second writing. Figure *gwam*.

Alternate Procedure: Work for speed as you take one 5' writing on all four ¶s combined. Figure *gwam*.

all letters used 1.4 si 5.3 awl 85% hfw

	gwam 1'	5'
Eventually, you will have to face the question about the kind of	13	3	49
career you will follow. You may have been advised already to choose a	27	5	52
career while you are still in school so that you can get ready for it.	42	8	55
Almost all jobs require some special training. Hopefully, you will	55	11	58
realize this fact before it is too late.	63	13	60
Just dreaming lazily about a career is not sufficient. Examine	13	15	62
yourself carefully. What can you do best? What do you enjoy doing?	27	18	65
Your parents and teachers have urged you to make a careful choice, and	41	21	68
then resolve to be the best in your field. This is wise advice. There	55	24	71
is room in any area if you are good enough.	64	26	72
As a general rule, you will be smart to avoid the trap that often	13	28	75
awaits those who know a little bit about a lot of things but not much	27	31	78
about anything in particular. The world has enough people like that.	41	34	81
Thousands of careers are available to almost anyone who wishes to	13	37	83
enter them. The problem is to discover the one that you can do well	27	39	86
and that you enjoy doing. If you cannot do it well, you'll fail. If	41	42	89
you dislike it, you'll miss one of the thrills life holds for you. You	55	45	92
certainly must select your career with care.	64	47	94

gwam 1' | 1 | 2 | 3 | 4 | 5 | 6 | 7 | 8 | 9 | 10 | 11 | 12 | 13 | 14 |
     5' | 1 | 2 | 3 |

123c ● Problem Typing: Business Letters in Block Style

Directions: Problem 1

1. Prepare a copy of the model letter shown on page 203.
2. Prepare the letter in block style with open punctuation. Set margins for a 50- space line; begin the dateline on line 18.
3. Address a small envelope. If a workbook is not available, use a small envelope or paper cut to size (6½ × 3⅝").

Directions: Problem 2

Retype the letter in Problem 1, but address the letter to:

Mrs. Marilyn Chmelka
10802 Ruggles Circle
Omaha, NE 68164-5743

Supply an appropriate salutation. Address a small envelope.

(continued on page 204)

LESSON 18

18a ● Keyboard Review

7 minutes **Directions:** Keyboard each line twice SS. DS between 2-line group.

keep eyes
on copy

```
b   bfb bfb bf bf bid bind bow bowl ban band bit built
p   ;p; ;p; p; p; par part up upon put post paid press
re  are care free great green press real red rest sure
    His new job in Mexico will require pluck and zeal.
alphabet
    I hope that Godfrey may receive her expert advice.
    |  1  |  2  |  3  |  4  |  5  |  6  |  7  |  8  |  9  | 10 |
```

18b ● Technique Builder: Typing Whole Words

5 minutes

Directions: Keyboard each line twice as your teacher dictates SS. DS between 2-line groups.

Do not type the lines between words.

think and
type whole
words

```
1  he|she|he did|she did|she did|she did it|I did the

2  and|and I|and if she|and if the|and if I|and if he

3  for|for|it is|it is|for it|for it is|for it is the

4  do|go|do go|do go to|and go|and do go|and do go to
```

18c ● Sentence Guided Writings

15 minutes

Directions: 1. Keyboard each sentence once for practice.
2. Take a 1′ writing with the call of the guide each 20″. Try to complete each sentence as the guide is called. (Your teacher will tell you how the guide will be called.)
3. Take two 1′ writings on the last sentence without the call of the guide.

		words in line	gwam 20″
keep arms and
wrists quiet

```
1  Work to the call of the guide.                        6   18

2  Sit erect if you wish to type well.                   7   21

3  Type with a keen mind and quick strokes.              8   24

4  Try to raise your rate by one word each line.         9   27

5  When work takes the place of words, we gain skill.   10   30
   |  1  |  2  |  3  |  4  |  5  |  6  |  7  |  8  |  9  | 10 |
```

Directions: Problem 1

1. Prepare a copy of the model letter shown on page 200.

2. Prepare the letter in modified block style with mixed punctuation. Set margins for a 50-space line; begin the dateline on line 18.

Directions: Problem 2

1. Keyboard/format the letter shown below in modified block style with mixed punctuation. Set margins for a 50-space

3. Address a small envelope. Envelopes are printed on the back of the letterhead paper in the workbook. If a workbook is not available, use a small envelope or paper cut to small envelope size (6½″ × 3⅝″).

line; begin the dateline on line 18.

2. Address a small envelope

	words
July 10, 19--	3
Mr. Robert Olivo	6
Public Works Director	11
819 Taylor Street	14
Fort Worth, TX 76102-3827	20
Dear Mr. Olivo:	23

Yesterday afternoon during a layover at Stapleton Airport in Denver, I happened to view a film made by the city of Fort Worth devoted to the problem of refuse collection in various cities. — 33 43 53 61

The film would be excellent for our public relations program in Greensboro because it provides a good explanation of different methods of waste disposal. — 72 81 92

If the film is available for rent or purchase, I would very much appreciate learning how I might order a copy. — 102 111 114

Sincerely yours, — 118

Note: In this letter and the remaining letters in the book, use your initials for the *xx* shown in the problem copy.

xx

Miss Nancy Enloe — 121
City Manager — 124

124

LESSON 123

70-space line

5 minutes

123a ● Keyboard Review

Directions: Keyboard each sentence three times SS. DS between 3-line groups.

keep your eyes on the copy as you return the carriage

alphabet A just, quick, but exact mind will help you develop a zest for living.

figure On June 30, 1899, Charles C. Murphy bicycled a mile in 57 4/5 seconds.

weak fingers I saw we were lax and had acquired lazy habits playing weak opponents.

easy The pitch that I missed was thrown right down the middle of the plate.

| 1 | 2 | 3 | 4 | 5 | 6 | 7 | 8 | 9 | 10 | 11 | 12 | 13 | 14 |

18d ● Continuity Practice

Directions: Keyboard both ¶s DS. Circle all errors. Repeat.

all letters used   1.1 si   *gwam* 1' | 2'

	gwam 1'	2'
It will pay you to think and type some of the	9	5
words in this copy as a whole. Just read and type	19	10
them as units. Do not spell them as you type.	29	14
Use quick, short, sharp strokes. Keep your	9	19
wrists low and firm. Relax, but sit erect. Have	19	24
a clear goal in mind; then work with zeal. You	28	29
can learn to type right.	33	31

gwam 1' | 1 | 2 | 3 | 4 | 5 | 6 | 7 | 8 | 9 | 10 |
     2' | 1 | 2 | 3 | 4 | 5 |

---

10 minutes   **18e ● Sustained Skill Building**

Directions: Keyboard a 1' writing on each ¶ in 18d. Figure *gwam*. Try to equal your 1' rate as you take two 2' writings on both ¶s combined.

LESSON 19   50-space line

7 minutes   **19a ● Keyboard Review**

Directions: Keyboard each line twice SS. DS between 2-line groups.

keep fingers
deeply curved

y   jyj jyj yj yj yet year you your yes yarn yearn eye
q   aqa aqa qa qa quart quire squire square quiet quit
nd   end send find land hand found friend second window

alphabet   Liz is quite right; I can do this wax job for Kim.
Paula will help you move their car out of the sun.

| 1 | 2 | 3 | 4 | 5 | 6 | 7 | 8 | 9 | 10 |

---

15 minutes   **19b ● Sentence Guided Writings**

Directions: 1. Keyboard each sentence once for practice.
2. Take a 1' writing on each sentence with the call of the guide each 20".
3. Take two 1' writings on the last sentence without the call of the guide.

	words in line	gwam 20"
return quickly; do not pause		
1 Do the job as well as you can.	6	18
2 *Hard work is the secret of success.*	7	21
3 Plan your work right if you wish to win.	8	24
4 *Plan to make some gain in your work each day.*	9	27
5 Now is the day to do these lines in the right way.	10	30

F. J. Schauf & Company

2709 Menlo Avenue
San Diego, CA 92105-5534
Tel: (619) 284-6166

*An Information
Network Center*

50-space line; mixed punctuation

	words
center point	
begin on line 18 → March 30, 19--	3
return 4 times	

letter address

Mr. Gilbert Gonzalez	5
United Services, Inc.	11
3419 Marian Way	15
San Diego, CA 92110-1310	20

DS

salutation Dear Mr. Gonzalez: 24

DS

body I am pleased to respond to your inquiry about the   34
services we provide at F. J. Schauf & Company.   43

DS

At F. J. Schauf & Company we can locate information   54
on virtually any topic. Because we have a wealth   64
of information available in the form of statistics,   74
reports, forecasts, news items, and directories,   84
we can tailor a search to your specifications.   94

DS

A search by Schauf & Company is fast and thorough,   104
enabling us to find in minutes what might otherwise   114
take hours or even days.   119

DS

If you need more information, please give me a call.   130

DS

complimentary
close   center point ⟶ Sincerely yours,   134

return 4 times

typed name and   Ms. Karen Brooks, Manager   139
official title   DS

reference initials sr   139

Business letter in modified block style

19c ● **Continuity Practice**

Directions: Keyboard the ¶ below DS. Circle all errors. As you repeat the exercise, try to make fewer errors.

all letters used 1.1 si   *gwam* 2' | 3'

		4		8			

return carriage quickly; resume typing at once

```
          .                 4            .            8
   If you want to add some zest to what could      4 |  3 | 22
        .          12          .              16        .
well turn out to be a dull summer, here are some   9 |  6 | 25
        20          .          24          .          28
quick ideas.  You can wax floors, mow lawns, make  14 |  9 | 28
        .          32          .          36          .
and sell jewelry or other crafts, sit with kids,   19 | 13 | 32
        40          .          44
cats, dogs, and birds, or even keep watch on a     24 | 16 | 35
    48          .          52          .          56
house on your street when the owners are away.     28 | 19 | 38
```

gwam 2' | 1 | 2 | 3 | 4 | 5 |
     3' | 1 | 2 | 3 | 4 . |

19d ● **Sustained Skill Building**

Directions: **1.** Take one 1' writing on the ¶ in 19c DS.
2. Circle all errors; figure *gwam*. Take one 2' and one 3' writing on the same ¶.

To figure *gwam* on the 1' writing, use the nearest figure above the copy from which you typed. For the 2' and 3' writings, use the columns and scales to figure *gwam*.

fingers deeply curved

hands upright over keys

LESSON 20

50-space line

20a ● **Keyboard Review**

Directions: Keyboard each line twice SS. DS between 2-line groups.

curve fingers; not wrists

x   sxs sxs xs xs lax lax mix mix fix fix box axe axle

p   ;p; ;p; p; p; play play plate plate plan plan pray

to to too told took top touch toward town total today

The two boys saw the young zebra near the big dam.

alphabet Jack Quay may get a prize for his next pole vault.

| 1 | 2 | 3 | 4 | 5 | 6 | 7 | 8 | 9 | 10 · |

LESSON 122

5 minutes

122a ● Keyboard Review

Directions: Keyboard each sentence three times SS. DS between 3-line groups.

reach with fingers;
keep hands and wrists
quiet

alphabet I'm amazed to know the fall gym party and major banquet are exclusive.

figure More than 6,000 people left between June 25, 1897, and March 24, 1923.

long reach Myrna succeeded in observing many subtle colors on a bright sunny day.

easy Change the shape of the figure and you can have it placed right there.

| 1 | 2 | 3 | 4 | 5 | 6 | 7 | 8 | 9 | 10 | 11 | 12 | 13 | 14 |

---

10 minutes

122b ● Skill Builder

Directions: 1. Take a 1' writing on the ¶ below. The last word typed will be your goal word.
2. Take a 5' writing with the return called after each minute. When the return is called, start the paragraph over again. Try to reach your goal each minute as the return is called.

1.3 si

Here is an exercise anybody can do quickly before playing tennis or zipping around the jogging track. Lie flat on your back and bend your knees. Using your arms, bring your knees to your chest. Slowly raise your head and shoulders off the floor toward your knees. Hold a few seconds before returning to your original position.

---

30 minutes

122c ● Problem Typing: Business Letters

General Information

Letter Styles: With slight variations, the modified block style shown on page 200 is the most commonly used style for business letters. Another style growing in usage is the block style illustrated on page 203.

Punctuation Styles: Two commonly used punctuation styles are open and mixed. In *open* punctuation, no punctuation marks are used after the salutation or the complimentary close. In *mixed* punctuation, a colon is placed after the salutation and a comma after the complimentary close.

Vertical Placement of Dateline: Vertical placement of the date varies with the length of the letter. However, for short to average business letters the date is placed on line 18. The address begins on the 4th line space (3 blank spaces) below the date.

Margins: The line length used for business letters varies according to the number of words in the letter. A 50-space line works well for most short letters; a 60-space line works well for most average-length letters. Or, if you prefer, set 2" side margins for a short letter, 1½" side margins for an average-length letter, or 1" side margins for a long letter.

Titles in Addresses: As a mark of courtesy to the person to whom a letter is addressed, you may use a personal or professional title on a letter, envelope, or card: *Mr. Robert Wertz, Dr. Ann Hendricks.* When a woman's preferred title is unknown, use *Ms.* as the personal title.

Abbreviations: Excessive abbreviations should be avoided. It is preferred, however, to use the two-letter state abbreviation in an address when using a ZIP Code. Leave two spaces between the state abbreviation and the ZIP Code.

Reference Initials: Reference initials of the typist should always be placed two line spaces below the typed name of the writer of the letter at the left margin.

Stationery: Most business letters are prepared on 8½" × 11" stationery that has a letterhead which includes the name and address of the company.

Envelopes: Either large or small envelopes may be used for one-page letters. Large envelopes should be used for two-page letters and in instances where materials are enclosed with the letters.

(continued on page 201)

20b ● Technique Builder: Typing Whole Words

Directions: Keyboard each line twice SS. DS between 2-line groups. Take a 1′ writing on each sentence. Figure *gwam*.

type each word
as a unit, not
letter by letter

1 he she then an and hand go got to torn he she they

2 end lend land fur for form fir firm me men man may

3 go got to torn do down she held did if so also rug

4 her half so is it with did or when than down field

5 I may pay the men to fix the torn fur rug for her.

6 All of the boys ran down the field after the game.

| 1 | 2 | 3 | 4 | 5 | 6 | 7 | 8 | 9 | 10 |

---

10 minutes **20c ● Continuity Practice**

Directions: Keyboard both ¶s twice DS. Repeat if time permits.

all letters used   1.1 si   *gwam* 2′ | 3′

use quick,
sharp strokes

We now know quite a lot about which jobs in   4   3 | 27

life are apt to cause the most stress. As a rule,   10   6 | 30

those which require one to meet and deal with the   15 10 | 34

public each day head the list.   18 12 | 36

    You need to give some extra thought to how you   22 15 | 39

may want to spend your working years. As you will   28 18 | 42

soon learn, the size of your paycheck each month   32 22 | 46

is not the only thing to think about.   36 24 | 48

gwam 2′ | 1 | 2 | 3 | 4 | 5 |
      3′ | 1 | 2 | 3 | 4 |

---

13 minutes **20d ● Sustained Skill Building**

Directions: **1.** Take a 1′ writing on each ¶. Circle errors and figure *gwam* on each writing.

2. Take a 2′ writing and a 3′ writing on the combined ¶s. Circle errors and figure *gwam* on each writing. Try to equal your 1′ rate on these writings.

121c ● Speed Ladder Paragraphs

Directions: 1. Take 1' writings on ¶1 DS until you complete the ¶ in 1'.
2. When you complete ¶1 in 1', continue on to ¶2. Repeat this procedure as you try to complete each of the five ¶s in the time given.

all letters used   1.4 si   *gwam 5'*

	3	55
As you have nearly completed your personal typewriting course, it's well to take a brief glance at what you have accomplished. The fact that you have typed this paragraph proves that some learning must have taken place. | 3 5 8 9 | 55 58 61 62 |

As you have nearly completed your personal typewriting course, it's well to take a brief glance at what you have accomplished. The fact that you have typed this paragraph proves that some learning must have taken place.

The reasons for entering this class likely differed from person to person. Some wanted to type because they felt it would help in their schoolwork. Others had an eye on the future, and they decided typing might be useful in getting a job.

Then, too, some students may have signed up because they felt that learning to operate a typewriter should be fun. Chances are good that they were not disappointed. It is fun to take a class in which you can actually see the results of what you have learned.

No matter what your reasons for taking typing might have been, you are sure to have gained enough basic skill to utilize this new tool to a great extent. The personal-use typist needs to have the same command of techniques as those students who take the class for vocational use.

It has required long hours of practice for you to reach your present level of ability. If you neglect to maintain your speed, it will gradually slip away from you. You have developed a skill that can be of great assistance in the future. Make good use of it in your classes and in your daily life.

gwam 5' | 1 | 2 | 3 |

121d ● Language Arts Skills: Composing at Your Machine

Directions: Compose a paragraph telling what the following quotation means to you.

"If it is to be, it is up to me."

Unit 3 ■ Learning the Figure Keys (Lessons 21–25)

General Directions

Use a 50-space line for all lessons in this unit (center − 25; center + 25 + 5). SS sentences and drill lines. DS between repeated groups of lines. DS paragraph copy. Set tabulator for a 5-space paragraph indention.

LESSON 21

7 minutes

21a ● Keyboard Review

Directions: Keyboard each sentence twice SS. DS between 2-line groups.

quick down-and-in
motion as you strike
the space bar

alphabet
Rex found the quartz in jagged rock in New Mexico.
Burton will pay for the ticket, so save it for me.

easy
She held her head down when she hit the golf ball.
Dick said that he laid the key there on the chair.

| 1 | 2 | 3 | 4 | 5 | 6 | 7 | 8 | 9 | 10 |

---

8 minutes

21b ● Location of 1, 3, and 7

Plan for Learning New Keys

1. Find new key on keyboard chart.
2. Locate key on your typewriter.
3. Place fingers over home keys.
4. Know what finger strikes each key.
5. Watch your finger as you make the reach to the new key.
6. Type each short drill twice on the same line. Be sure to use the correct finger.

In some instances, the lower case l may be used for the number 1. Your instructor will tell you if you can use the letter l.

4 \ 3 \ 2 \ 1   1 \ 2 \ 3 \ 4
left fingers   right fingers

Reach to 3

1. Find 3 on the chart.
2. Find it on your keyboard.
3. Place your fingers over the home keys.

4. Reach to 3 with the d finger.
5. Touch 3d lightly without moving the other fingers from their typing position.
6. Keyboard the drill below twice on the same line.

d3d d3d d3d 3d 3d 3d d3d

Reach to 7

1. Find 7 on the chart.
2. Find it on your keyboard.
3. Place your fingers over the home keys.

4. Reach to 7 with the j finger.
5. Touch 7j lightly without moving the other fingers from their typing position.
6. Keyboard the drill below twice on the same line.

j7j j7j j7j 7j 7j 7j j7j

The lessons in Cycle 4 introduce you to some of the keyboarding/formatting duties performed in a typical business office. Cycle 4 also provides material to help you improve your basic keyboarding skills.

Business Letters: The two basic letter styles introduced in Cycle 2 (block style and modified block style) are again presented in Cycle 4, this time as they are commonly used in business correspondence. You will learn how to format letters of different lengths so that they are placed properly on the page.

Business Forms: Interoffice memorandums and invoices are introduced in Unit 16.

Improving Basic Skills: By this time you have acquired considerable keyboarding speed and control. Increases in speed do not come so rapidly now as they did early in the year. The skill-building material provided in this cycle will put the finishing touches on your keyboarding skill.

Extra-Credit Assignments: Problems are given at the end of units for students who finish early and wish extra credit.

Unit 15 ■ Learning to Format Business Letters (Lessons 121–130)

General Directions

Use a 70-space line (center − 35; center + 35 + 5) for drills and timed writings in this unit. SS sentences and drill lines. DS paragraph copy. Much of the problem copy that you will keyboard will be set in lines either longer or shorter than those for which your margins are set. It will be necessary for you to listen for the bell, use the margin release, and divide long words coming at the ends of lines.

Your teacher will tell you whether or not to correct errors when formatting problems. As your teacher directs, prepare the problems on special forms provided in the workbook or on plain paper.

LESSON 121

5 minutes

121a ● Keyboard Review

Directions: Keyboard each sentence three times SS. DS between 3-line groups.

begin slowly;
increase speed
as you repeat
the sentences

alphabet	Pale, excited men inquired about a few objects hovering in a hazy sky.
figure	The 27 students in Room 139 raised a total of $46.85 during the drive.
s/w	Shrewd witnesses will wisely swear they saw shadows on the white snow.
easy	It is not right to talk when your mouth is full or your head is empty.

| 1 | 2 | 3 | 4 | 5 | 6 | 7 | 8 | 9 | 10 | 11 | 12 | 13 | 14 |

10 minutes

121b ● Speed Ladder Sentences

Directions: Take two 1' writings on each sentence. Your teacher will call the guide at 15", 12", or 10" intervals. As time permits, repeat sentences on which you were not able to complete a line with the call of the guide.

		guide 15"	12"	10"
1	Decide what level of skill you believe you can acquire.	44	55	66
2	Be determined to attain the level you have set for yourself.	48	60	72
3	During every practice session, keep this goal fixed in your mind.	52	65	78
4	If you heed these suggestions, your typing ability is sure to improve.	56	70	84

| 1 | 2 | 3 | 4 | 5 | 6 | 7 | 8 | 9 | 10 | 11 | 12 | 13 | 14 |

21c ● Location Drills 3, 7, and 1

Directions: Keyboard each line twice SS. DS between 2-line groups.

Reach to 3

Reach to 7

3
d3d d3d d3d 3d 3d 3d 33 days, 333 hours, 33 and 33
Give us 333 feet. Take 3,333 gallons. I have 33.

7
j7j j7j j7j 7j 7j 7j 77 jars, 77 jolts, 77 and 777
Send 77 sets. Paint 777 frames. Ship 7,777 pens.

1
ala ala ala la la la 11 ages, 11 after, 11 and 111
We won 111 games in 11 years. I went 111.1 miles.

number
fluency
I sent you 33 feet of wire and 77 pounds of nails.
Only 37 of the 73 boys were at the game on May 13.
| 1 | 2 | 3 | 4 | 5 | 6 | 7 | 8 | 9 | 10 |

---

6 minutes **21d ● Technique Builder**

Directions: Keyboard each line three times SS. DS between 3-line groups.

do not pause
before or after
the return

1 and I│and go│and look│and grade│and limp│and right

2 to jump│to show│to start│to save│to have│to regard

3 the fee│the boy│the man│the date│the rest│the time

---

12 minutes **21e ● Continuity Practice**

Directions: Keyboard both ¶s DS. Circle   no more than four errors per writing.
all errors. Repeat the exercise. Try to make

all letters used   1.1 si   gwam 1'   3'

keep your eyes
on the copy

	gwam 1'	3'
When you sit down to type each day, take a	9	3 | 33
second or so to decide just what it is you want	18	6 | 36
to do. Your goal may be to improve your stroking	28	9 | 39
speed, or it may be to make fewer errors than you	38	13 | 43
made the last time.	42	14 | 44
One thing we know for sure is that you will do	9	17 | 47
your best if you work on only one skill at a time.	20	21 | 51
It is quite hard to make your fingers fly and still	30	24 | 54
have all the words come out right. When you zip	40	27 | 57
along, you can expect to make a few mistakes.	49	30 | 60

gwam 1' | 1 | 2 | 3 | 4 | 5 | 6 | 7 | 8 | 9 | 10 |
3' | 1 | 2 | 3 |

CYCLE FOUR

Introduction to Business Communications

LESSON 22

22a ● Keyboard Review

7 minutes

Directions: Keyboard each line twice SS. DS between 2-line groups.

keep arms and
wrists quiet

alphabet

Requiring better helmets can help reduce injuries.
Mickey Lopez won five prizes in the exciting race.

3   d3d d3d 3d 3d 313 desks, 33 sets, 33 and 33 and 13

7   j7j j7j 7j 7j 717 pints, 77 pens, 77 and 77 and 17

easy   They will be done with their work in a short time.

| 1 | 2 | 3 | 4 | 5 | 6 | 7 | 8 | 9 | 10 |

---

5 minutes   ## 22b ● Location of 5 and 9

Reach to 5

1. Find 5 on the chart.
2. Find it on your keyboard.
3. Place your fingers over the home keys.
4. Reach to 5 with the f finger.
5. Touch 5f lightly without moving other fingers from their typing position.

4 3 2   1   1   2 3 4
left fingers   right fingers

Reach to 9

1. Find 9 on the chart.
2. Find it on your keyboard.
3. Place your fingers over the home keys.
4. Reach to 9 with the l finger.
5. Touch 9l lightly without moving other fingers from their typing position.

f5f f5f f5f 5f 5f 5f f5f   Type twice on same line   191 191 191 91 91 91 191

---

6 minutes   ## 22c ● Location Drills 5 and 9

Reach to 5

Directions: Keyboard each line twice SS. DS between 2-line groups.

5   f5f f5f f5f 5f 5f 5f 55 files, 551 feet, 55 and 55
    Sell 515 sets.   Order 5,551 books.   Mail 515 pins.

9   191 191 191 91 91 91 99 lakes, 919 lids, 99 and 99
    Buy 19 dozen.   Sell 191 sets.   Pay for 19 and 991.

Reach to 9

22d ● Continuity Practice   6 minutes

Directions: Keyboard the ¶ as many times as you can in the time allotted.

words

Our team should be one of the best in the city.   10

Most of the girls played on the squad last season.   20

The fact that we have a good coach will help too.   30

| 1 | 2 | 3 | 4 | 5 | 6 | 7 | 8 | 9 | 10 |

120d ● Problem Measurement: Report and Outline

Directions: Problem 1 Unbound Report
Keyboard the one-page unbound report

below. Place the footnote in the correct position at the bottom of the page

Directions for formatting an unbound report are given on page 144. Directions for footnotes are given in 83c, page 143. Refer to these pages if necessary.

stroke keys
with a flowing
rhythm

MAKING USE OF THE LIBRARY

When you go to the library to study or read for pleasure, you go to a room with something more than just four walls and a number of tables. No other room in your school is quite like it. It is here that you can find the key that opens the door to a whole new world for you. It is here that you can meet the wisest and wittiest people of all time.

Plato will not mind at all if you want to turn back the pages of time to get his views on philosophy--neither will Mozart mind if you want his help in composing an opera. On the other hand, if you feel like laughing, Bennett Cerf will be glad to oblige with some of the funniest stories ever told.

The contents of libraries have changed so much through the years that the word library itself is really inaccurate today. It comes from the Latin word liber, which means book. Modern libraries contain a wide variety of materials in addition to books. A few examples are recordings, films, photographs, micro-reproductions, musical scores, and computerized information.[1]

Our information society is creating a great many challenges for librarians. You will find them rising to these challenges and working hard to make the library of even greater use to you.

---

[1]"Library," The World Book Encyclopedia (1984), XII, p. 211.

If necessary, refer to 57d, page 100, for spacing directions.

Directions: Problem 2 Topic Outline
Keyboard the topic outline below on a half sheet of paper. Indent, space, capitalize,

and punctuate the outline correctly. Place it in the exact vertical center of the page.

using an encyclopedia

I introduction
  A importance of encyclopedia as a reference
  B rules for library use
II body
  A how to locate information
    1 look first in the regular alphabetical place
    2 always look for last names of persons
  B miscellaneous hints
III conclusion

120e ● Extra Credit Typing

Directions: Problem 1
Keyboard a note of regret to a friend who has asked you to a play. Look at 117c, Problem 2, page 190 for ideas, but write the message in your own words.

Directions: Problem 2
Keyboard a postal card announcement for a club in your school. If necessary, refer to 117c, Problem 1, page 190, for help in arranging the material.

22e ● Sentence Guided Writings

Directions: 1. Take a 1' writing on each sentence with the call of the guide each 20". Try to complete each sentence as the guide is called.

2. Take two 1' writings on the last sentence without the call of the guide.

		words	in line	gwam 20"
1	Try to type each line as time is called.	8	24
2	*Type with a keen mind and quick strokes.*	8	24
3	I must try to type with quiet hands and arms.	9	27
4	*Try to raise your rate by one word each line.*	9	27
5	If I type well, I can win the prize of high speed.	10	30
6	*When work takes the place of words, we gain skill.*	10	30

---

11 minutes **22f ● Sustained Skill Building**

Directions: 1. Take one 1' writing on each ¶ in 21e, page 35.
2. Take one 2' writing and two 3' writings on both ¶s combined. Figure *gwam*.

3. For the 2' rate, use the 1' column and scale to get total words; divide by 2.
4. Try to equal your 1' rate on the longer writings.

LESSON 23

50-space line

7 minutes **23a ● Keyboard Review**

Directions: Keyboard each line twice SS. DS between 2-line groups.

keep eyes
on copy

alphabet	Mike W. Cruz gave up his tax job and left quickly.
5, 9	f5f 191 f5f 191 5f 91 55 fans, 99 lads, 191 and 55
3, 7	They sold 373 cars. Our tour covered 3,737 miles.
easy	Jane and she both did their own work with no help.

| 1 | 2 | 3 | 4 | 5 | 6 | 7 | 8 | 9 | 10 |

---

8 minutes **23b ● Technique Builder**

Directions: Keyboard each line three times from dictation SS. DS between 3-line groups.

type smoothly;
do not pause
between phrases

1 if it did|if it did look|and if they were|to trade

2 it is the|it is the best|and if she reads|and pull

3 to do the|to do the best|for if they fear|they are

4 if we are|if we are free|and if they look|she sees

119e ● Learn to Make Division and Plus Signs

Directions: 1. To make the *division sign*, type the colon; backspace and strike the hyphen. **2.** To make the *plus sign*, type the diagonal; backspace and strike the hyphen. **3.** Keyboard each sentence 3 times SS; DS between 3-line groups.

```
Here are my three problems:  96 ÷ 8 = 12.  96 ÷ 4 = 24.  248 ÷ 8 = 31.
Here are two addition problems:  24 + 62 = 86 and 1,098 + 701 = 1,799.
```

LESSON 120

70-space line

5 minutes **120a ● Keyboard Review**

Directions: Keyboard each sentence three times SS. DS between 3-line groups.

alphabet Even Mike expected to enjoy a cheery fire blazing in our new quarters.

figure They reported (in 1986) that 265 of the 1,743 names were listed there.

long reaches The executive secretary is probably aware of my terminated exemptions.

easy It is a shame that more folks are not able to laugh at their problems.

| 1 | 2 | 3 | 4 | 5 | 6 | 7 | 8 | 9 | 10 | 11 | 12 | 13 | 14 |

5 minutes **120b ● Language Arts Skills: Number Expression Guides**

Directions: The following are number expression guides and sentences that illustrate those guides. Study each guide. Keyboard the sentences that illustrate the guides twice SS; DS between 2-line groups.

Use figures to type dates. If a day comes before a month, use a figure and follow it with *th*, *st*, or *d*.
We moved on May 26, 1980. I started to work on the 15th of September.

Spell a number beginning a sentence even if figures are used later in the sentence.
Fifty more were needed; only 25 applied. Eighty dollars is the price.

5 minutes **120c ● Speed Builder**

Directions: 1. Take a 1' writing on the ¶ below. The last word typed will be your goal word. **2.** Take a 3' writing with the return called after each minute. When the return is called, start the ¶ over again. Try to reach your goal each minute as the return is called.

1.4 si

sit erect;
feet flat
on the floor

         •   4   •   8   •   12
If you are looking for a relaxing new hobby, one that will enable
  •   16   •   20   •   24
you to remain sharp and alert, look into the art of juggling. Keeping
28   •   32   •   36   •   40
several items in the air at once is not only challenging, it is also
  •   44   •   48   •   52   •
good for you. Think how much exercise you will get by bending over to
56   •   60
retrieve your mistakes.

23c ● Location of 4, 8, and : (colon)

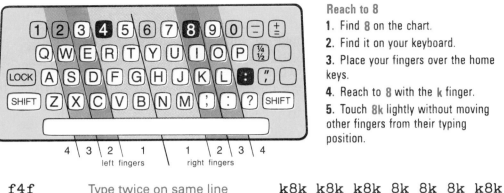

Reach to 4
1. Find **4** on the chart.
2. Find it on your keyboard.
3. Place your fingers over the home keys.
4. Reach to **4** with the **f** finger.
5. Touch **4f** lightly without moving other fingers from their typing position.

Reach to 8
1. Find **8** on the chart.
2. Find it on your keyboard.
3. Place your fingers over the home keys.
4. Reach to **8** with the **k** finger.
5. Touch **8k** lightly without moving other fingers from their typing position.

4 \ 3 \ 2 \ 1   1 \ 2 \ 3 \ 4
left fingers   right fingers

f4f f4f f4f 4f 4f 4f f4f   Type twice on same line   k8k k8k k8k 8k 8k 8k k8k

> The : is the shift of the ;. Touch ;:; three times.
> Space twice after : used as punctuation.

---

12 minutes   **23d ● Location Drills 4, 8 and : (colon)**

Directions: Keyboard each line twice SS. DS between 2-line groups.

Reach to 4

Reach to 8

4
f4f f4f f4f 4f 4f 4f 44 firs, 414 fans, 4,414 feet
Pay in 44 days. Mark 4,414 tags. Send 14 and 44.

8
k8k k8k k8k 8k 8k 8k 88 kits, 18 kites, 8,818 ties
Dig 818 feet. Walk 18 miles. Buy 8,188 new sets.

:
;:; ;:; :; :; Dear Sir: Note: To: Dear Dr. Yue:
This is why: These are the items: The girl said:

number fluency
A note stated: Sell the 37 axes we have in stock.
In 1985, 54,918 fans were at the opening day game.

23e ● Paragraph Guided Writings   10 minutes

Directions: 1. Take a 1' writing on the ¶ below. Figure *gwam*. Add four words to your *gwam* for a new goal.

2. Take three 1' writings. Strive to reach your goal on each writing.
3. Take one 1' writing on the ¶. Compare *gwam* on this writing to your first 1' writing.

all letters used   1.1 si

When you see a new word in print, try to guess
what it means. The way it is used in the sentence
should give you a hint. To find the real meaning,
though, you will need to look it up. Then put your
new word to work at once when you speak or write.

119b ● Language Arts Skills: Apostrophe Guides

Directions: The following are apostrophe guides and sentences that illustrate those guides. Study each guide. Keyboard the sentences that illustrate the guides twice SS; DS between 2-line groups.

The apostrophe denotes possession. Do not use it merely to form the plural of a noun.
There were only three boys in each room.   There is the new boy's room.

Add 's to form the possessive of any singular noun.
According to my son-in-law's father, Ana's pin was found in Hal's cap.

Add 's to form the possessive of a plural noun that does *not* end in *s*.
Two women bought two women's coats, but six men bought ten men's ties.

Add only an apostrophe after the *s* if a plural noun does end in *s*.
Ten girls shared six girls' books; eight boys shared four boys' books.

To show possession, add an apostrophe and *s* to a proper name of one syllable which ends in *s*.
The Jones's land is several miles down the road from the Sims's ranch.

To show possession, add only an apostrophe to a proper name of more than one syllable which ends in *s*.
Aunt Virginia enjoyed reading the story to Mrs. Roberts' son, William.

---

10 minutes **119c ● Paragraph Guided Writings**

Directions: **1.** Set goals of 40, 50, and 60 words a minute. Take two 1' writings at each rate. Try to reach your goal word as time is called.

2. Your teacher may call the quarter or half minutes to guide you.

3. Keyboard additional writings at the 50- and 60-word rate as time permits.

all letters used   1.4 si

keep a steady, even rhythm

It is amazing that so many people are lax about using the proper techniques when making a telephone call.   There are two major points to remember.   First, always give your name to the person who answers the phone.   Second, when you make the call, you should also be the one who ends the conversation.

---

10 minutes **119d ● Skill Comparison**

Directions: Take two 1' writings on each sentence SS. DS between 2-line groups. Compare your rate on the lowest syllable intensity sentence to your rate on each of the other sentences.

1.0 si   To know how to do work well and to know that you know is a good thing.

1.2 si   We can learn to work, as there are many ways open to the right person.

1.3 si   Everyone should learn to work well with others on many kinds of tasks.

1.4 si   The people who really like their work lead much more satisfying lives.

| 1 | 2 | 3 | 4 | 5 | 6 | 7 | 8 | 9 | 10 | 11 | 12 | 13 | 14 |

LESSON 24

24a ● Keyboard Review

7 minutes

Directions: Keyboard each line twice SS. DS between 2-line groups.

sit erect;
keep your eyes
on the copy

alphabet	Max was picking five dozen bright yellow jonquils.
4, 8	f4f k8k f4f k8k 4f 8k 44 firs, 88 kits, 881 and 44
: colon	Use the colon with numbers: 7:45, 8:15, and 7:35.
easy	He held the signs for us at just the right height.

| 1 | 2 | 3 | 4 | 5 | 6 | 7 | 8 | 9 | 10 |

---

5 minutes ## 24b ● Location of 2 and 0 (zero)

Reach to 2

1. Find **2** on the chart.

2. Find it on your keyboard.

3. Place your fingers over the home keys.

4. Reach to **2** with the **s** finger.

5. Touch **2**s lightly without moving other fingers from their typing position.

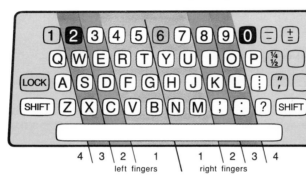

4 3 2   1   1   2 3 4
left fingers   right fingers

Reach to 0 (zero)

1. Find **0** on the chart.

2. Find it on your keyboard.

3. Place your fingers over the home keys.

4. Reach to **0** with the **;** finger.

5. Touch **0**; lightly without moving other fingers from their typing position.

s2s s2s s2s 2s 2s 2s s2s   Type twice on same line   ;0; ;0; ;0; 0; ;0 0; ;0;

---

7 minutes ## 24c ● Location Drills: 2 and 0 (Zero)

Directions: Keyboard each line twice SS. DS between 2-line groups.

Reach to 2

2 s2s s2s s2s 2s 2s 2s 22 suits, 212 slides, 22 sets
   I am 22. I walked 212 miles in 22 days, 12 hours.

0 ;0; ;0; ;0; 0; 0; 0; 100 pets, 110 pints, 909 tons
   We may have 20, 30, 40, or 50 of these long forms.

Reach to 0

24d ● Script Builder   14 minutes

Directions: **1.** Practice the ¶ twice DS. Take two 1' writings. Figure *gwam*.   **2.** Take two 1' writings on 23e, page 38. Compare rates on the two ¶s.

all letters used 1.2 si   *gwam* 1'

Do you realize that not all firms require one 9
to go to work five days a week? Some of them will 19
let people put in extra hours so they can finish 29
their jobs in only four days. 35

118c ● Problem Measurement

Directions: Problem 1 Personal/Business Letter

Keyboard the letter below on a full sheet, 50 space line. Use modified block style, mixed punctuation. Begin the return address on line 18. Prepare a carbon copy. Address an envelope. Fold and insert letter in envelope.

Return Address: 115 Orange Drive│ Pekin, IL 61554-7295│ Today's date │ Letter Address: Miss Karen Fleming│ Karen's Specialty Shop│ 64 Clover Avenue│ Chicago, IL 60641-6584│ Dear Miss Fleming

Thank you very much for sending me the special birthday candle I ordered when I was in your shop last Saturday.

I am glad to learn that in the future I shall be able to order these candles by mail. They make such unique birthday gifts.

Enclosed is the list of names I promised to send you. You will find all these people potential customers, I am sure.

Sincerely yours│ Miss Lorraine Johnson│ Enclosure

Directions: Problem 2 Keyboarding a Poem

Keyboard the poem in the exact vertical center on a half sheet of paper DS. TS after the heading. Center the copy horizontally by the second line of the first verse.

space quickly with down-and-in motion of thumb

Loco-Motive

Down at the station I like to see the trains
Sticking out their chests and coming down the lanes
Dinging and a-hooing, reaching out their light--
How I wish that trains wouldn't cry at night.

Out in the country, rushing through the grass,
Trains seem happy, purring as they pass,
Or across the highway, clatter-banging by--
Why in the nighttime do the trains cry?
--Augusta Towner Reid

Directions: Problem 3 Personal/Business Letter

Using a full sheet, 50-space line, keyboard the letter in Problem 1 again. Use block style, open punctuation.

LESSON 119

5 minutes **119a ● Keyboard Review**

Directions: Keyboard each sentence three times SS. DS between 3-line groups.

alphabet Even now, a dozen more expect to qualify for those kinds of good jobs.

figure During that day--May 29, 1962--the market average rose over 27 points.

left hand Tatsu Baba saw six dozen square zinc plates and a quilt at the bazaar.

easy Some nations of the world used quantities of such coal for their fuel.

| 1 | 2 | 3 | 4 | 5 | 6 | 7 | 8 | 9 | 10 | 11 | 12 | 13 | 14 |

24e ● Continuity Practice

Directions: Keyboard both ¶s DS. Circle all errors. Repeat the exercise. Try to make no more than four errors per writing.

all letters used 1.2 si

	gwam 1'	3'

keep elbows in; feet flat on floor

	gwam 1'	3'	
A good grade is the prize you get when you bet	9	3	34
on yourself. You can collect the prize if you lay	20	7	37
your talents and your will to learn each lesson on	30	10	41
the line. Your efforts must be equal to the prize	40	13	44
if you expect to win.	44	15	46
Do not forget that the grade is just a symbol.	9	18	49
What counts are the things you learn and the new	19	21	52
skills you acquire. These are the lasting rewards	28	25	55
of learning. A poor grade is the only thing you	39	29	59
can get in this world without working for it.	48	31	62

gwam 1' | 1 | 2 | 3 | 4 | 5 | 6 | 7 | 8 | 9 | 10 |
3' | 1 | 2 | 3 |

LESSON 25

7 minutes

25a ● Keyboard Review

Directions: Keyboard each line twice SS. DS between 2-line groups.

alphabet The people have really acquired a taste for pizza.
Many also go there to listen to their new jukebox.

2 s2s s2s 2s 2s 22 sets, 221 slides, 22 or 222 suits

0 ;0; ;0; 0; 0; 10 pans, 101 plans, 10 or 100 plants

easy More than half of the men here paid their own way.

| 1 | 2 | 3 | 4 | 5 | 6 | 7 | 8 | 9 | 10 |

---

5 minutes

25b ● Technique Builder

Directions: Keyboard each line three times from dictation SS. DS between 3-line groups.

do not pause between phrases

1 and the sets│and the seat│and the ink│and the oil

2 if they were│if they look│if they bet│if they get

3 for the rest│for the inn│for the cats│for the pup

Directions: Problem 3 Postal Card Announcement
Follow the directions given in Problem 1.   telephone number as the chairperson.
Use your own name, address, and

LESSON 118

70-space line

5 minutes   **118a ● Keyboard Review**

Directions: Keyboard each sentence three times SS. DS between 3-line groups.

keep fingers
deeply curved

alphabet	To move enough zinc for export would require buying trucks and a jeep.
figure	In the period 1951-1974, Lucille Ball starred in 495 television shows.
both hands	Kate Dark had a knack for finding all kinds of kindling on their dike.
easy	It is better to get in the first thought than to get in the last word.

| 1 | 2 | 3 | 4 | 5 | 6 | 7 | 8 | 9 | 10 | 11 | 12 | 13 | 14 |

10 minutes   **118b ● Speed Builder**

Directions: Take two 1' writings on each ¶; try to increase speed on the second writing. Figure *gwam*.

Alternate Procedure: Work for speed as you take one 5' writing on all four ¶s combined. Figure *gwam*.

all letters used   1.3 si   gwam 1' | 5'

When youngsters write home from camp next summer, they may not be   13 | 3 | 47
scribbling their news on a plain piece of paper.   They could be writing   28 | 6 | 50
in a slightly different way.   The required note to mom and dad from the   42 | 8 | 52
modern camper is likely to be mailed on a computer printout.   54 | 11 | 55

There are now quite a few summer and vacation programs from coast   13 | 13 | 57
to coast that bill themselves as computer camps.   They offer the chance   28 | 16 | 60
to learn more about computers, yet they still take some time for such   42 | 19 | 63
things as arts and crafts, hiking, and learning how to avoid poison ivy.   56 | 22 | 66

These camps are not limited to computer junkies either.   You don't   13 | 25 | 69
have to be a whiz kid to attend.   Some even cater to the whole family,   28 | 28 | 72
where toddlers are turned over to a sitter.   At the present time boys   42 | 30 | 74
have been outnumbering the girls about three to one.   52 | 32 | 76

Most of the time campers are divided into groups by experience or   13 | 35 | 79
age and allowed to learn at their own pace.   Those who are new at this   27 | 38 | 82
sort of thing often start out by playing programmed games.   Some will   41 | 41 | 85
learn computer music, which could mean that songs around the campfire   55 | 43 | 87
will never be the same.   60 | 44 | 88

gwam 1' | 1 | 2 | 3 | 4 | 5 | 6 | 7 | 8 | 9 | 10 | 11 | 12 | 13 | 14 |
5' | 1 | 2 | 3 |

5 minutes **25c ● Location of 6 and 1**

Reach to 6
1. Find **6** on the chart.
2. Find it on your keyboard.
3. Place your fingers over the home keys.
4. Reach to **6** with the **j** finger.
5. Touch **6j** lightly without moving other fingers from their typing position.

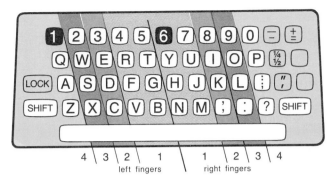

```
4 \ 3 \ 2 \  1      1 \ 2 \ 3 \ 4
     left fingers    right fingers
```

Reach to 1
1. Find **1** on the chart.
2. Find it on your keyboard.
3. Place your fingers over the home keys.
4. Reach to **1** with the **a** finger.
5. Touch **1a** lightly without moving other fingers from their typing position.

j6j j6j j6j 6j 6j 6j j6j   Type twice on same line   ala ala ala la la la ala

---

6 minutes **25d ● Location Drills: 6 and 1**

Reach to 6

Reach to 1

Directions: Keyboard each line twice SS. DS between 2-line groups.

```
6   j6j  j6j  j6j  6j  6j  6j  66 jolts, 66,666 jets, 6 or 6
    I weigh 66 pounds.  Send 666 now.  Collect 66 now.

1   ala ala ala la la la either 11, 111, or 1,111 rods
    Go north for 11 miles; then go east for 111 miles.
    | 1 | 2 | 3 | 4 | 5 | 6 | 7 | 8 | 9 | 10 |
```

25e ● Sentence Guided Writings   8 minutes

Directions: Keyboard each sentence for a 1' writing with the call of the guide each 20". Try to complete each sentence as the guide is called.

		words in line	gwam 20"
1	We hope to sell 1,600 tickets.	6	18
2	She will be 16 years old on May 10.	7	21
3	Kay said the number was either 60 or 61.	8	24
4	Joe made the trip in 16 hours and 10 minutes.	9	27
5	They live just 160 miles north of here on Route 1.	10	30

```
| 1 | 2 | 3 | 4 | 5 | 6 | 7 | 8 | 9 | 10 |
```

---

14 minutes **25f ● Sustained Skill Building**

Directions: **1.** Take two 1' writings on each¶ in 24e, page 40. Figure *gwam*.
2. Take two 3' writings on both ¶s combined. Circle errors. Figure *gwam* on the better writing.
3. Compare your 3' rate with your 1' rate.

Lesson 25   **41**

LESSON 117

117a ● Keyboard Review

5 minutes

Directions: Keyboard each sentence three times SS. DS between 3-line groups.

alphabet We planned to move the six wagons quickly to Arizona before next July.

figure The Dodgers' Koufax walked only 71 men while striking out 382 in 1965.

adjacent keys Sandra has always assumed that her necessary assistance was available.

easy Always keep your goal in view, and you can reach the top in your work.

| 1 | 2 | 3 | 4 | 5 | 6 | 7 | 8 | 9 | 10 | 11 | 12 | 13 | 14 |

117b ● Concentration Practice

10 minutes

Directions: Keyboard the ¶ below as many times as possible in the time given SS. DS each time you begin the paragraph over.

words

Age has little to do with accomplishments. Mickey Mantle hit 23 — 13
home runs at the age of 20; Ted Williams slammed a homer at age 42 in — 27
his last official time at bat. Mozart played the harpsichord at 3 and — 41
published his first composition at 7. George Bernard Shaw had a play — 55
produced when he was 94. — 60

| 1 | 2 | 3 | 4 | 5 | 6 | 7 | 8 | 9 | 10 | 11 | 12 | 13 | 14 |

117c ● Problem Measurement

30 minutes

Directions: Problem 1 Postal Card Announcement
1. Insert a postal card or paper cut to size (5½″ × 3¼″) into your machine.
2. Center the announcement at the right horizontally and vertically. (If necessary, refer to 40c, page 67 for finding the center of odd-size paper.)
3. Address the card to yourself on the opposite side (no return address needed).

EDUCATION COMMITTEE MEETINGS
TO BE AT HIGH SCHOOL

Please watch bulletin for dates and times

For further information, call:

Mrs. Myra Young, Chairperson
3982 East Gettysburg Avenue, 225-4850

Directions: Problem 2 Informal Regret
1. Keyboard the informal regret note at the right on a half sheet of paper with the short side up as you did in 73c, page 127.
2. Use modified block style with open punctuation. Use your address as the return address and sign your name.

Current date | Dear Carol

You were so thoughtful to ask us to attend the Community Theater performance on Wednesday evening. Unfortunately, Ken has to work late that week, and we cannot accept your kind invitation.

Thanks for thinking of us, Carol. I hope we can take a rain check for a future time. | Sincerely

continued on next page

Unit 4 ■ Improving Your Basic Skills (Lessons 26–30)

General Directions

Use a 50-space line for all lessons in this unit (center − 25; center + 25 + 5). SS sentences and drill lines. DS between repeated groups of lines. DS paragraph copy. Set tabulator for a 5-space paragraph indention.

Follow the procedures that are given throughout this unit for the tabulator control, the margin release key, and the shift lock.

LESSON 26

7 minutes **26a ● Keyboard Review**

Directions: Keyboard each sentence twice SS. DS between 2-line groups.

sit erect;
keep arms and
wrists quiet

alphabet   We all hope the speaker will tell some good jokes.

Quite a number of citizens have to pay more taxes.

3, 7   Please add 33 and 77.   She is 73; her niece is 37.

at   at great water rather matter attend nation station

easy   Jan says she will work with me on the paper route.

| 1 | 2 | 3 | 4 | 5 | 6 | 7 | 8 | 9 | 10 |

15 minutes **26b ● Sentence Guided Writings**

Directions: 1. Take a 1' writing on each sentence with the call of the guide each 20".

2. Try to complete each sentence as the guide is called.

3. Take two 1' writings on the last two sentences without the call of the guide.

	words	in line	gwam 20"

return quickly;
no pauses

1 He made sure the job was well done.   7 | 21

2 Leave the papers lying on the desk.   7 | 21

3 Their group left today for a field trip.   8 | 24

4 They asked how much a ticket would cost.   8 | 24

5 The speed of the new computer will amaze you.   9 | 27

6 She plans to ride her new bike in the parade.   9 | 27

7 Some of them spent their time playing video games.   10 | 30

8 We hurried to the library after our morning break.   10 | 30

| 1 | 2 | 3 | 4 | 5 | 6 | 7 | 8 | 9 | 10 |

116d ● Speed Ladder Paragraphs

Directions: Take a 1' writing on ¶1 DS until you complete the ¶ in 1'. When you complete ¶1 in 1', continue on to ¶2. Repeat this procedure as you try to complete each of the ¶s in the given time.

Alternate Procedure: Take a 1' writing on ¶1 DS. Move to the second and succeeding ¶s only when you have completed each one within the error limit specified by your teacher.

all letters used   1.3 si

gwam 5'

use quick, sharp strokes

	gwam 5'	
If you are one of the millions who enjoy bike riding, you know	3	55
it offers good exercise plus a lot of fun. Moreover, it is a sport in	5	57
which the whole family can be involved, from grandpa right on down to	8	60
the little ones.	9	61
To be sure that you will be riding until a ripe old age, you should	12	64
make safety a prime consideration every time you get on a bike. This	14	66
is a true statement whether you are going on an overnight tour or just	17	69
taking a spin around the block.	18	70
Believe it or not, a helmet is a must for all bike riders, not just	21	73
those who take long trips. Eighty percent of all injuries that require	24	76
one to be hospitalized are due to a blow on the head. If more cyclists	27	79
wear helmets, this figure can be greatly reduced.	29	81
To make sure you can be seen by car drivers, wear bright or light	31	83
colors. Stitch reflective tape on your clothing, and also apply it to	35	87
the wheels and pedals of your bike. Another good plan is to wear a	37	89
vest as it will make you more visible to traffic going in both direc-	40	92
tions.	40	92
For riding at night, a good front light is essential. If it's one	43	95
you can remove, you can use it as a flashlight too. You might want to	46	98
consider buying a lightweight light to strap on your arm or leg. Its	48	100
advantage, of course, is that the movement of the light will attract	51	103
attention as you pedal.	52	104

gwam 5' | 1 | 2 | 3 |

26c ● **Tabulator Control**

Directions: **1.** Clear all tab stops. (Refer to page 20).
2. Set four tab stops at 5-space intervals from left margin.

3. Keyboard each sentence once as shown DS. Strike tab key or bar sharply and return finger to home position as you tab for the sentences.

return quickly
without pauses

They can learn to use the tab bar or key by touch.

tab once   5⟶Just complete each line without slowing down.

tab twice   10⟶Move your hand to home position quickly.

tab 3 times   15⟶Indent when starting each new line.

tab 4 times   20⟶Do not look back at your keys.

---

10 minutes   **26d** ● **Paragraph Guided Writings**

Directions: **1.** Take a 1' writing on the ¶ below. Figure *gwam*. Add four words to your *gwam* for a new goal.
2. Take three 1' writings. Strive to reach

your goal on each writing.
3. Take one 1' writing on the ¶. Compare *gwam* on this writing to your first 1' writing.

all letters used   1.1 si

          •   4   •   8
No one should say that a mule lacks good sense.
  •   12   •   16   •   20
In a burning barn, a horse will freeze and have to
    •   24   •   28   •
be led out with a blindfold over its eyes. A cow
   32   •   36   •   40
will walk out quietly with a little help. A mule
    •   44   •   48
will just kick the door down to make an exit.

LESSON 27

50-space line

7 minutes   **27a** ● **Keyboard Review**

Directions: Keyboard each line twice SS. DS between 2-line groups.

type with a
steady rhythm

alphabet   Julie asked her to buy me a dozen quarts of punch.
We are expecting a more exact count very soon now.

5, 9   My number is 55; hers is 99. Subtract 59 from 95.

ha   has had hand hard have chance change happy perhaps

easy   He may also throw their ball down the field to me.

| 1 | 2 | 3 | 4 | 5 | 6 | 7 | 8 | 9 | 10 |

Unit 14 ■ Improving Your Basic Skills—Measurement

(Lessons 116–120)

General Directions

Use a 70-space line for all lessons in this unit (center − 35; center + 35 + 5) unless otherwise directed. SS sentences and drill lines; DS paragraphs.

This unit includes measurement of straight-copy and problem typing skills similar to problems covered in Cycle 3. You will be expected to format/keyboard these problems with less directional material by applying what you have learned in previous lessons.

LESSON 116

5 minutes **116a ● Keyboard Review**

Directions: Keyboard each sentence three times SS. DS between 3-line groups.

alphabet	Elizabeth very quickly solved the sixth problem again just for Weston.
shift	Don Ruiz and Lucy Wong saw both Mickey and Minnie Mouse at Disneyland.
figure	From mid-1982 to mid-1983 the world population rose 83 million people.
easy	They liked to sit by the side of the lake and throw rocks at the fish.

| 1 | 2 | 3 | 4 | 5 | 6 | 7 | 8 | 9 | 10 | 11 | 12 | 13 | 14 |

10 minutes **116b ● Paragraph Guided Writings**

Directions: 1. Set goals of 40, 50, and 60 words a minute. Take two 1' writings at each rate. Try to reach your goal word as time is called.

2. Your teacher may call the quarter or half minutes to guide you.

3. Keyboard additional writings at the 50- and 60-word rate as time permits.

1.4 si

type without pauses between words

If you are planning to enter one certain trade or profession, it is important to study your fitness for such work. If you find that you are weak in certain traits, you will know where to concentrate your efforts to improve yourself. You may find that you have greater aptitude for some other work.

10 minutes **116c ● Technique Builder: Stroking**

Directions: Take two 1' writings on each sentence SS. DS between 2-line groups.

1st finger	That runner had run too far to return to first base after Beth's bunt.
2d finger	Did Dick and Eddie Decker pick up all the kids' kites from their deck?
3d finger	I saw an old notice about Lois Olson's solo in the school talent show.
4th finger	Gonzalez is puzzled about whether to write a paper or take a pop quiz.

| 1 | 2 | 3 | 4 | 5 | 6 | 7 | 8 | 9 | 10 | 11 | 12 | 13 | 14 |

27b ● **Technique Builder: Stroking**

Directions: Take two 1' writings on each sentence SS.

strike keys
with quick,
sharp strokes

1 Our words are to our minds what keys are to doors.

2 *Time is on the side of those who will plan for it.*

3 He must think the words as he types to gain speed.

4 *Give her time, and she will do the work all right.*

5 Use your head and your hands to learn how to type.

---

16 minutes

27c ● **Paragraph Guided Writings**

Your instructor may call the ½'
guide on the 1' writings to aid
you in checking your rate.

Directions: **1.** Take a 1' writing on ¶1.
Figure *gwam*. Add four words to your
gwam for a new goal.
2. Take two 1' writings on the same ¶ as
you strive to reach your new goal.

3. Repeat Steps 1 and 2 for ¶2.
4. Take a 3' writing on both ¶s combined.
Figure *gwam*. Compare your new rate to
your 1' writing.

all letters used

gwam 3'

			gwam 3'
	• 4 • 8		
¶1 1.1 si	One of the most offbeat jobs around these	3	30
	12 • 16		
	days has to be that held by a fellow out west who	6	33
	20 • 24 • 28		
	is the head of a unique school for jumping frogs.	10	37
	32 • 36		
	He says he can make them think they are the best	13	40
	40 • 44		
	in the world at their trade.	15	42
	• 4 • 8		
¶2 1.2 si	He even lets them do something that you and	18	45
	12 • 16		
	I might think a bit crazy or at least strange.	21	48
	20 • 24 • 28		
	The frogs are allowed to hop into a bubble bath	24	51
	32 • 36		
	to relax and then to dine on bees dipped in honey.	27	55

gwam 3' | 1 | 2 | 3 | 4 |

To type all-cap items,
depress the shift lock with
the left little finger (No.
30) and type.

To release the shift lock,
depress either the right or
left shift key.

27d ● **Typing in All Capital Letters**   7 minutes

Directions: Keyboard the sentences below two times SS.

Teachers read the WEEKLY BULLETIN to ALL students.

We BOTH read THE SHINING, a novel by Stephen King.

115b ● **Timed Writings**

Directions: **1.** Take two 1' writings on ¶1, 101d, page 170. Figure *gwam* on the better writing.

2. Take a 5' writing on all five ¶s combined. Circle errors and figure *gwam*.

115c ● **Problem Typing**

Directions: **Problem 1 Notice and Agenda of a Meeting**

1. Keyboard the notice and agenda in 97c, Problem 1, page 164, as directed in the problem.

2. Use the new center point and keyboard the page number.

Directions: **Problem 2 Minutes of Meeting**

1. Keyboard the minutes in 98c, page 166, following the directions in the problem.

2. Use the new center point and place the page number in the correct position.

After you complete the minutes, assemble your style guide in the correct order. Staple the report together at the left.

115d ● **Extra-Credit**

Directions: **1.** Keyboard the unbound report below on a full sheet of paper; 60-space line DS.

2. Leave a 2″ top margin; center an

appropriate heading using the backspace from center method.

3. Make corrections as indicated.

words

keep eyes and mind on copy

In 1869, an ᴀ*early* explorer ~~entered~~ *wrote* the following descrip- | 11

tion of ᴧ*#* an amazing ve i̷w from a mountain ᴧ*top* in north eastern | 23

Utah: "From this point, I can look away to the north and | 34

see in the ᴧ*dim* distance the sweetwater and wind river moun- | 46

tains, more *#* than a hundred miles away." | 54

Touri sts streaming through this same region today may find | 66

that the pure air and beautiful ve i̷ws ~~have not vanished~~ *are vanishing* | 76

beneath clouds of smog. Some areas in the mountain states | 88

now fail to meet federal air quality standards intended | 99

to pro tect ᴧ ~~our~~ *human* health. | 104

LESSON 28

7 minutes

28a ● Keyboard Review

Directions: Keyboard each line twice SS. DS between 2-line groups.

alphabet
Judy now plans to take her driving quiz next week.
Most kids cannot get there before the end of June.

4, 8 Multiply 44 by 88. They saw 48 girls and 84 boys.

is is his list miss wish visit discuss furnish island

easy They can make a big profit by working eight hours.

| 1 | 2 | 3 | 4 | 5 | 6 | 7 | 8 | 9 | 10 |

10 minutes

28b ● Continuity Practice: Numbers

Directions: Keyboard the ¶ two times DS

all numbers used   gwam 3'

The only woman ever to cross Niagara Falls on   3 | 27

a tightrope did so in 1876. Maria Spelterina, 23   6 | 30

years old, walked 1,104 feet across the deadly gorge   10 | 34

at a height of 165 feet. After this initial walk   13 | 37

on July 8 she made a second trip on July 12, with a   17 | 40

peach basket strapped to each foot. On July 19 she   20 | 44

tried it again, this time with her eyes blindfolded.   24 | 47

gwam 3' | 1 | 2 | 3 | 4 |

12 minutes

28c ● Typing Outside the Right and Left Margins

The position of the backspace key varies from machine to machine. On some, it is on the right side of the keyboard. On others, it is on the left side. Reach for the backspace key with the little finger.

Directions: **1.** Right margin. Using an exact 50-space line (center − 25; center + 25), keyboard the first sentence.
2. Find the margin release key (No. 32) on your typewriter. When the carriage or carrier locks, use the correct little finger to depress the margin release key and complete the sentence. Repeat.

3. Left Margin. Return the carriage or carrier to the left margin.
4. Depress the margin release key; backspace five spaces into the left margin, and keyboard the second sentence. Repeat.

right margin   Your typewriter has useful gadgets. Learn to use them.

left margin   Your typewriter has useful gadgets. Learn to use them.

113c, continued

Directions: Problem 2 Leftbound Report
1. Keyboard the report in 60c, pp. 104–105, in the form illustrated.

2. Use the new center point and place the page number in the correct position.

LESSON 114

70-space line

5 minutes **114a ● Keyboard Review**

Directions: Keyboard each sentence three times SS. DS between 3-line groups.

alphabet — The woman gave hazy explanations for both of Judge Mackey's questions.

fig/sym — Dan's note for $3,270 (due June 1) bears interest at the rate of 9.8%.

adjacent keys — We were extremely thankful her proposal was passed by three districts.

easy — Our city papers are rushed to neighboring towns when they are printed.

| 1 | 2 | 3 | 4 | 5 | 6 | 7 | 8 | 9 | 10 | 11 | 12 | 13 | 14 |

---

10 minutes **114b ● Timed Writings**

Directions: 1. Take two 1' writings on ¶1, 96d, page 163. Figure *gwam* on the better writing.

2. Take a 5' writing on all five ¶s combined. Circle errors and figure *gwam*.

---

30 minutes **114c ● Problem Typing: Outlines**

Directions: Problem 1 Sentence Outline
1. Keyboard the outline in 57d, Problem 1, page 100, according to the directions given.

2. Use the new center point; keyboard the page number.

Directions: Problem 2 Topic Outline
1. Keyboard the outline in 87c, Problem 1, page 150, following the directions given.

2. Use the new center point and keyboard the page number.

LESSON 115

70-space line

5 minutes **115a ● Keyboard Review**

Directions: Keyboard each sentence three times SS. DS between 3-line groups.

alphabet — My box was packed with five dozen jars of apple, fig, and quince jams.

fig/sym — The admission for adults is $2.50; children 5-9, $0.75; under 5 free.

long reaches — Bret announced that Lanny would hire many new musicians in the summer.

easy — Remember that you can't be blamed for advice which you have not given.

| 1 | 2 | 3 | 4 | 5 | 6 | 7 | 8 | 9 | 10 | 11 | 12 | 13 | 14 |

28d ● Paragraph Guided Writings

Directions: **1.** Take a 1' writing on ¶1. Figure *gwam*. Add four words to your *gwam* for a new goal.

2. Take two 1' writings on the same ¶ as you strive to reach your new goal.

3. Repeat Steps 1 and 2 for ¶2.

4. Take a 3' writing on both ¶s combined. Figure *gwam*. Compare your new rate to your 1' writing.

gwam 3'

all letters used

¶1 1.1 si

Those who pull their own weight seldom have	3	34
any left to throw around. While they are quick to	6	37
do their share, they do not bother others. This	10	40
fact is as true in school or on the playing fields	13	44
as it is on the job.	14	45

¶2 1.2 si

Look about and you will soon find that busy	17	48
folks just do not get into trouble. They lack the	21	51
time to find it. The lazy people are always the	24	55
ones who seem to have an axe to grind. The first	27	58
rule of teamwork, then, is to pull your own weight.	31	61

gwam 3' | 1 | 2 | 3 | 4 |

LESSON 29

50-space line

7 minutes   **29a ● Keyboard Review**

Directions: Keyboard each line twice SS. DS between 2-line groups.

keep fingers curved; arms and wrists still

alphabet The Bijou marquee lists names of six famous stars.
Fonz was picked by one girl as her favorite actor.

2, 0 Place 00 in column 22. I said to divide 20 by 20.

it it its city permit unit profit write either little

easy I believe their game is going to be action packed.

| 1 | 2 | 3 | 4 | 5 | 6 | 7 | 8 | 9 | 10 |

7 minutes   **29b ● Technique Builder**

Directions: Keyboard each line three times from dictation SS. DS between 3-line groups.

return carriage quickly

1 to do the|to do the work|and it did|and it did the

2 if it is|if it is the|if the duty is|if they do go

3 and it|and it is|and it is the|and they did go the

4 in the|in the time|in the end|in their town|in the

112b ● Timed Writings

Directions: **1.** Take two 1' writings on ¶1, 86d, page 149.

2. Take a 5' writing on all 5 ¶s combined. Circle errors and figure *gwam*.

---

30 minutes **112c ● Problem Typing: Formatting/Keyboarding Letters**

Directions: Problem 1 Personal/Business Letter in Block Style

1. Keyboard the letter in 78d, Problem 1, page 135. Follow the directions given in the problem.

2. Place the page number in the correct position.

3. Remember that the center point should be 3 spaces to the right of the point normally used.

Directions: Problem 2 Personal Letter

1. Keyboard the letter in 75c, page 129. Follow the directions given for the problem.

2. Place the page number in the correct position.

3. Staple the letter on an 8½" × 11" sheet of paper, placed so it appears centered when bound at the left margin.

LESSON 113

70-space line

5 minutes **113a ● Keyboard Review**

Directions: Keyboard each line three times SS. DS between 3-line groups.

keep wrists and arms quiet

alphabet Karla expected me to realize that use of jargon was very questionable.

figure The winner of an 1895 car race drove 53 miles in 10 hours, 23 minutes.

combination if it is to pull, if it is to trace, if it is to join, if it is to get

easy It is tough for us to keep our minds and mouths open at the same time.

| 1 | 2 | 3 | 4 | 5 | 6 | 7 | 8 | 9 | 10 | 11 | 12 | 13 | 14 |

---

10 minutes **113b ● Timed Writings**

Directions: **1.** Take two 1' writings on ¶1, 91c, page 156. Figure *gwam* on the better writing.

2. Take a 5' writing on all five ¶s combined. Circle errors and figure *gwam*.

---

30 minutes **113c ● Problem Typing: Reports**

Directions: Problem 1 One-Page Report

1. Keyboard the report on page 94. Follow the directions given in 53c, page 93.

2. Use the new center point and place the page number in the correct position.

continued on next page

29c ● **Skill Comparison**

Directions: Keyboard two 1' writings on each sentence SS. DS between 2-line groups. Compare *gwam* on the four sentences.

type without
pauses

easy Some things have to be believed to be seen at all.

one-hand Dexter Lyon saw Milo pull a beaver in a red crate.

figures Nearly all 25 girls on their teams are already 16.

script *A pound of pluck is worth more than a ton of luck.*

10 minutes **29d** ● **Timed Writings**

Take two 3' writings on Lesson 28d, page 46. Circle all errors. Figure *gwam*. Submit the better writing.

10 minutes **29e** ● **Listening for the Bell: Right Margin Release**

Directions: 1. Set an exact 50-space line (center − 25; center + 25).
2. Move the right margin stop 5 to 8 spaces farther to the right. Doing this will give your copy better horizontal balance.
3. Type the ¶ below, listening for the bell. When the bell rings, finish the word you are typing and return to the next line. If the carriage locks before you are finished, depress the margin release key and complete the word.
4. Set a 60-space line by moving your left and right margin stops out five spaces beyond your margin for a 50-space line. Type the ¶ as you did for a 50-space line.

all letters used 1.2 si   words

While they will not set an exact date, some   9

say the time when we will drive electric cars is   18

just around the corner. It may be quicker than   28

that if the present cars guzzle too much gas.   37

| 1 | 2 | 3 | 4 | 5 | 6 | 7 | 8 | 9 | 10 |

LESSON 30   50-space line

7 minutes **30a** ● **Keyboard Review**

Directions: Keyboard each line twice SS. DS between 2-line groups.

keep wrists
low and still

alphabet Jeff was easily the best running back on our team.
The movie was explained in the quarterly magazine.

6, 1 Take Route 66, not Route 11. Next, add 61 and 16.

he he her here head help she when where neither other

easy Both of them were able to hold their balance well.

| 1 | 2 | 3 | 4 | 5 | 6 | 7 | 8 | 9 | 10 |

Directions: Problem 2 Table of Contents

1. Keyboard the table of contents below for your style guide.

2. Set your margins for a 60-space line. (Remember that the center point should be 3 spaces to the right of the point normally used.)

3. Leave a 2″ top margin. TS between the title and the heading; DS between items.

4. Insert leaders as you did in 103c, page 173.

Note: Align periods with those in the first line, noting whether you start the periods on an odd or even number.

                    TABLE OF CONTENTS
                           TS

Personal Business Letter in Modified Block Style 1
                                                        DS
Personal Business Letter in Block Style 2

Personal Letter in Semibusiness Form 3

One-Page Report 4

First Page of Report with Footnotes 5

Sentence Outline 6

Topic Outline 7

Notice and Agenda of a Meeting 8

Minutes of a Meeting 9

Directions: Problem 3 Personal/Business Letter in Modified Block Style

1. Keyboard the letter in 47e, Problem 1, page 81. Use the directions given for the problem.

2. Set margins for a 50-space line using the new center point.

3. Refer to the style guide general information given on page 183 for the placement of the page number.

LESSON 112

70-space line

5 minutes

112a ● Keyboard Review

Directions: Keyboard each line three times SS. DS between 3-line groups.

keep fingers deeply curved

alphabet Excited crowds enjoy big trapeze events and frequently clap them back.

figure While Maury Wills stole 104 bases in 1962, he was thrown out 13 times.

4th finger was upon saw polite warm zone zeal police quake quack quit pay pad paw

easy They who spend their leisure time in the right way are sure to profit.

| 1 | 2 | 3 | 4 | 5 | 6 | 7 | 8 | 9 | 10 | 11 | 12 | 13 | 14 |

30b ● Timed Writings

Directions: Take two 3-minute writings on the ¶ below DS. Circle errors. Figure *gwam*. Submit the better writing.

all letters used 1.2 si

	gwam 1'	3'
It has been said that the only sure and safe	9	3	29
way for people to double their money is to fold it.	20	7	33
While this remark was likely made in jest, there is	30	10	36
more than a little truth in it. Before you decide	40	13	39
where to invest the money you earned, give a good	50	17	43
deal of thought to the task. You may want to quiz	61	20	46
an expert in these matters. Money comes too hard	71	24	50
for you to squander it in the wrong place.	79	26	52

gwam 1' | 1 | 2 | 3 | 4 | 5 | 6 | 7 | 8 | 9 | 10 |
3' | 1 | 2 | 3 | 4 |

30c ● Tabulator Control

Directions: 1. Clear all tab stops.
2. Check to see that margin stops are set for a 50-space line.
3. Set the tab stop for the second column 21 spaces from the left margin. Set the tab stop for the third column 21 spaces from the first tab stop. Return the carriage or carrier to the left margin.
4. Keyboard each line DS; tab between words. Repeat if time permits.

margin	tab	tab
|←—— 21 spaces ——→| |←—— 21 spaces ——→|
buffer	memory	program
computer	modem	software
diskette	network	storage
keyboard	printer	terminal

30d ● Listening for the Bell

Directions: Keyboard the ¶ below with a 50-space line, then with a 60-space line. Let the bell guide you in returning the carriage or carrier. Use the margin-release key to allow you to type beyond your margin stop.

all letters used 1.2 si

words

keep fingers deeply curved

	words
States that require auto inspections say half	9
of the cars fail to pass the first time. This means	20
that about half the cars driven on the roads are	30
faulty in some way. Think about this the next time	40
a car zooms by or you are caught in a traffic jam.	50

Unit 13 ■ Preparing a Student-Writer's Style Guide

(Lessons 111–115)

General Directions

Use a 70-space line for all lessons in this unit (center − 35; center + 35 + 5) unless otherwise directed. SS sentences and drill lines; DS paragraphs.

LESSON 111

5 minutes

111a ● Keyboard Review

Directions: Keyboard each line three times SS. DS between 3-line groups.

alphabet	I was quite lucky that my jams won five prizes at today's big exhibit.
fig/sym	My projector has an f/1.2 lens, 406-foot take-up reel, and costs $375.
direct reaches	herb bramble breeze bum tumble grumble stumble mumble peck wreck cedes
easy	Signs of rising profits will be found in most firms during the spring.

| 1 | 2 | 3 | 4 | 5 | 6 | 7 | 8 | 9 | 10 | 11 | 12 | 13 | 14 |

10 minutes

111b ● Timed Writings

Directions: **1.** Take two 1' writings on ¶1, 81d, page 140. Figure *gwam* on the better writing.

2. Take one 5' writing on all five ¶s combined. Circle errors and figure *gwam*.

5 minutes

111c ● Problem Typing: Student Writer's Style Guide

General Information:

1. In the problems in this unit, you will prepare a booklet entitled STUDENT WRITER'S STYLE GUIDE. Keep the pages you prepare until the entire booklet is finished. The booklet will contain 11 pages in all.

2. Correct all errors.

3. The booklet will be stapled at the left side. Refer to leftbound reports, 84b, page 145, for formatting procedures, if necessary.

4. Number the pages as indicated in the table of contents. Keyboard page numbers on the fourth line space from the top, 1" from the right edge of the paper.

5. The center point for all pages in the booklet is 3 spaces to the right of the point normally used. Use this center point in centering titles and in setting margins when the directions call for setting a certain space line, such as a 50-space line.

25 minutes

Directions: Problem 1 Title Page of Style Guide

Prepare a title page similar to the one shown in 85c, page 147. Keyboard the title, STUDENT WRITER'S STYLE GUIDE, your name, and the current date on the page.

continued on next page

Unit 5 ▪ Learning the Basic Symbol Keys (Lessons 31–35)

General Directions

Use a 60-space line for all lessons in this unit (center − 30; center + 30 + 5). SS sentences and drill lines. DS between repeated groups of lines. DS paragraph copy. Set tabulator for a 5-space paragraph indention.

LESSON 31

5 minutes   **31a ● Keyboard Review**

Directions: Keyboard each sentence twice SS. DS between 2-line groups.

alphabet   They flew D. G. Chavez home quickly by jet at their expense.

figures   Yoki bought 24 dozen streamers and 350 balloons for a party.

easy   Make sure that the fuel is kept where there will be no risk.

| 1 | 2 | 3 | 4 | 5 | 6 | 7 | 8 | 9 | 10 | 11 | 12 |

---

7 minutes   **31b ● Location of $ (dollar), # (number or pounds), and / (diagonal)**

Reach to $ (dollar sign)
1. Shift, then reach up to $ with the f finger.
2. Touch $f lightly without moving other fingers from their typing position.

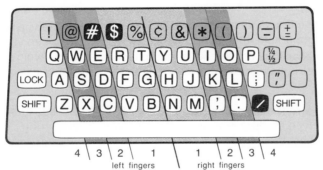

4 \ 3 \ 2 \ 1   1 \ 2 \ 3 \ 4
left fingers   right fingers

Reach to # (number sign)
1. Shift, then reach up to # with the d finger.
2. Touch #d lightly without moving other fingers from their typing position.

f4f f$f f4f f$f $f $f $4   Type twice on same line   d3d d#d d3d d#d #d #d #3

Reach to $

Reach to /

Reach to / (diagonal)
1. Reach down to / with the ; finger.
2. Touch /; lightly without moving other fingers from their typing position.

;/; ;/; ;?; ;/; /; /; ;/

Reach to #

31c ● Location Drills $, #, and /   8 minutes

Directions: Keyboard each line twice SS. DS between 2-line groups.

Note: Do not space between $, #, or / and a figure.

$ They paid $4.40, $4.50, $4.80, and $4.90 for the four books.

Number 134 is written as #134. They wrote 33 pounds as 33#.

/   Use the / to type fractions, as 1/3, 1/5, 1/6, 11/16, 15/16.

LESSON 110

110a ● Keyboard Review

Directions: Keyboard each sentence three times SS. DS between 3-line groups.

alphabet My first objective is plainly to make a good showing on the next quiz.

figure Attendance at all our home games increased 115% between 1984 and 1986.

adjacent keys As they walked past in review, Terry joined the last column of troops.

easy Your smile is one thing that is worth more when it is given to others.

| 1 | 2 | 3 | 4 | 5 | 6 | 7 | 8 | 9 | 10 | 11 | 12 | 13 | 14 |

110b ● Timed Writings

Directions: **1.** Take two 5′ writings on 106c, page 177. Work for best possible speed with a minimum of errors.

2. Figure *gwam*; submit the better of the two writings to your teacher.

110c ● Problem Typing: Justifying the Right Margin

School newspapers prepared on duplicating machines are sometimes typed so that all the lines, except the last line in a paragraph, are even at the right margin. The copy then has the appearance of a printed page.

Note: If you are using a machine that automatically justifies the right margin, *do not* use the automatic function. Learn to justify the right margin in the typewriter mode.

Directions for justifying right margin:
1. Type a line of diagonals to indicate maximum line length (pica 30; elite, 36).
2. Keyboard the article. Add diagonals to the short lines to make them even with the line of diagonals at the top.
3. Retype the article. Add one extra space between words for each diagonal in the line. Avoid putting extra spaces in one line under extra spaces in the line above.

Directions: Problem 1 Article with Justified Right Margin
1. Prepare the article below on 4¼″ × 11″ paper. Type the first draft with diagonals for short lines; then type the final draft with justified lines.

2. Use directions in 108c, page 180, for preparing newspaper copy, but justify right margin. Use the title for this article: WHAT'S YOUR TITLE?

```
/////////////////////////////
    No matter what kind of///
job you have these days, you//
can be sure someone will give/
it a title that sounds impor-/
tant.  A janitor is an engi-//
neer of sanitation; an usher//
is an audience guide; and a///
dog catcher is a supervisor of
missing canines.
```

```
    No matter   what   kind  of
job you have  these days,  you
can be  sure someone will give
it a title that  sounds impor-
tant.   A janitor is  an engi-
neer of  sanitation;  an usher
is  an audience  guide;  and a
dog catcher is a supervisor of
missing canines.
```

Directions: Problem 2 Article with Justified Right Margin
Prepare 94c, page 160, in a form suitable for a school newspaper. Justify the right margin; use as the title KEEP YOUR HOUSE COOL.

110d ● Extra Credit

Directions: Prepare the two topics you *did not* use in Problem 2 of 109c, page 181, as feature stories for your newspaper. Use proper newspaper format.

31d ● **Comparison Sentence Skill Builder**

Directions: Keyboard two 1' writings on each sentence SS.   Compare rates on the three sentences.

easy   Some of the girls also thought that her goals were too high.
fig/sym Beginning on 10/17/86, the cost of Item #465 will be $23.95.
shift   Tom Doyel, Michelle Dunn, and R. C. Jan won the Lacy awards.

| 1 | 2 | 3 | 4 | 5 | 6 | 7 | 8 | 9 | 10 | 11 | 12 |

15 minutes   **31e** ● **Speed Ladder Paragraphs**

Your teacher may call half minute guides. You should be at or past the first . at 30" to finish the ¶ in 1'.

Directions: **1.** Take a 1' writing on ¶1 DS. **2.** When you complete ¶1 in 1', continue on to ¶2. Repeat this procedure as you try   to complete all five ¶s in the given time. **3.** Take three 1' writings on any ¶ you cannot finish in 1'.

all letters used   1.2 si   gwam 1' | 3'

return
carriage
quickly

	gwam 1'	3'
One bit of advice you should heed is to keep your sense	11	4
of humor, even when things look their worst.	20	7
In fact, being able to laugh at oneself may well be the	11	10
secret to a good life and real success. That is no joke	24	14
either.	25	15
A good laugh can make living much easier. A joke cuts	11	19
problems down to size. It lowers tension if tempers start to	23	23
flare and things get out of hand.	30	25
Humor brings out the best in other folks too. It helps	11	29
them relax so they can enjoy being with you. They respond	23	33
in kind when facts are given to them in a clever, funny way.	35	37
The greatest thing about a sense of humor, however, is	11	40
that it is so good for your health. A quip can do as much	23	44
for how a person feels as jogging around the block. People	36	49
who laugh, they say, last.	40	50

gwam 1' | 1 | 2 | 3 | 4 | 5 | 6 | 7 | 8 | 9 | 10 | 11 | 12 |
     3' | 1 | 2 | 3 | 4 |

31f ● **Extra-Credit Typing**

Directions: Try to keyboard each of the ¶s in 31e without any errors. You will not be   timed on these ¶s. When you complete a ¶ without error, move on to the next.

LESSON 109

109a ● Keyboard Review

5 minutes

Directions: Keyboard each sentence three times SS. DS between 3-line groups.

alphabet	Vickie Morgan did an excellent job of sewing the skirt zipper quickly.
fig/sym	Average farmland in New Jersey is $2,057/acre; it's $93 in New Mexico.
left hand	We saw brave crews steer fast craft as great westward breezes started.
easy	When the road on which you go is straight, it is not easy to get lost.

| 1 | 2 | 3 | 4 | 5 | 6 | 7 | 8 | 9 | 10 | 11 | 12 | 13 | 14 |

---

10 minutes

109b ● Skill Builder from Rough Draft Copy

Directions: Take two 1' writings on each sentence.

words

1 we now we can see others some of of our own traits--good or bad.   14

2 The quick way gain your goals is to help another gain his.   14

3 Always choose those words which give life to your thoughts.   14

4 All of us must listen about 4 times a a person talks.   14

---

30 minutes

109c ● Problem Typing: Preparing Newspaper Copy

Directions: Problem 1 Items of Special Interest

1. Keyboard an article entitled (*Use Your Name*) SAYS--. Make the article consist of the items listed below.

2. Follow the directions for preparing newspaper copy given in 108c, page 180. Compose an appropriate side heading for each item.

86c	Skill Builder from Script	page 148
87b	Skill Builder	page 150
102b	Skill Builder from Script	page 171

Directions: Problem 2 Feature Story

1. Compose on a full sheet in rough-draft form a feature story on one of the following topics. The reference following each topic is to a similar article in the textbook. You may get ideas from these articles, but do not copy them; compose your own story.

2. Make a final copy of your feature article on 4¼" × 11" paper in the same form you used for keyboarding the other items for the school newspaper.

3. Use your name as the author; give your story an appropriate title.

The Energy Crisis (61e Paragraph Guided Writings page 107)

Is College For Me? (73b Speed Builder page 126)

How Many People? (98b Speed Builder page 165)

LESSON 32

32a ● Keyboard Review

5 minutes   **Directions:** Keyboard each sentence twice SS. DS between 2-line groups.

alphabet   Zelda expects to be in Quincy for a visit with Jack Goodman.

fig/sym   Our hours will be from 9:30 a.m. to 6:30 p.m. after June 15.

easy   Their first goal is to make enough to own their own bicycle.

| 1 | 2 | 3 | 4 | 5 | 6 | 7 | 8 | 9 | 10 | 11 | 12 |

7 minutes   ## 32b ● Location of % (percent), & (ampersand), and - (hyphen) or --(dash)

Reach to % (percent)
1. Shift, then reach up to % with the f finger.
2. Touch %f lightly without moving other fingers from their typing position.

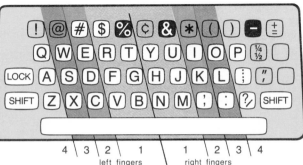

4 \ 3 \ 2 \ 1   1 / 2 / 3 / 4
left fingers   right fingers

Reach to & (ampersand)
1. Shift, then reach up to & with the j finger.
2. Touch &j lightly without moving other fingers from their typing position.

f5f f%f f5f f%f %f %f %5   Type twice on same line   j7j j&j j7j j&j &j &j &7

Reach to %

Reach to -

Do not space before or after - (hyphen) or --(dash).

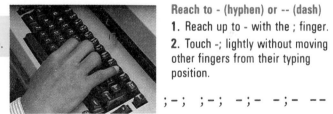

Reach to - (hyphen) or -- (dash)
1. Reach up to - with the ; finger.
2. Touch -; lightly without moving other fingers from their typing position.

;-; ;-; -;- -;- -- -; ;-

Do not space between a figure and %.

32c ● Location Drills %, &, and -   8 minutes

Directions: Keyboard each line twice SS. DS between 2-line groups.

%   Rate increases were as follows: 17%, 15%, 9%, 23%, and 17%.

&   The Day & Night Market ordered 77 sets from Johnson & Gomez.

-   Our 7-story building--the one in Reno--was sold in mid-June.

Reach to &

Space before and after the &, which may be used in place of the word *and*.

32d ● Script Skill Builder   10 minutes

Directions: Keyboard the following ¶ twice DS. Take two 1' writings. Figure *gwam*.

all letters used   1.2 si

gwam 1'

Quite a few people would be just amazed if they   10
knew that the penguin is the only bird that can swim   20
yet cannot fly. The fact is, experts say, this odd   31
creature can move through the water a lot faster   40
than you or I can.   44

108c ● Problem Typing: Preparing Newspaper Copy

In the next three lessons, you will prepare copy for an editor. The copy will be part of a newspaper duplicated on 8½″ × 11″ paper.

Many schools, clubs, and other organizations prepare and issue newspapers and newsletters of the type you will prepare in the next 3 lessons. Items of interest are composed and prepared in accordance with

set rules and are submitted to an editor. The editor checks the items and arranges the copy on plan sheets. When all copy is arranged, the paper is duplicated or printed, assembled, and distributed.

Directions for Preparing Newspaper Copy: **1.** Cut several sheets of paper in half lengthwise (4¼″ × 11″).

2. Make a rough-draft copy of your item on a separate sheet of paper. Proofread; mark errors.

To review centering lines on odd size paper, refer to page 67.

3. Prepare your final copy on 4¼″ × 11″ paper. Set margins for a 3″ line (pica, 30 spaces; elite, 36 spaces). If the right margin is to be justified (see page 182), the

maximum line length is 30 or 36 spaces.

4. Center and type main headings in all capitals. If a side heading is used, capitalize the initial letter of each main word in the heading. Triple space above a side heading; double space below the heading. Single space paragraph copy; double space between paragraphs. Indent paragraphs 3 spaces. Leave a 1″ top margin on each sheet.

Directions: Problem 1 Feature Article

1. Prepare a copy of 101d, page 170, as a feature story for your school newspaper. Use the following heading: THE PERFECT GIFT.

2. When preparing your copy, follow the general directions given above. Your copy should look like the copy in the partial illustration at the right.

```
          THE PERFECT GIFT

    The next time you are faced
with the problem of what to
buy the person who has every-
thing, why not consider buying
a mule?  While this idea might
sound odd at first, you should
realize the many advantages of
such a gift.

    Here are just a couple of
them.  First of all, a mule
requires much less upkeep than
```

Directions: Problem 2 Special Items

1. The second sentence in many Keyboard Reviews in Cycle 3 is a factual statement of general interest. Select six or more of these sentences for an article. Use the following heading: FACTS OF LIFE. Use your name as the author.

2. Your copy should look like the copy in the partial illustration at the right.

```
         FACTS OF LIFE

          Use Your Name

    As of September 1, 1983,
the nation was importing only
28% of its oil.

    A 1964 Civil Rights Act
filibuster took up 77 days
(March 26-June 10).
```

Directions: Problem 3 Short Item

Prepare the paragraph in 77b, page 132, as an item for your newspaper. Give the item

a suitable title; use your name as the author.

10 minutes **32e ●** **Timed Writings**

Directions: Keyboard two 3' writings on Lesson 31e, page 50. Figure *gwam*. Submit the better of the two writings.

---

5 minutes **32f ●** **Technique Builder**

Directions: Keyboard each line twice SS. DS between 2-line groups.

1 three happy jetty room bill week inn message sleep mood well
2 issue guess look good less rubber apply proof speed too free
3 buzz allow apply feel fall soon funny offer muzzle add bluff

---

LESSON 33   60-space line

5 minutes **33a ●** **Keyboard Review**

Directions: Keyboard each sentence two times SS. DS between 2-line groups.

alphabet Phil Singer wanted Liza to fly Jack to Quebec next November.

fig/sym The increase--20%--raised the price of a $6 ticket to $7.20.

easy I know for sure which items are on sale at the market today.

| 1 | 2 | 3 | 4 | 5 | 6 | 7 | 8 | 9 | 10 | 11 | 12 |

---

5 minutes **33b ●** **Location of (and) (parentheses)**

Reach to ((parenthesis)

1. Shift, then reach up to (with the l finger.

2. Touch (l lightly without moving other fingers from their typing position.

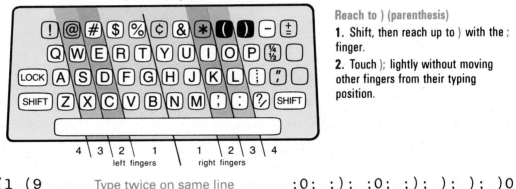

4 \ 3 \ 2 \ 1   1 / 2 / 3 / 4
left fingers   right fingers

Reach to) (parenthesis)

1. Shift, then reach up to) with the ; finger.

2. Touch); lightly without moving other fingers from their typing position.

191 1(1 191 1(1 (1 (1 (9   Type twice on same line   ;0; ;); ;0; ;);););)0

Reach to (

Reach to)

33c ● **Location Drills: (and)**   10 minutes

Directions: Keyboard each line twice SS. DS between 2-line groups.

Note: Do not space between ( ) and the words they enclose.

(To type (, shift and strike the 9.   Type 9; then (9 and (99.

) To type), shift and strike the 0.   Type 0; then 0) and 00).

Most of the students (190 to be exact) passed all the tests.

( ) The report (handwritten) is quoted in full.   (See page 124.)

The record (206.9 miles per hour) was held by Brown (Paris).

Directions: Problem 2
On a half sheet, prepare the notice shown below. Center the notice vertically; set a 70-space line and begin the first entry at left margin; center second entry; make third entry end at right margin. Space copy vertically as you did in Problem 1.

To review centering items under headings, refer to page 117.

P H Y S I C A L   F I T N E S S   A W A R D S

Seventh Grade Winner	GRAND SLAM AWARD	Eighth Grade Winner
Chris Greyfeather	Patty Bryan	Lowell Reynolds

P H Y S I C A L   F I T N E S S   A W A R D S

LESSON 108

70-space line

5 minutes

108a ● Keyboard Review

Directions: Keyboard each sentence 3 times SS. DS between 3-line groups.

strike keys with quick, crisp, short strokes

alphabet Mark will require five dozen big boxes for the apricots early in July.

figure Charles Lindbergh crossed the Atlantic in 33 hours 39 minutes in 1927.

direct reach I doubt that Brad brought my Uncle Cecil an unusually carved umbrella.

easy They thought that six or eight of their firms would make a big profit.

| 1 | 2 | 3 | 4 | 5 | 6 | 7 | 8 | 9 | 10 | 11 | 12 | 13 | 14 |

10 minutes

108b ● Speed Builder

Directions: Take two 1' writings on each ¶; try to increase speed on the second writing. Figure *gwam*.

Alternate Procedure: Work for speed as you take one 5' writing on all three ¶s combined. Figure *gwam*.

all letters used 1.3 si

	gwam 1'	5'
The problem of too much noise is drawing quite a bit of attention	13	3 / 33
from people who are concerned with quality of life these days. We know	28	6 / 36
that prolonged exposure to high noise levels can cause deafness, and	41	8 / 39
doctors now tell us it affects nearly all the functions of the body.	55	11 / 42
As crazy as it may sound, some experts suggest that we add more	13	14 / 44
noises to drown out the racket around us. One firm even sells a gadget	27	17 / 47
which makes a constant hum, like a breeze blowing in the trees, to mask	42	19 / 50
out unwanted sounds.	46	20 / 51
Such an idea may have some merit, but not all authorities think	13	23 / 54
this solution is a sensible one. They say adding more noise may just	27	26 / 57
make a bad problem worse. In their view, the only real answer is to	41	28 / 59
find the source of the noise and take steps to reduce it.	52	31 / 62

gwam 1' | 1 | 2 | 3 | 4 | 5 | 6 | 7 | 8 | 9 | 10 | 11 | 12 | 13 | 14 |
5' | 1   2   3 |

33d ● Continuity Practice

Directions: 1. Keyboard the ¶ below one time DS. Circle all errors.
2. Try to type correctly three times the words in which you made an error.

3. Try to type the entire ¶ without errors as many times as you can in the time remaining.

all letters used 1.2 si

words

keep fingers deeply curved

Since wages can rise only so fast, firms try quite 10

hard to keep workers pleased in other ways. Some let them 22

take extra time off; or they may offer low cost loans or 33

even prizes to help make sure people like their jobs. 44

| 1 | 2 | 3 | 4 | 5 | 6 | 7 | 8 | 9 | 10 |

17 minutes **33e ● Timed Writings**

Directions: 1. Take one 3' writing. Figure *gwam*.
2. Take two 1' writings on each ¶.

3. Take one 3' writing. Figure *gwam*. Compare this rate with your first 3' writing.

gwam 1' | 3'

¶1 1.2 si

Mistakes might be a sign of progress. They are made when 12 | 4 | 33

we try out new or better ways of doing a job. The people who 24 | 8 | 37

succeed do not make the same mistake twice; they try to make 36 | 12 | 41

some new ones. 39 | 13 | 42

¶2 1.1 si

The world is full of willing people: some are willing to 11 | 17 | 45

work; the rest are willing to let them. You may know that 23 | 21 | 49

there is no such thing in this world as something for nothing. 36 | 25 | 54

We must all be willing to work for the things we want. 47 | 29 | 57

gwam 1' | 1 | 2 | 3 | 4 | 5 | 6 | 7 | 8 | 9 | 10 | 11 | 12 |
3' | 1 | 2 | 3 | 4 |

LESSON 34

60-space line

5 minutes **34a ● Keyboard Review**

Directions: Keyboard each sentence twice SS. DS between 2-line groups.

keep arms and wrists quiet

alphabet Kim required only five major exercises with the big trapeze.
fig/sym On June 15, Flight #59 left at 7:35 with 7 men and 39 women.
easy It will pay them to take some time to plan for their visits.

| 1 | 2 | 3 | 4 | 5 | 6 | 7 | 8 | 9 | 10 | 11 | 12 |

LESSON 107

107a ● Keyboard Review

5 minutes | **Directions:** Keyboard each sentence three times SS. DS between 3-line groups.

do not pause
between words

alphabet	We explorers quickly made several journeys through Zimbabwe last fall.
figure	Ted Williams, who hit .406 in 1941, was the last player to reach .400.
adjacent keys	Treats were served in class prior to a talk on the topic of mnemonics.
easy	If they spend their time working in the right way, they can type more.

| 1 | 2 | 3 | 4 | 5 | 6 | 7 | 8 | 9 | 10 | 11 | 12 | 13 | 14 |

10 minutes

107b ● Language Arts Skills: Punctuation Guides (Quotation Marks)

Directions: The following are guides for the use of quotation marks and sentences that illustrate the use of those guides. Study each guide; then keyboard the sentence that illustrates the guide. Keyboard each sentence twice SS; DS between groups.

reach to the
shift key
quickly and
firmly

Place quotation marks around the exact words of a speaker.
Professor Cole said, "Only 29 percent of the earth's surface is land."

When the quotation is broken to identify the speaker, put quotation marks around each part.
"The deepest mine in the world," they continued, "is 9,811 feet deep."

If the second part of the quotation is a new sentence, use a capital letter.
"We are going to Hawaii," she replied softly. "Here are our tickets."

Use no quotation marks with an indirect quotation.
David said he thinks that the Grand Coulee is the world's biggest dam.

Use quotation marks around the titles of articles, songs, poems, themes, short stories, and the like.
Gayle Sobolik wrote the report entitled, "Automation Isn't Automatic."

Always place the period or comma inside the closing quotation mark.
"Sweden," the first speaker insisted, "has the highest literacy rate."

30 minutes

107c ● Problem Typing: Bulletin Board Notices

Directions: Problem 1
On a half sheet, prepare the bulletin board notice shown below. Center the notice vertically and horizontally; set margins at each side of the main heading; align third line of notice at each margin.

To review spread headings, refer to page 139.

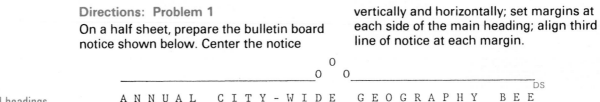

```
                              O
                        O  O
                                                              DS
ANNUAL  CITY-WIDE  GEOGRAPHY  BEE
                                                              SS
                              O  O
                           O
                          TS
```

Notice to All Contestants
DS
BUS LEAVES FOR IRWIN JUNIOR HIGH SCHOOL
DS
Faculty Parking Lot   Wednesday, May 18
DS
              8:30 a.m.

(continued on next page)

7 minutes **34b** ● **Location of ' (apostrophe) and ! (exclamation point)**

MANUAL KEYBOARD

Reach to ' (apostrophe)

1. Shift, then reach up to ' with the **k** finger.

2. Touch 'k lightly without moving other fingers from their typing position.

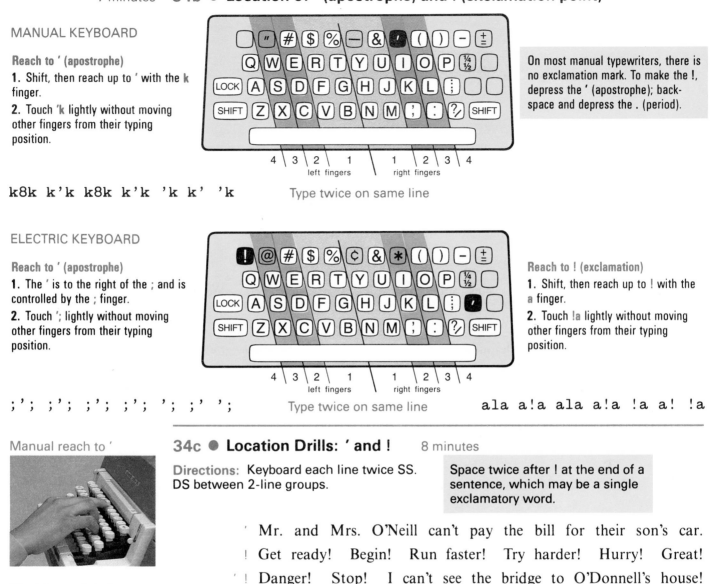

4 \ 3 \ 2 \ 1   1 / 2 / 3 / 4
left fingers   right fingers

On most manual typewriters, there is no exclamation mark. To make the !, depress the ' (apostrophe); backspace and depress the . (period).

k8k k'k k8k k'k 'k k' 'k

Type twice on same line

ELECTRIC KEYBOARD

Reach to ' (apostrophe)

1. The ' is to the right of the ; and is controlled by the ; finger.

2. Touch '; lightly without moving other fingers from their typing position.

Reach to ! (exclamation)

1. Shift, then reach up to ! with the **a** finger.

2. Touch !a lightly without moving other fingers from their typing position.

4 \ 3 \ 2 \ 1   1 / 2 / 3 / 4
left fingers   right fingers

;'; ;'; ;'; ;'; '; ;' ';

Type twice on same line

ala a!a ala a!a !a a! !a

Manual reach to '

Electric reach to '

Reach to !

34c ● **Location Drills: ' and !**   8 minutes

Directions: Keyboard each line twice SS. DS between 2-line groups.

Space twice after ! at the end of a sentence, which may be a single exclamatory word.

' Mr. and Mrs. O'Neill can't pay the bill for their son's car.

! Get ready! Begin! Run faster! Try harder! Hurry! Great!

' ! Danger! Stop! I can't see the bridge to O'Donnell's house!

34d ● **Continuity Practice: Numbers and Symbols**   10 minutes

Directions: Keyboard the ¶ below once DS.

all letters used   words

Bits and pieces of news (called trivia) make interesting 11
reading. Did you realize that the 1903 Thomas automobile had 24
a tilt steering wheel, or that Al Capone's gross income in 36
1927 was $105 million? The Baskin (Louisiana) High School 47
girls' basketball team won 218 games in a row (1947-1953). 59
Each day the average American household has a TV set playing 72
for 6 hours and 44 minutes. 77

| 1 | 2 | 3 | 4 | 5 | 6 | 7 | 8 | 9 | 10 | 11 | 12 |

106c ● Speed Ladder Paragraphs

Directions: Take 1' writings on each ¶ as you did in 96d, page 163.

all letters used   1.3 si

gwam 5'

For thousands of years now, ever since the beginning of history 3 | 55
in fact, people have searched far and wide for gold. To locate this 5 | 58
most precious metal, they have moved and crushed enough rock to build 8 | 61
a mountain range. 9 | 61

While gold was first discovered on or near the ground, today the 11 | 64
majority of it is mined far beneath the surface. It is found buried in 14 | 67
quartz veins often more than two miles deep. We dig deeper for gold 17 | 70
than for any other mineral we use. 19 | 71

Despite this constant searching, however, we have been able to 21 | 73
accumulate only a modest supply. Hard as it may be to believe, all the 24 | 76
gold in the world could be placed in a cube about fifty feet high. It 27 | 79
could be stored on the first floor of the White House. 29 | 81

Gold has been used in many different ways throughout the years. 32 | 84
It serves quite well for money because it lasts a long time and can be 34 | 87
shaped easily into coins. Since it is much desired for its beauty, 37 | 90
it is often made into jewelry. Much gold also goes into fillings for 40 | 92
teeth. 40 | 93

Although no one knows for certain exactly how much more gold is 43 | 95
left to be discovered, experts say there is not a lot. It now appears 46 | 98
that gold may well be in short supply before the end of this century. 49 | 101
If these predictions are accurate, gold will become even more precious 51 | 104
to us than it is today. 52 | 105

gwam 5' | 1 | 2 | 3 |

106d ● Composing at Your Machine

Directions: Compose a paragraph, telling in your own words what the following quotation means to you.

"The best place to find a helping hand," Banks said, "is at the end of your arm."

34e ● Speed Ladder Paragraphs

Directions: **1.** Take a 1' writing on ¶1 DS. **2.** When you complete ¶1 in 1', continue on to ¶2. Repeat this procedure as you try to complete all five ¶s in the given time. **3.** Take three 1' writings on any ¶ you cannot finish in 1'.

Your teacher may call half minute guides. You should be at or past the first . at 30" to finish the ¶ in 1'.

strike keys with quick, sharp strokes

all letters used   1.2 si   gwam 1' | 3'

	1'	3'
Friends fill a vital role in life. They provide comfort	11	4
as they let you know you are not all alone.	20	7
With every new friend you explore a new path in life.	11	10
You will learn more and more the wider your circle of friends	23	14
becomes.	25	15
You might just hit it off with someone right away, or	11	19
it may take months before you do so. Recognize that each	22	22
new friendship moves at its own speed.	30	25
One of the very best times to meet new people is when	11	29
the school year begins. Then you have some good chances to	23	33
get acquainted with those outside your circle of old friends.	35	37
While we know how important our friends are to us, this	11	40
discussion will not be complete without some words of caution.	24	45
The advice may be trite, but it's true. To have a friend,	36	49
you must also be one.	40	50

gwam 1' | 1 | 2 | 3 | 4 | 5 | 6 | 7 | 8 | 9 | 10 | 11 | 12 |
       3' | | 1 | | 2 | | 3 | | 4 |

LESSON 35   60-space line

5 minutes

35a ● Keyboard Review

Directions: Keyboard each sentence twice SS. DS between 2-line groups.

alphabet Jeff expects to have two dozen big aprons made very quickly.

fig/sym A. Tangora (1923) typed 147 net words a minute--for an hour!

easy He knows you can locate all eight of the islands on the map.

| 1 | 2 | 3 | 4 | 5 | 6 | 7 | 8 | 9 | 10 | 11 | 12 |

105c ● Problem Typing: Luncheon Program and Menu

Directions: Keyboard the Luncheon Program and Menu shown below. Follow the directions given in 104d, page 174.

Space and arrange the copy attractively on both pages of the fold-over sheet.

Cover Page

L U N C H E O N   M E E T I N G

JUNIOR ACHIEVEMENT ASSOCIATION

```
        XX
       X  X
      X    X
     X  JA  X
      X    X
       X  X
        XX
```

Crystal Dining Room

Granada Inn

November 5, 19--

Inside Page

P R O G R A M

Presiding	Terry McDonald, President
Introductions	Sandra Nagai, Vice President
Keynote Address	"Partners in Progress" R. A. Flam, Chairperson Industry-Education Council
Awards	Inga Pietrowski, Manager Garabedian Enterprises

L U N C H E O N   M E N U

Tossed Salad	Green Bean Casserole
Veal Cordon Bleu	Rolls, Butter, and Jelly
Baked Potato	Bavarian Cream Pie

Coffee, Tea, Milk

LESSON 106

70-space line

5 minutes **106a ● Keyboard Review**

Directions: Keyboard each sentence three times SS. DS between 3-line groups.

alphabet Everybody expected a big kid my size to qualify for the javelin throw.

figure Robin could have purchased a Model 27F-205 for less than $314 in 1985.

balanced/one-hand We saw their pals. Read my theme at noon. We saw them work and rest.

easy Turn your book so that it is at the right angle for you when you type.

| 1 | 2 | 3 | 4 | 5 | 6 | 7 | 8 | 9 | 10 | 11 | 12 | 13 | 14 |

---

10 minutes **106b ● Skill Comparison**

Directions: Take two 1' writings on each sentence. Compare *gwam*. Try to match your "easy" sentence speed on the other sentences.

easy Do not rest your fingers on the keys if you wish to reach a high rate.

fig/sym Each person's share (according to the 1985 figures) was less than $15.

rough draft the people who work always seem to get the most out of the life.

shift Madge saw June and Mildred Avery at the Georgia State Fair in Atlanta.

35b ● **Location of " (quotation marks), * (asterisk), and _ (underline)**

Manual reach to "

MANUAL KEYBOARD

4 \ 3 \ 2 \ 1   1 / 2 / 3 / 4
left fingers   right fingers

Manual reach to _

Reach to " (quotation)

1. Shift, then reach up to " with the s finger.

2. Touch "s lightly without moving other fingers from their typing position.

s2s s"s s2s s"s "s s" "s

Type each drill twice

Reach to _ (underline)

1. Shift, then reach up to _ with the j finger.

2. Touch _j lightly without moving other fingers from their typing position.

j6j j–j j6j j–j –j j– –j

Manual reach to *

Reach to * (asterisk)

1. Shift, then reach up to * with the ; finger.

2. Touch *; lightly without moving other fingers from their typing position.

;–; ;*; ;–; ;*; *; ;* *;

Electric reach to "

ELECTRIC KEYBOARD

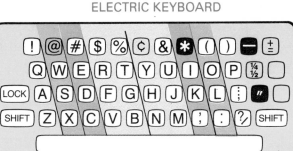

4 \ 3 \ 2 \ 1   1 / 2 / 3 / 4
left fingers   right fingers

Electric reach to _

Reach to " (quotation)

1. The " is the shift of the ' and is controlled by the ; finger.

2. Touch "; lightly without moving other fingers from their typing position.

;'; ;"; ;'; ;"; "; ;" ";

Type each drill twice

Reach to _ (underline)

1. Shift, then reach up to _ with the ; finger.

2. Touch _; lightly without moving other fingers from their typing position.

;–; ;–; ;–; ;–; –; ;– –;

Electric reach to *

Reach to * (asterisk)

1. Shift, then reach up to * with the k finger.

2. Touch *k lightly without moving other fingers from their typing position.

k8k k*k k8k k*k *k k* *k

104d, continued | **To center lines on paper of odd size,** refer to directions on page 67 if necessary. | **To type spread headings,** refer to directions on page 139 if necessary.

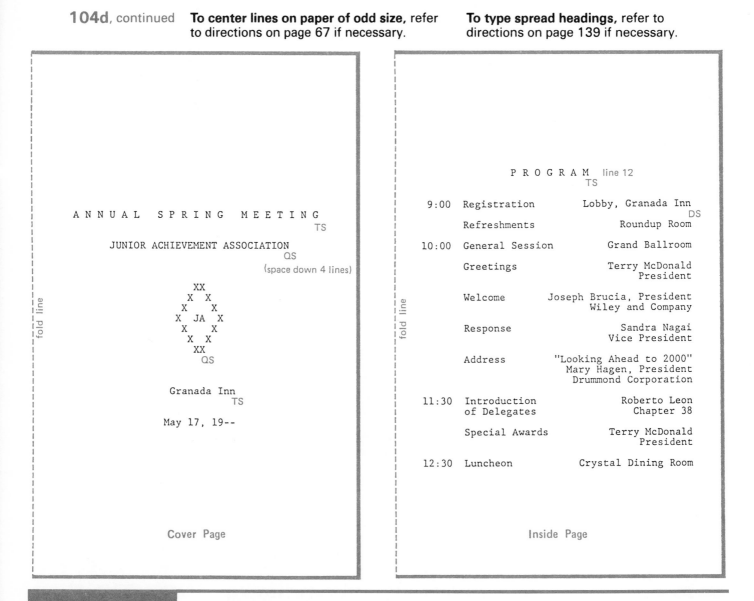

```
                ANNUAL  SPRING  MEETING
                            TS
           JUNIOR ACHIEVEMENT ASSOCIATION
                        QS
                (space down 4 lines)

                       XX
                      X  X
                     X    X
                     X  JA  X
                      X    X
                       X  X
                       XX
                       QS


                   Granada Inn
                       TS
                  May 17, 19--
```

Cover Page

```
        P R O G R A M   line 12
                    TS
9:00  Registration       Lobby, Granada Inn
                                   DS
      Refreshments          Roundup Room

10:00 General Session       Grand Ballroom

      Greetings           Terry McDonald
                              President

      Welcome        Joseph Brucia, President
                           Wiley and Company

      Response            Sandra Nagai
                          Vice President

      Address       "Looking Ahead to 2000"
                     Mary Hagen, President
                     Drummond Corporation

11:30 Introduction          Roberto Leon
      of Delegates          Chapter 38

      Special Awards      Terry McDonald
                              President

12:30 Luncheon         Crystal Dining Room
```

Inside Page

LESSON 105

70-space line

5 minutes **105a ● Keyboard Review**

Directions: Keyboard each line three times SS. DS between 3-line groups.

sit erect as you keyboard the copy

alphabet	Wendy bought an exquisite Navajo necklace for me on a trip to Arizona.
figure	About 49% of the men and women aged 20 or more now exercise regularly.
long reach	numb doubt sum any zebra hunt myself ace nurse mystery curve zany cent
easy	The officers thought it was their duty to visit with the past members.

| 1 | 2 | 3 | 4 | 5 | 6 | 7 | 8 | 9 | 10 | 11 | 12 | 13 | 14 |

---

15 minutes **105b ● Timed Writings**

Directions: Take two 5' writings on 101d, page 170. Work for best possible speed with a minimum of errors.

2. Figure *gwam*; submit the better of the two writings to your teacher.

35c ● Location Drills: ", *, and _

Directions: Keyboard each line twice SS. DS between 2-line groups.

To *underline*. Type the material, then backspace to the first letter, shift and strike the underline. Use the shift lock if several words are to be underlined. The underline is not broken between words unless each word is to be considered separately.

" Type "forty," not "fourty." Ken typed "ninty" for "ninety."

Hannah typed "advice" for "advise" and "libel" for "liable."

* You can use * for some footnotes. We quoted Ronald Reagan.*

_ Type slowly. Work for control. Keep your eyes on the copy.

"_ They were told to read "Building for a Bigger Role" in Time.

_ The title of their required text was Business Communication.

---

7 minutes **35d ● Technique Builder**

Directions: Keyboard each line three times SS. DS between 3-line groups.

type with a steady rhythm

1 if she gets | if he sees | if she reads | if he cares | if they were

2 he did see | she did look | he did get | she did pull | they did set

3 if they join | if they trade | if they jump | to my | if it only did

4 she may set | he may oil | he may rest | she may draw | she may wear

---

8 minutes **35e ● Timed Writings**

Directions: Keyboard two 3' writings on   the better writing.
Lesson 34e, page 55. Figure *gwam*. Submit

Punctuation Guide

1. Space twice after end-of-sentence punctuation.

2. Do not space after a period within an abbreviation. Space once after an abbreviation; twice if that period ends a sentence.

3. Space once after a comma.

4. Space twice after a colon. Do *not* space before or after a colon when stating time.

5. Type the dash with two hyphens; do not space before or after.

6. Do not space before or after the hyphen in a hyphenated word.

35f ● Spacing After Punctuation Marks: Review   10 minutes

Directions: Keyboard each line one time SS.

1 Joan heard the bell. It rang at night. Al did not hear it.

2 Will they go? Can he drive? Where does he live? Who's it?

3 Dash to the nearest exit! Hurry! Beware! This is madness!

4 I saw him at 11 a.m. They will leave on the 10 p.m. flight.

5 She bought statues, jewelry, and other gifts in Rome, Italy.

6 I used these figures: 39, 58, and 20. He left at 4:16 p.m.

7 Ridicule is thus the first--and the last--argument of fools.

8 The well-known skin diver could not find the life preserver.

| 1 | 2 | 3 | 4 | 5 | 6 | 7 | 8 | 9 | 10 | 11 | 12 |

LESSON 104

104a ● Keyboard Review

5 minutes

Directions: Keyboard each sentence three times SS. DS between 3-line groups.

keep fingers deeply curved

alphabet	Jack got zero on his final exam simply because we have hard questions.
figure	One giant Sequoia is 272 feet 4 inches tall with a girth of 79.1 feet.
home row	Eight jewelers finally agreed to make sketches of my flashy jade ring.
easy	We should not spend so much time asking others to do this and do that.

| 1 | 2 | 3 | 4 | 5 | 6 | 7 | 8 | 9 | 10 | 11 | 12 | 13 | 14 |

104b ● Language Arts Skills: Punctuation Guides (Dash and Parentheses)

5 minutes

Directions: The following are guides for the use of the dash and parentheses and sentences that illustrate the use of the guides. Study each guide; then keyboard the sentence that illustrates the guide. Keyboard each sentence twice SS; DS between 2-line groups.

Use a dash to show a sudden break in thought.
Time may be what all of us want most--but what we often use the worst.

Use a dash before the name of an author when it follows a direct quotation.
"We have nothing to fear but fear itself."--Franklin Delano Roosevelt.

Use parentheses to enclose an explanation.
They will start typing on the 13th line space (2 inches) from the top.

104c ● Skill Builder from Rough Draft

5 minutes

Directions: Take four 1' writings on the ¶; try to increase speed with each writing.

gwam 1'

Being able to type we sill for one minute is one thing;	11
being able to type do well on a longer writings is quite	21
another. Your must, of course, learn to be a study steady	32
learner and wroker. In a way, this is writing is a	41
text of you staying power. how will are you meeting	52
the this test?	54

104d ● Problem Typing: Program of a Meeting   30 minutes

To align items at the right margin, set a tab stop at the right margin. After typing copy in the line beginning at the left margin, tab to the right margin; backspace for each letter or space in the item; begin typing where backspacing ends.

Directions: **1.** Fold an 8½" × 11" sheet of paper in half to 5½" × 8½".

2. Insert the folded sheet with the fold at the left (against the paper guide).

3. Arrange the copy for the cover page shown on page 175. Center all copy vertically; center each line horizontally; use spacing guides on the model.

4. After you finish the cover, remove the paper, reverse the fold, and reinsert the paper with the fold at the left.

5. Arrange the copy for the inside page as illustrated on page 175. Center all copy vertically; use ½" side margins. Items at the right of the page are aligned at the right margin.

(continued on next page)

CYCLE TWO

Basic Personal Applications

Directions: On a full sheet, keyboard the school organization budget shown below. Leave a 2″ top margin; center copy vertically as directed on the model. Center each heading horizontally; center the body copy using the longest item in each column; leave 10 spaces between columns. Use leaders to separate the two columns.

Leaders: Type the first line of the first column; space once and note whether the printing point indicator is on an odd or even number. Type a period, space, period in turns across the line; stop 2 or 3 spaces before the second column. On lines that follow, align the periods with those in the first line, typing on odd or even numbers.

Dollar Signs: Place a dollar sign before the first amount in a column and before the total. Align the dollar sign 1 space to the left of the longest amount in the column. Type an underline under the last item in the column. Then DS and type the total line. Indent the word "Total" 5 spaces from the left margin.

Double Lines: To type double lines, type the first underline; then move the cylinder forward slightly and type the second underline.

ASSOCIATED STUDENT BODY BUDGET
                                                    DS
                    19-- to 19--
                                    TS

                Anticipated Income
                                        DS
Security Bank, Interest . . . . $ 40.00
                                            DS
Student Body Card Sales 1,500.00

Vending Machines 350.00

        Total $1,890.00
                                                TS

              Anticipated Expenditures
                                        DS
Activities . . . . $ 625.00
                                            DS
Awards 140.00

Yearbook 250.00

Newspaper 400.00

Student Body Cards 50.00

Equipment and Supplies 125.00

        Total $1,590.00
                                                TS

Total Budgeted Income $1,890.00
                                            DS
Total Budgeted Expenses 1,590.00

Total Budgeted Balance . . . . $ 300.00

You are now ready to build upon and apply the basic skills you learned in Cycle 1. The following is a preview of some of the problems you will be working on in Cycle 2.

Notices, Personal Notes, and Letters

You will learn procedures for keyboarding announcements, personal notes, and personal business letters in acceptable form.

Themes, Outlines, and Tables

These papers are an important part of school work. The guides that you will be given are those most commonly used in keyboarding themes, outlines, and tables.

Language Arts Development

One of your goals in this course is to be able to compose school and personal papers at the keyboard. The drills, spelling aids, and capitalization guides included in this cycle will help you achieve this goal.

Extra-Credit Assignments

Problems are given at the end of each unit for students who finish assignments ahead of schedule. Type these problems as time permits. You will be given extra-credit for these assignments.

Building Basic Skills

The more you improve your keyboarding skills, the easier it will be for you to concentrate on the papers you are preparing.

Help Yourself to Improve

Much of what you get out of the lessons in Cycle 2 will depend upon you. Here are some points to keep in mind as you prepare your lessons:

1. Have the desire to improve. You learn best when you really want to learn.
2. Have a clear goal in mind for each exercise. You cannot learn if you do not know what you should be learning. Keep your goals in mind as you keyboard the drills and problems.
3. Learn to plan your work. Part of this job requires you to read and hear directions correctly. In order to accomplish your goals, you must learn to follow directions carefully.

Unit 6 ■ Centering Notices and Announcements (Lessons 36–40)

General Directions

Use a 60-space line for all lessons in this unit (center − 30; center + 30 + 5). SS sentences and drill lines. DS between repeated groups of lines. DS paragraph copy.

Instructions for making corrections are given in Lesson 39 of this unit. Your instructor will tell you whether or not you are to correct errors on problems in Lessons 39 and 40.

LESSON 36

5 minutes   36a ● **Keyboard Review**

Directions: Keyboard each sentence three times SS. DS between 3-line groups.

use quick, sharp strokes

alphabet   I'm amazed Dave Kowing expects to qualify in the broad jump.

symbol   She assigned us three books: <u>Poland</u>, <u>Space</u>, and <u>Gorky Park</u>.

easy   At least eight of their members work there in the same firm.

| 1 | 2 | 3 | 4 | 5 | 6 | 7 | 8 | 9 | 10 | 11 | 12 |

Directions: Problem 2

1. On a half sheet, center the graph shown below.
2. Center both lines of the main heading

SS; TS between 2-line main heading and body of graph. Space body of graph as you did in Problem 1.

```
        FIRST-SEMESTER TYPING SPEED GROWTH
                FOR KRISTIE ROYAL

        September    xxx
        October      xxxxxx
        November     xxxxxxxxxxxxxx
        December     xxxxxxxxxxxxxxxxxxxxxx
        January      xxxxxxxxxxxxxxxxxxxxxxxxxx

            GWAM     10        20        30
```

LESSON 103

5 minutes **103a ● Keyboard Review**

Directions: Keyboard each line three times SS. DS between 3-line groups.

alphabet We couldn't give any excuse for most of the crazy quips and bad jokes.

figure Mariner 4 flew a total distance of 325 million miles in only 228 days.

4th finger lamp palm quiz zipper pail lap soap group pupil people palace pit quit

easy We can do good work if we have a goal for each bit of work that we do.

| 1 | 2 | 3 | 4 | 5 | 6 | 7 | 8 | 9 | 10 | 11 | 12 | 13 | 14 |

10 minutes **103b ● Speed Builder**

Directions: Take two 1' writings on each ¶; try to increase speed on the second writing. Figure *gwam*.

Alternate Procedure: Work for speed as you take one 5' writing on all three ¶s combined. Figure *gwam*.

all letters used 1.3 si   *gwam* 1' | 5'

	1'	5'
In one ad, a son returns home a college dropout. In another, a	13	3 | 35
small child stands in front of a blackboard, unable to work a math prob-	27	5 | 38
lem written there. These children are, the two ads suggest, doomed to	41	8 | 41
fail because they do not have computer skills.	51	10 | 43
Parents are subjected to a barrage of ads such as these each day.	13	13 | 46
They also see computers being used in more and more offices, stores,	27	16 | 48
and banks. It is only normal that they would want their children to	41	18 | 51
have all of the benefits a home computer can give them.	52	21 | 53
Learning how to do math through exposure to a machine is not quite	13	23 | 56
so simple as it might sound, however. While a computer can tell when	27	26 | 59
you have memorized the right answers, it will not really know if you	41	29 | 62
understand what you have done. For this kind of help, a good teacher	55	32 | 64
is pretty hard to beat.	60	33 | 65

gwam 1' | 1 | 2 | 3 | 4 | 5 | 6 | 7 | 8 | 9 | 10 | 11 | 12 | 13 | 14 |
5' | | 1 | | 2 | | 3 |

5 minutes **36b ● Technique Builder: Stroking**

Directions: Keyboard each sentence three times SS. DS between 3-line groups.

keep fingers deeply curved

top row Will you try to keep up my treatment as so many others have?

direct reaches They are doubtful I will be able to collect many place mats.

bottom row We know that the girl held the big soap box when she met us.

| 1 | 2 | 3 | 4 | 5 | 6 | 7 | 8 | 9 | 10 | 11 | 12 |

---

8 minutes **36c ● Language Arts Skills: Spelling and Proofreading Aid**

Directions: **1.** Keyboard each line three times SS. DS between each 3-line group. **2.** Note the spelling of each word as you keyboard this drill.

3. Proofread carefully. Check any word about which you are uncertain against the original copy. Circle all errors.

type without pauses between words

1 attempt coming fourth library prior finally until using paid

2 quantity excellent privilege particular substantial mortgage

3 efficient continuing guarantee superintendent accommodations

---

17 minutes **36d ● Paragraph Guided Writings**

Directions: **1.** Take a 1' writing on ¶1. Figure *gwam*. Add four words to your *gwam* for a new goal. **2.** Take two 1' writings on the same ¶. Try to reach your goal on each writing.

3. Take a 1' writing on the same ¶. Drop back two to four *gwam*. Your goal is to keyboard without errors. **4.** Repeat Steps 1, 2, and 3 for the second and third ¶s.

all letters used 1.2 si   *gwam* 3'

keep wrists and arms quiet

One thing most experts agree on is the need for a warmup   4 | 35
before starting any sport. Though it may seem like a chore   8 | 39
at first, it pays off in results.   10 | 41

No matter what your size, a routine that requires you to   14 | 45
stretch your muscles is said to be the best. It will help   18 | 49
avoid major aches and pains later.   20 | 51

Be sure to combine the stretching with ten minutes of   24 | 55
movement like that used in your sport. If you are a bike   27 | 58
rider, for instance, pump your legs up and down.   31 | 62

gwam 3' | 1 | 2 | 3 | 4 |

LESSON 102

102a ● Keyboard Review

5 minutes

return carriage
quickly

Directions: Keyboard each sentence three times SS. DS between 3-line groups.

alphabet   The objective was to organize and make plans for an exquisite display.

figure   Check 3904 (dated June 7) for $68 was sent to Brown and Company today.

double letter   Bill succeeded in getting the committee's message to the office staff.

easy   Most of our team members do hard work to keep their body weights down.

| 1 | 2 | 3 | 4 | 5 | 6 | 7 | 8 | 9 | 10 | 11 | 12 | 13 | 14 |

---

5 minutes

102b ● Skill Builder from Script

Directions: Take four 1' writings on the ¶; try to increase speed with each writing.

gwam 1'

For the sake of good health you should walk more.   10
Walking is one of the best ways to improve overall fitness.   22
It uses more muscles in a steady, uniform action than   33
most other forms of exercise. One of the greatest things   49
about walking is that it can be done throughout life.   55

---

5 minutes

keep locations of
symbol keys fixed
in your mind

102c ● Building Skill on Figures and Symbols

Directions: Keyboard each sentence three times SS. DS between 3-line groups.

1   The article entitled "Tributes and Tears" appeared in <u>Time</u> on June 18.

2   Their current rate on a 1-year, tax-deferred IRA investment is 11.25%.

3   My new car (purchased at Craig & Cochrane) gets 38.5 miles per gallon.

---

30 minutes

102d ● Problem Typing: Horizontal Bar Graphs

Directions: Problem 1

1. On a half sheet, center the graph shown below. Use the directions on the model as a guide for spacing.

2. To determine the left margin, center the carriage and backspace once for each 2 letters in the longest name, in the longest bar, and for spaces between names and bars. Set left margin. Space forward once for each letter in the longest name and for spaces between names and bars. Set a tab here to begin the bars.

3. Each *x* represents one word a minute, beginning with 30 *gwam*. Place an apostrophe under the first *x* in each group of ten as shown. Center the figures under the apostrophe by depressing the backspace key or incremental spacer key if your machine has one.

```
              TOP TYPEWRITING SPEEDS IN 1ST PERIOD CLASS
                                                         DS
                        April 10, 19--
                                         TS
                    6 spaces
        Basso, John         xxxxxxxxxxxxxxxxxxxxxxx
                                                       DS
        Clark, Dennis       xxxxxxxxxxxxxxxxxx
        Johnson, Marilyn    xxxxxxxxxxxxxxxxxxxxxxxxxx
        Ortiz, Robin        xxxxxxxxxxxxxxxxxxxxxxxxxxxxxxxxxxx
                            '         '         '         '
        GWAM                30        40        50        60
```

36e ● **Language Arts Skills: Composing at the Typewriter**

Directions: **1.** Keyboard an answer to each question. Use complete sentences as shown in the sample answer.

2. If time permits, retype any sentences in which you made errors.

Questions

1. What is your favorite sport?
2. What is your favorite subject?
3. What is the name of your school?
4. What is your typewriting teacher's

name?
5. Name the state in which you live.
6. Name the city in which you were born.

Sample Answer: My favorite sport is basketball.

LESSON 37

5 minutes **37a** ● **Keyboard Review**

Directions: Keyboard each sentence three times SS. DS between 3-line groups.

keep arms and wrists quiet

alphabet Ms. W. C. Jung may have kept her botany quiz and final exam.

fig/sym Only 24 of the 95 students who completed the test passed it!

easy The students wanted to visit all the towns shown on the map.

| 1 | 2 | 3 | 4 | 5 | 6 | 7 | 8 | 9 | 10 | 11 | 12 |

5 minutes **37b** ● **Language Arts Skills: Typing from Dictation and Spelling Checkup**

Directions: Your teacher will dictate the words in 36c, page 60. Keyboard the words from dictation. Check your work for correct spelling. Retype any words in which you made an error.

10 minutes **37c** ● **Timed Writings**

Directions: Take two 3' writings on 36d, page 60. Figure *gwam*.

Submit the better of the two writings.

25 minutes **37d** ● **Learn to Center Vertically**

Centering material so that it will have uniform top and bottom margins is called vertical centering.

Step 1 Count the lines in the copy to be centered. If your copy is to be double-spaced, remember to count the spaces between the lines. There is only 1-line space following each line of copy when material is double-spaced.

Step 2 Subtract the total lines to be used from the lines available on the paper you are using. (There are 33 lines on a half sheet, 66 on a full sheet).

Step 3 Divide the number of lines that remain by 2. The answer gives you the number of lines in the top and bottom margins. If the result contains a fraction, disregard it.

Step 4 Insert your paper so that the top edge is exactly even with the aligning scale (No. 21). Bring the paper up the proper number of line spaces. Start typing one line-space below the number you calculated for your top margin.

(continued on next page)

101d ● Speed Ladder Paragraphs

Directions: Take 1' writings on each ¶ as you did in 96d, page 163.

all letters used   1.3 si

gwam 5'

The next time you are faced with the problem of what to buy the | 3 | 55
person who has everything, why not consider buying a mule? While this | 5 | 58
idea might sound odd at first, you should realize the many advantages | 8 | 61
of such a gift. | 9 | 62

Here are just a couple of them. First of all, a mule requires | 11 | 64
much less upkeep than a nifty sports car and has fewer moving parts | 14 | 67
than a wristwatch. To be perfectly frank, I must admit that sometimes | 17 | 69
a mule has absolutely no moving parts. | 19 | 71

Mules are smart, stubborn, and not the least bit choosy when it | 21 | 74
comes to eating. They will eat whatever is in sight, including wooden | 24 | 76
fences. Mule lovers claim their favorite animals have good sense since | 27 | 79
they won't do anything that will end up hurting them. | 29 | 81

Mules, which often live to be about thirty years old, work until | 32 | 84
the day they die. They are used in national parks, in the movies, in | 34 | 87
fishing camps, and down on the farm. Armies have used mules to carry | 37 | 90
ammunition. West Point football games would never be the same without | 40 | 93
one. | 40 | 93

Surely you are interested by now. Therefore, it is only fair to | 43 | 95
warn you of one minor problem. A mule's stubborn streak can sometimes | 46 | 98
be troublesome. If the ears go down, you had better watch out. You | 49 | 101
can always take comfort in the fact, however, that a mule won't kick | 51 | 104
you unless you deserve it. | 52 | 105

gwam 5' | 1 | 2 | 3 |

101e ● Continuity Practice

Directions: Type the last ¶ of 101d as many times as you can in 5'. Work for even, continuous stroking.

Vertical Centering

Directions: Problem 1

1. Center the ¶ below vertically on a half sheet of paper (long side up).
2. Keyboard the ¶ line-for-line. Use a 60-space line DS.

Directions: Problem 2

1. Center the ¶ below vertically on a full sheet of paper.
2. Keyboard the ¶ line-for-line. Use a 60-space line DS.

1	
2	
3	
4	
5	
6	
7	
8	Start on
9	Line 9

words

Start on Line 9

A half sheet of paper contains 33 lines; a full sheet — 11

has 66 lines. It does not make any difference what kind of — 23

typewriter you are using. All are the same on this point. — 35

To center copy vertically, up and down, count the lines in — 46

the copy. Subtract this total from 33 if you are using a — 58

half sheet or 66 if you are using a full sheet. Divide the — 70

difference by 2 to get top and bottom margins for exact cen- — 82

tering. If the result contains a fraction, just disregard — 94

it. Type the copy. You will find that it is neatly placed. — 100

Lines on half sheet 33
Lines and line spaces in copy 17
Line spaces in top and bottom margins 16
Divide by 2. Top margin 8*
Bottom margin 8
* Start typing on the 9th line space from the top

(line numbers in left margin: 1–33)

LESSON 38

60-space line

5 minutes   **38a ● Keyboard Review**

Directions: Keyboard each sentence three times SS. DS between 3-line groups.

keep feet flat on floor

alphabet   Jack Walder bought five exquisite topaz pins in Mexico City.

symbol   Fifty-nine votes were cast for vice-president--a new record!

easy   They said she should get a bid from more than one rock band.

| 1 | 2 | 3 | 4 | 5 | 6 | 7 | 8 | 9 | 10 | 11 | 12 |

Directions: Problem 3 Postal Card from Script Copy

1. Prepare another postal card containing the message given in Problem 1, page 168.

2. Address the card to Chris Van Elswyk,

2947 Herndon Avenue, Ellensburg, WA 98926-3016.

LESSON 101

70-space line

101a ● Keyboard Review

5 minutes

Directions: Keyboard each sentence three times SS. DS between 3-line groups.

keep key locations fixed in your mind

alphabet	Juan B. Ramirez has received a plaque for his exceptionally good work.
figure	Among our 70.8 million households, 83.6% have at least one automobile.
e,i	They were relieved when neither of the scientists believed their news.
easy	Place all eight chairs on the field where they will be handy for them.

| 1 | 2 | 3 | 4 | 5 | 6 | 7 | 8 | 9 | 10 | 11 | 12 | 13 | 14 |

101b ● Language Arts Skills: Punctuation Guides (Colon)

5 minutes

Directions: The following are guides for the use of the colon and sentences that illustrate the use of those guides. Study each guide; then keyboard the sentence that illustrates the guide. Keyboard each sentence twice SS; DS between 2-line groups.

keep feet flat on the floor

Use a colon to introduce a list of items or expressions.
They will ship these items: uniforms, shoes, gloves, bats, and balls.

Use a colon to separate hours and minutes when expressed in figures.
Lori left from Seattle at 7:15 p.m.; she arrived in Butte at 9:20 p.m.

Use a colon to introduce a question or long quotation.
The question before us is this: Can we complete the projects in time?

101c ● Sentence Control Builder

10 minutes

Directions: Take two 1' writings on each sentence. Try to complete each writing without error.

space quickly with a down-and-in motion

1 We will not expect to lead others farther than we have gone ourselves.

2 Folks who think too much of themselves usually aren't thinking enough.

3 If they get half their wishes, they will likely double their troubles.

4 You have the right to risk those things if no one else will be harmed.

| 1 | 2 | 3 | 4 | 5 | 6 | 7 | 8 | 9 | 10 | 11 | 12 | 13 | 14 |

38b ● Paragraph Guided Writings

Directions: **1.** Take a 1' writing on ¶1. Figure *gwam*. Add four words to your *gwam* for a new goal.
2. Take two 1' writings on the same ¶. Try to reach your goal on each writing.

3. Take a 1' writing on the same ¶. Drop back two to four *gwam*. Your goal is to keyboard without errors.
4. Repeat Steps 1, 2, and 3 for the second and third ¶s.

all letters used   *gwam* 3'

			gwam 3'	
Packed up tight in a traffic jam or alone on the open | | | 4 | 39
road, cars have left their tracks on all aspects of our lives. | | | 8 | 43
It almost seems as if we measure progress in miles per gallon. | | | 12 | 47
It was but a few years back that one of every six who | | | 16 | 51
were in the labor force could trace his or her income to this | | | 20 | 55
machine.   Its impact was felt far beyond the assembly line. | | | 24 | 59
They built cars in small sizes in those days too; the | | | 27 | 62
compacts of today are not unique.   In fact, a famous cartoon | | | 31 | 66
showed one of the first small cars stuck to a wad of chewing | | | 35 | 70
gum. | | | 36 | 71

gwam 3' | 1 | 2 | 3 | 4 |

38c ● Learn to Center Horizontally

Centering material so there will be equal left and right margins is called horizontal centering.

Step 1 Check the placement of the paper guide. Turn to page vii, and read the directions for adjusting the paper guide.

Step 2 Clear tab stops. Set tab at center point of paper (elite 51; pica 42) for paper 8½ inches wide.

Step 3 Backspace from center point once for every 2 characters or spaces in the line to be centered. If there is one character left, do not backspace for it. Begin to type at the point where the backspacing is completed.

Directions: Problem 1

1. Keyboard the announcement below on a half sheet of paper following the directions above.
2. TS below the heading; DS between all

other lines
3. Begin on Line 14. When you complete the line, return to center point and repeat the steps for each line.

FINAL GAME OF THE SEASON
                             TS

See the Blue and Gold Warriors in Action!
                                              DS

Saturday, November 10, 2 p.m.
                                    DS

Surprise Stunts at Halftime

(continued on next page)

LESSON 100

100a ● Keyboard Review

5 minutes

Directions: Keyboard each sentence three times SS. DS between 3-line groups.

think each word as you type

alphabet	Toxic waste is a major problem all good citizens have to face quickly.
figure	Wall Street had 16,410,000 shares of stock traded on October 29, 1929.
long reach	No doubt a number of ceramic mugs and many curved saucers were broken.
easy	The one who uses few words does not have to take so many of them back.

| 1 | 2 | 3 | 4 | 5 | 6 | 7 | 8 | 9 | 10 | 11 | 12 | 13 | 14 |

100b ● Timed Writings

15 minutes

Directions: **1.** Take two 5' writings on 96b, page 163. Work for best possible speed with a minimum of errors.

2. Figure *gwam*; submit the better of the two writings to your teacher.

100c ● Problem Typing: Postal Cards

25 minutes

Directions: Problem 1 Postal Card from Script Copy

1. Prepare the following message on a postal card or on paper cut to size (5½" × 3¼"). Use modified block style.

2. Insert the card into your machine with short side at left. Determine horizontal center; set margins 4 spaces in from each side of card.

3. Address the card to Ms. Joy Palmquist, 129 Chestnut Drive, Ellensburg, WA 98926-4751.

4. Type the following return address in the upper left corner of the address side of the postal card: Doug Calhoun, 15 Poe Street, Seattle, WA 98101-2478.

July 1, 19- -
Dear Service Club Member

We are making plans for Orientation Day in the fall. We need help from as many of our returning members as we can get.

Please let me know if you can serve as a guide for new students on September 5.
Doug Calhoun, Secretary

Directions: Problem 2 Composing a Postal Card

1. Assume the message in Problem 1 has been mailed to you. Compose an answer and prepare it in proper form on a postal card.

2. Explain that you can work as a guide during the morning of September 5 but that you have to work in the testing office in the afternoon.

(continued on next page)

Learn to Center Horizontally

Directions: Problem 2
1. Center 38c, Problem 1, page 63 vertically on a half sheet of paper (long side up).
2. Center each line horizontally.
3. TS below the heading; DS between all other lines.

Directions: Problem 3
1. Center the announcement below vertically on a half sheet of paper (long side up).
2. Center each line horizontally.
3. TS below the heading; DS between all other lines.

CAMERA CLUB MEETING

TS

Tuesday, November 13, 2:30 p.m.

DS

Room 242

DS

Prizes for Outstanding Photographs

DS

Refreshments

LESSON 39

60-space line

5 minutes

39a ● Keyboard Review

Directions: Keyboard each sentence three times SS. DS between 3-line groups.

alphabet Five or six Jersey cows grazed quietly back among the pines.

fig/sym In 1985, the prices ranged from $364.50 to more than $1,270.

easy Both of them asked to take their autos to the new body shop.

| 1 | 2 | 3 | 4 | 5 | 6 | 7 | 8 | 9 | 10 | 11 | 12 |

8 minutes

39b ● Speed Ladder Sentences

Directions: 1. Take 1' writings on each sentence. Try to keyboard each sentence four times within the minute.
2. Your instructor will call the return each

15 seconds to guide you.
3. The rate increases 5 words a minute with each succeeding sentence.

keep your
eyes on
the copy

		gwam 15"	words
1	To type right, sit erect.	20	5
2	Use guides as you type these lines.	25	7
3	Try typing with the call of the guide.	30	8
4	The aim is to type this line with the guide.	35	9
5	Few of us know what a big job a little job can be.	40	10

| 1 | 2 | 3 | 4 | 5 | 6 | 7 | 8 | 9 | 10 |

LESSON 99

99a ● Keyboard Review

5 minutes

Directions: Keyboard each sentence three times SS. DS between 3-line groups.

alphabet Julia got very few dark boxes of any size in the shipment from Quincy.

figure All 34 eighth graders did Spelling Lesson 1-B on page 368 for Tuesday.

u,i They required us to build a building suitable for a public sanitarium.

easy To write a good report, you should learn all you can about your topic.

| 1 | 2 | 3 | 4 | 5 | 6 | 7 | 8 | 9 | 10 | 11 | 12 | 13 | 14 |

---

10 minutes

99b ● Control Builder

Directions: Keyboard the ¶ twice at the control level. Repeat if time permits.

Goals: 2 or fewer errors per writing.

think the letters
and figures as
you type them

words

On June 9, 1985, that famous quacking fowl, Donald Duck, celebrated   14

his 51st birthday.   He is younger than his pal Mickey Mouse, who was 56   28

in November, 1984.   Donald produced revenues of up to $100 million from   42

130 cartoons, 4 feature films, and various books and products.   During   57

World War II, more than 400 military patches had Donald as their symbol.   71

| 1 | 2 | 3 | 4 | 5 | 6 | 7 | 8 | 9 | 10 | 11 | 12 | 13 | 14 |

---

30 minutes

99c ● Problem Typing: Preparing Copy on 5″ × 3″ cards

Directions: Problem 1 Admission Tickets

1. Prepare three tickets of the kind illustrated below. Use 5″ × 3″ cards or paper cut to size. DS the copy and arrange it neatly as directed on the illustration below.

2. Note that some of the lines are centered and some are flush with the left and right margins. (See page 67 to review finding center point on odd-size paper).

3. Number your three cards in sequence beginning with No. 150.

Directions: Problem 2 Membership Cards

1. Prepare three membership cards of the kind illustrated below. Use 5″ × 3″ cards or paper cut to size. Arrange the copy neatly as directed on the illustration below.

2. After you finish the last line of centered copy, return 4 times and keyboard 1½″ underlines flush with each margin for the signature lines. Center the titles under the underlines.

3. Number your three cards in sequence beginning with No. 75. Membership will last to June 1 of next year. Use the correct year on your cards.

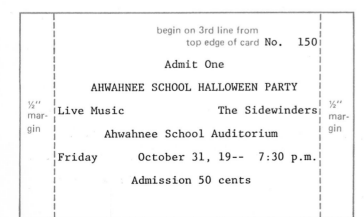

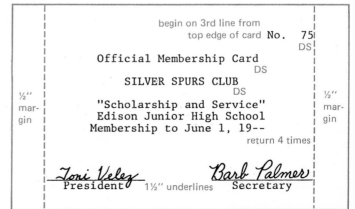

39c ● **Continuity Practice from Script**

Directions: Keyboard the ¶ below at least two times on a 60-space line DS.   Repeat if time permits.

all letters used   1.2 si

	words
A late quote from the College Board states	9
that the broad major field of health ranks	18
first choice of many high school students	26
from both sexes who plan to go to college.	34
Business now receives a fair-sized interest	43
too.	44

39d ● **Problem Typing: Centering Paragraphs**

Directions: 1. Center the report below vertically on a full sheet of paper. Use a 60-space line. Keyboard the copy line-for-line.

2. Center the heading horizontally.
3. TS below the heading; DS between all other lines.

Correcting Errors

Learn to use the basic methods for correcting typing errors. Three of these methods are explained in the ¶s at the right.

words

CORRECTING ERRORS   4

TS

Unless the typewriter has a special correcting ribbon,   15
you may correct errors with a typing eraser, with correction   27
fluid, or with correction tape.   33

When using a typing eraser, move the carriage to one   44
side to keep the crumbs from falling into the machine. Roll   56
your paper up two or three spaces, then hold the paper firmly 68
against the platen while making the erasure.   77

To correct an error with correction fluid, just paint   88
over the incorrect letter. Make sure the fluid is dry before 101
typing the correct letter.   106

Correction tape should be placed between the ribbon and   117
your error. Simply retype your error, allowing powder from   129
the tape to cover the incorrect letter.   137

98c ● Problem Typing: Minutes of Meetings

Directions: **1.** On a full sheet, prepare the minutes of a meeting from the copy below.
2. Leave a 2″ top margin; use the directions on the model as a guide for spacing copy. Set a 1½″ left margin and a 1″ right margin because the minutes will be kept in a binder.

AHWAHNEE SCHOOL SERVICE CLUB

Minutes of Meeting

Date: September 24, 19--
Time: 12:10 p.m.
Place: Room 119, Ahwahnee School
Present: About 35 students in addition to the advisers, Mr. Holmes and Miss Code

1. Dennis Kerns, President, presided. He introduced the officers and our two advisers.

2. The president outlined the goals of the club and the requirements for membership. Dues are 50 cents per member.

3. Mr. Holmes explained that the principal would like the Service Club to sponsor after-school movies once a month. The cost to students will range from 25 cents to 50 cents depending upon the rental cost of the film.

4. Miss Code asked for volunteers to help paint trash cans after school on September 26.

5. Pat Anderson reported that the Halloween costume party would be held Friday evening, October 31.

6. The president asked members to list their free periods when they would be available to act as guides for school visitors.

7. A decision was made to hold meetings on the first Wednesday of each month at 12:10 p.m.

8. The president appointed two committees:
   a. Program committee: Jennifer Jones, Chairperson; Becky Brunn; Tim Mar
   b. Refreshments committee: Jim Lundeen, Chairperson; Dorothy Voss; Roger Clark

9. The meeting was adjourned at 12:55 p.m.

Wendy Sniffin, Secretary

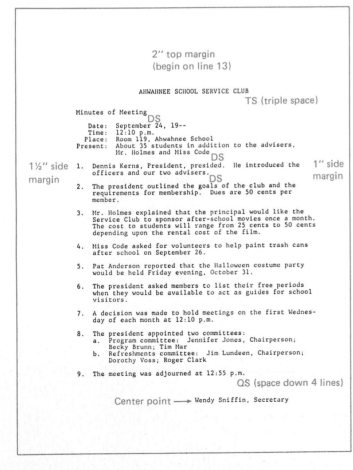

39e ● Learn to Correct Rough Draft

Copy that has been typed or printed may be corrected by the use of proofreader's marks. Study the proofreader's marks explained here; then follow the directions below for typing the announcement.

Common Proofreader's Marks

∧	insert	✗	delete	lc	lowercase
⩚	insert comma	⊐	move right	tr ∿	transpose
⩗	insert period	⊏	move left	#	add space
◡	close up	Cap	capitalize	¶	paragraph

Directions: 1. Center the announcement vertically on a half sheet of paper (long side up).
2. Center each line horizontally. Backspace once for 2 characters or spaces as they will appear in the corrected copy.
3. TS below the heading; DS between all other lines.
4. Make the corrections as you keyboard the announcement.

```
            YOU ARE INVITED

               by the

      Junior Pep Varsity club

         to attend the
           Annual SwimFest

       Madisonville YMCA

  Saturday December 12, 7:30 p. m.
```

LESSON 40

40a ● Keyboard Review

Directions: Keyboard each sentence three times SS. DS between 3-line groups.

use quick, sharp strokes

alphabet Gail required me to fix every brown jacket with new zippers.
fig/sym Janice said, "Meet me at Paul's house at 83901 Verna Drive."
easy All of the big towns are right there at the end of the lake.

| 1 | 2 | 3 | 4 | 5 | 6 | 7 | 8 | 9 | 10 | 11 | 12 |

97c, continued   **Directions: Problem 2**

Use a full sheet; 50-space line; follow Problem 1 directions.

AHWANEE SCHOOL "A" CLUB
Notice of Regular Meeting

October 15, 19--   3:30 p.m.

Room 126
AGENDA

1. Approval of September 12 minutes
2. Report of Treasurer, Chris Combs
3. Discussion of new business
   a. Need to raise money for club activities
   b. Volunteers to work at October 25 PTA meeting

LESSON 98

5 minutes

98a ● Keyboard Review

Directions: Keyboard each sentence three times SS. DS between 3-line groups.

type with a flowing rhythm

alphabet	I have been lucky to exceed my first high quota and win a major prize.
figure	In 1884, a champion ice skater went 10 miles in 31 minutes 11 seconds.
shift key	Steven, Janet, Scott, and Ted all liked Mrs. Severson's English class.
easy	Riding the bus to games in neighboring towns is fun for all of us now.

| 1 | 2 | 3 | 4 | 5 | 6 | 7 | 8 | 9 | 10 | 11 | 12 | 13 | 14 |

---

10 minutes

98b ● Speed Builder

Directions: Take two 1' writings on each ¶; try to increase speed on the second writing. Figure *gwam*.

Alternate Procedure: Work for speed as you take one 5' writing on all three ¶s combined. Figure *gwam*.

all letters used 1.3 si   *gwam* 1' | 5'

	1'	5'
A subject receiving a good bit of thought these days is what we	13	3	35
might refer to as the people explosion. The number of people who now	27	5	37
inhabit the earth has passed the four billion mark. At present growth	41	8	40
rates, there will be two billion more people by the end of the century.	55	11	43
In the millions of years of human life on earth, this number was	13	14	46
not half that size until about sixty years ago. That is in the life-	27	16	49
times of people who are still living. Experts say that a quarter of	41	19	51
all the people who ever lived on this planet are alive today.	53	22	54
While estimates vary, of course, we know that a great many of the	13	24	56
people do not receive enough of the right kinds of food to function at	27	27	59
their best. Because of this fact, a great debate now rages as to how	41	30	62
many people the resources of the earth can support.	52	32	64

gwam 1' | 1 | 2 | 3 | 4 | 5 | 6 | 7 | 8 | 9 | 10 | 11 | 12 | 13 | 14 |
     5' | 1 | 2 | 3 |

Lessons 97 & 98

40b ● Timed Writings

Directions: Keyboard two 3' writings on 38b, page 63. Figure *gwam*. Submit the better of the two writings.

40c ● Finding Horizontal Center Point

In order to center headings on paper or cards of different sizes, you must learn how to find the center point.

Step 1 Insert the paper you will use to type 40d into your machine.

Step 2 Add the numbers on the line-of-writing scale at the right and left edges of the paper.

Step 3 Divide the sum by 2. The resulting figure is the horizontal center point of the paper.

40d ● Problem Typing on Odd-Size Paper or Cards

Directions: Problem 1

1. Insert a half sheet of paper (5½ × 8½") with the short side up.

2. From the top edge of the paper, space down to the 19th line for the heading.

3. Find the horizontal center of the half sheet following directions in 40c. Set a tab stop at this point.

4. Keyboard the announcement below, centering each line horizontally. TS below the heading; DS between all other lines.

There are six vertical line spaces to an inch. An 8½ inch sheet contains 51 vertical line spaces: 8½ × 6 = 51.

Lines available 51
Lines required 14
Lines remaining 37
Top margin 18
Begin on line 19

THE COMPUTER CLUB

Announces

a Lecture/Demonstration

"Today's Personal Computer"

Dr. James M. Highsmith

Thursday, March 10, 2:30 p.m.

Room 382

Directions: Problem 2

1. Insert a half sheet of paper with the short side up.

2. Center the announcement at the top of the page 68 vertically; center each line horizontally. TS below the heading; DS between all other lines.

(continued on next page)

LESSON 97

97a ● Keyboard Review

5 minutes

Directions: Keyboard each sentence 3 times SS. DS between 3-line groups.

keep your eyes on
the copy as you
return the carriage

alphabet   The quickness and dexterity of this juggler amazed the viewing public.

figure   The population of Alaska grew from 302,583 in 1970 to 400,481 in 1980.

long words   A correspondent should study the environment and location of the firm.

easy   All of them spent some of their time doing social work on the islands.

| 1 | 2 | 3 | 4 | 5 | 6 | 7 | 8 | 9 | 10 | 11 | 12 | 13 | 14 |

---

10 minutes

97b ● Control Ladder Paragraphs

Directions: 1. Take 1' writings on each ¶ in 96d, p. 163. Circle errors and figure *gwam*. 2. When you keyboard a ¶ within the error limit specified by your teacher, move to the next ¶. Use control as you keyboard this exercise.

Note: To type an item flush with the right margin, tab to the right margin and backspace once for each character or space in the item. Begin typing where backspacing ends.

97c ● Problem Typing: Notices and Agendas of Meeting   30 minutes

Directions: Problem 1

1. On a full sheet, 50-space line, prepare the notice and agenda of a meeting from the copy below. Leave a 2" top margin; use the directions on the model as a guide for spacing copy.

2. The items in the third line (date and time) are to be typed flush with left and right margins.

AHWAHNEE SCHOOL SERVICE CLUB

Notice of the First Meeting

September 24, 19--   12:10 p.m.

Room 119

AGENDA

1.   Introduction of officers and advisers
2.   Discussion of Service Club organization
    a.   Aims
    b.   Membership requirements
3.   Discussion of major projects for the year
    a.   Sponsoring of monthly movies
    b.   Club's role in the "Beautify Your School" campaign
    c.   Halloween costume party
    d.   Guide service for school visitors
4.   Decision on meeting dates and time
5.   Appointment of program committee
6.   Appointment of refreshments committee
7.   Adjournment by 12:55 p.m.

2" top margin
(begin on line 13)

AHWAHNEE SCHOOL SERVICE CLUB
                      TS (triple space)
Notice of the First Meeting
          TS
September 24, 19--   12:10 p.m.
                  TS
      Room 119
          QS (space down 4 lines)

      AGENDA
        TS
1.   Introduction of officers and advisers
                    DS
2.   Discussion of Service Club organization
    a.   Aims
    b.   Membership requirements
                    DS
3.   Discussion of major projects for the year
    a.   Sponsoring of monthly movies
    b.   Club's role in the "Beautify Your School" campaign
    c.   Halloween costume party
    d.   Guide service for school visitors
4.   Decision on meeting dates and time
5.   Appointment of program committee
6.   Appointment of refreshments committee
7.   Adjournment by 12:55 p.m.

(continued on next page)

RED WAVE BAKE SALE

at Cafeteria Entrance
Thursday, November 8
Donuts, Cookies, Cakes, Pies
High Quality and Low Prices
Send the Red Wave to the District Tournament

Directions: Problem 3

1. Insert a half sheet of paper with the short side up. TS below the heading; DS between all other lines.

2. Center the problem vertically; center each line horizontally.

Do not keyboard lines within the copy. They indicate return points.

JOIN THE EXPLORERS' CLUB | Meetings on Fridays, 2 to 3 p.m. | Dues Only $1 a Semester | Tours, Exhibits, Demonstrations | First Meeting, Friday, September 28 | Movie: "Undersea Secrets"

40e ● Extra-Credit: Typing from Rough Draft

When rough draft copy must be centered vertically, you may wish to keyboard the corrected copy on practice paper first.

You can then count the number of lines required and follow the usual procedure for vertical centering.

Directions: 1. Center the exercise vertically on a full sheet of paper, using a 60-space line.

2. Provide an appropriate heading. TS below the heading; DS between all other lines.

(Provide appropriate heading)

While folks generally take the university of Okoboji seriously, this "College for Every one" is all in fun. Located in the lakes region of Northwest Iowa, it considers all the residents and those who vacation there as its student body. Although you may not know anyone who played foot ball at this particular institution, you might have seen one of the University T-shirts. its insignia includes the school motto and small representations of sports the area is noted for.

96d ● Speed Ladder Paragraphs

Directions: **1.** Take a 1' writing on ¶1 DS until you complete the ¶ in 1'.

2. When you complete ¶1 in 1', continue on to ¶2. Repeat this procedure as you try to complete each of the five ¶s in the given time.

3. Take three 1' writings on any ¶ you cannot finish in the given time.

all letters used   1.3 si   *gwam* 5'

```
        •        4        •        8        •        12
    If you spend less than two whole years of your life talking on the      3 | 51
        •      16        •      20        •      24        •      28
telephone, you are just not average.  At least that is the claim of some    6 | 54
        •      32        •      36        •      40
who have studied the use of this popular communication tool.                8 | 56
        •        4        •        8        •        12
    A cynic might say that the teenage years account for a large part       11 | 59
        •      16        •      20        •      24        •
of this time.  Such a statement certainly would not be fair, though,       13 | 62
      28        •      32        •      36        •      40
as we know our growing dependence on the telephone involves people in      16 | 65
        •      44
all age groups.                                                            17 | 65
        •        4        •        8        •        12
    It is not likely the inventor of this device could have foreseen       20 | 68
        •      16        •      20        •      24        •
the great impact it has had on our lives.  Bell, the inventor of the       22 | 71
      28        •      32        •      36        •      40
telephone, even had phones banned from his study when he needed quiet      25 | 74
        •      44        •      48
in order to work on his experiments.                                       27 | 75
        •        4        •        8        •        12
    Now, of course, the telephone can be used for a good deal more         29 | 78
        •      16        •      20        •      24        •
than simply talking to someone.  Phones enable computers to talk to one    32 | 80
      28        •      32        •      36        •      40
another.  They help us send written messages as well as spoken ones.       35 | 83
        •      44        •      48        •      52
We can use them to do our banking and to pay our bills.                    37 | 86
        •        4        •        8        •        12
    As if all this is not amazing enough, consider the fact that the       40 | 88
        •      16        •      20        •      24        •
telephone can control the rest of our home appliances and serve as an      43 | 91
      28        •      32        •      36        •      40
intercom system.  So far no one has been able to get one to walk the       45 | 94
        •      44        •      48        •      52        •
dog or run the bath water, but don't say it won't be done one of these     48 | 97
      56
days.                                                                      49 | 98
```

gwam 5' | 1 | 2 | 3 |

96e ● Continuity Practice

Directions: Keyboard the last paragraph of 96d as many times as you can in 5'.

Technique Goals: Work for continuous stroking, with eyes on copy, and with wrists and arms quiet.

Unit 7 ■ Keyboarding Personal Notes and Letters (Lessons 41–50)

General Directions

Use a 60-space line for all lessons in this unit unless otherwise directed. SS sentences and drill lines. DS between repeated groups of lines. DS paragraph copy. Set tabulator for a 5-space paragraph indention. Your teacher will tell you whether or not to correct errors when typing problems.

LESSON 41

5 minutes

41a ● Keyboard Review

Directions: Keyboard each sentence 3 times SS. DS between 3-line groups.

keep feet
on the floor

alphabet	How can Bud mix five quarts of gray paint for Jack and Liza?
fig/sym	Room rates will now be $1,309--for just 8 days and 7 nights!
easy	We bought some more land down the road from their old house.

| 1 | 2 | 3 | 4 | 5 | 6 | 7 | 8 | 9 | 10 | 11 | 12 |

10 minutes

41b ● Technique Builder: Flowing Rhythm

Directions: Keyboard each line 3 times SS from dictation. DS between 3-line groups.

stroke keys
with a flowing
rhythm

1 for him | if the cases | and they were | and the date | for the text
2 and the set | to do my | only for the | we see you | and read | to act
3 she saved | and look | for them | and read | if you | they saw | to join
4 and they join | and she sees | she did care | may go after | for him

5 minutes

41c ● Sentence Skill Builder from Script

Directions: Take a 1′ writing on each sentence. Figure *gwam*.

words

Our school newspaper is now being published every two weeks. 12
All news items have to be submitted to the advisor's office. 12
The editor was chosen because of her ability and experience. 12
One or two important jobs on the staff have not been filled. 12

5 minutes

41d ● Language Arts Skills: Spelling and Proofreading Aid

Directions: Keyboard each line 3 times SS. DS between 3-line groups.

type each word
letter by letter

1 toward   similar   practice   valuable   salary   acknowledge   hesitate
2 dollar   financial   procedure   situation   separate   volume   session
3 convenient   responsibility   circular   calendar   specific   license

Unit 12 ■ Keyboarding for Club and Community Activities

(Lessons 96-110)

General Directions

Use a 70-space line for all lessons in this unit (center − 35; center + 35 + 5) unless otherwise directed. SS sentences and drill lines; DS paragraphs. Your teacher will tell you whether or not you are to correct errors on the problems in this unit.

LESSON 96

5 minutes

96a ● Keyboard Review

Directions: Keyboard each sentence three times SS. DS between 3-line groups.

keep wrists and elbows still

alphabet	We have just realized Gib's black picture frame is not exactly square.
figure	A $1 bet on a race horse, "Wishing Ring," won $1,213 on June 17, 1912.
exa	I wasn't exactly exalted, but exasperated, at the exaggerated example.
easy	They were to type their last names right below the title of the theme.

| 1 | 2 | 3 | 4 | 5 | 6 | 7 | 8 | 9 | 10 | 11 | 12 | 13 | 14 |

5 minutes

96b ● Making Times and Equal Signs

Times sign: Use a small letter *x* with a space before and after it.

Equal sign: If your machine does not have an equal key, type two hyphens, one slightly below the other. Turn the cylinder knob slightly away from you to type the second hyphen. Leave a space before and after the hyphen.

Directions: Keyboard each sentence 3 times SS following the directions for making the *times* or *equal* signs. DS between 3-line groups.

1 She determined the interest rate like this: $6,890 × .1425 = $981.82.

2 This is the way he should figure his earnings: $739 × .0865 = $63.92.

96c ● Language Arts Skills: Punctuation Guides (Semicolon) 10 minutes

think of the rules as you type the sentences

Directions: The following are guides for the use of the semicolon and sentences that illustrate the use of those guides. Study each guide; then keyboard the sentence(s) that illustrates the guide. Keyboard each sentence or group of sentences twice SS; DS between groups.

Use a semicolon between the clauses of a compound sentence when no conjunction is used.
Kathy Denin arrives in Chicago today; she will be in Detroit tomorrow.
Our fine softball team won easily; they will play again next Thursday.

If a conjunction is used to join the clauses, use a comma between them.
Dave plans to be in Memphis today, but he will go to Atlanta tomorrow.

Use a semicolon between the clauses of a compound sentence that are joined by such words as *also, however, therefore,* and *consequently.*
This is the current plan; however, it is subject to Martha's approval.
Laura and Don plan to go; consequently, they will need the automobile.

Use a semicolon to separate groups of words or figures if one or more of the groups contains a comma.
We saw Linda Bell, Ogden; Henry Abels, Reno; and Renee Freeman, Provo.

41e ● Paragraph Guided Writings

Directions: 1. Take a 1' writing on ¶1. Figure *gwam*. Add four words to your *gwam* for a new goal.
2. Take two 1' writings. Try to reach your goal on each writing.

3. Take a 1' writing on the same ¶. Drop back two to four *gwam*. Your goal is to keyboard the ¶ without errors.
4. Repeat Steps 1, 2, and 3 for the second and third ¶s.

all letters used   1.2 si   *gwam* 3'

keep wrists low and arms quiet

	gwam 3'
Before you start to look for your first job, you will be	4 | 43
wise to consider some techniques of job seeking that have been	8 | 47
helpful to others. They can also pay off for you.	11 | 50
For example, show that you are not lazy by listing the	15 | 54
kinds of work you have done. You might have delivered papers	19 | 58
or taken care of children. Be sure to include work for which	23 | 62
you did not get paid.	25 | 64
The strong points of your school record should be noted,	29 | 67
of course. It will help if you can say you missed only two	33 | 71
days of school in three years or that your typing rate was	37 | 75
one of the best in the class.	39 | 77

gwam 3' | 1 | 2 | 3 | 4 |

41f ● Language Arts Skills: Composing at the Typewriter

Directions: Compose answers to as many of the questions below as time permits.

Use complete sentences as you type your answers.

1. How many vertical line spaces are there on a full sheet of paper?
2. How many vertical line spaces are there on a half sheet of paper?

3. How many horizontal spaces (elite type) are there on a full sheet (8½" × 11") of paper?
4. How many horizontal spaces (pica type) are there on a full sheet of paper?

LESSON 42   60-space line

42a ● Keyboard Review

Directions: Keyboard each sentence 3 times SS. DS between 3-line groups.

sit erect; keep feet flat on floor

alphabet Her big objective was to set a complex zone defense quickly.
fig/sym The club's meeting dates are March 30, April 17, and May 24.
easy Terry thinks they would be smart to visit that island today.

| 1 | 2 | 3 | 4 | 5 | 6 | 7 | 8 | 9 | 10 | 11 | 12 |

LESSON 95

95a ● Keyboard Review

5 minutes

Directions: Keyboard each sentence three times SS. DS between 3-line groups.

alphabet One excited gazelle jumped the river before us and quickly raced away.

fig/sym The stocks that sold for $104.37 in 1929 had risen to $568.60 by 1969.

direct reaches My brother Bunkichi and I hunted quail at a curve by a munitions dump.

easy Some of them had questions about the amount of work done in the class.

| 1 | 2 | 3 | 4 | 5 | 6 | 7 | 8 | 9 | 10 | 11 | 12 | 13 | 14 |

10 minutes

95b ● Timed Writings

Directions: Take a 1' writing on 91c, page 156, with as few errors as possible. Take a 5' writing on the same ¶s. Circle errors and figure *gwam*.

30 minutes

95c ● Problem Typing: Writing a Report

Directions: Problem 1 Title Page
Use the information at the right to format/keyboard the title page for your leftbound report. If necessary, refer to 85c, page 147.

```
WRITING A REPORT

    Your Name
  Typewriting II

  Current Date
```

Directions: Problem 2 Bibliography
Format/keyboard the bibliography for your leftbound report from the information given below. If necessary, refer to page 148.

After you complete the bibliography, assemble your report. Place the title page on top, followed by the final outline, the body of the report, and the bibliography. Bind the pages together at the left.

Bartky, Joyce and Yvonne Kuhlman, Spectrum of English. Encino: Glencoe Publishing Company, Inc., 1979.

Fraier, Jacob J. and Flora Morris Brown, Effective English 7. Morristown: Silver Burdette Company, 1979.

Glatthorn, Allan A. Composition Skills. Chicago: Science Research Associates, Inc., 1980.

James, T. F. "Hemingway at Work." Cosmopolitan, August, 1957, p. 54.

Roberts, F. "A Revolution in Writing." Parents, October, 1983, p. 52.

Warriner, John E., and Sheila Laws Graham. English Grammar and Composition, Second Course. New York: Harcourt Brace Jovanovich, Inc., 1977.

95d ● Extra-Credit

Directions: Problem 1
Format/keyboard a short unbound report based on the outline in 87c, Problem 1, page 150.

Directions: Problem 2
Format/keyboard a short leftbound report based on the outline in 87c, Problem 2, page 151.

42b ● Language Arts Skills: Keyboarding from Dictation and Spelling Checkup

Directions: **1.** Your teacher will dictate words in 41d, page 69. Keyboard the words from dictation.

2. Check your work for correct spelling. Retype any words in which you made an error.

---

10 minutes **42c ● Timed Writings**

Directions: **1.** Take two 3' writings on 41e, page 70. Proofread; circle errors.

2. Figure *gwam*; submit the better writing.

---

25 minutes **42d ● Problem Typing: Personal Notes in Block Style, Open Punctuation**

Directions: Problem 1

1. Set margins for a 50-space line.
2. On a half sheet of paper, keyboard the personal note below.

Begin the date on the 7th line from the top edge of the paper. Begin the salutation on the 4th line below the date.

begin 7 lines from
top edge of paper

words

Date May 8, 19--	2

4th line (return 4 times)
below date

Salutation Dear Michelle	5

DS

Body Congratulations on being elected as our new Student — 15
Body President. I know from experience that you — 25
will be the busiest person on campus next year. — 35

DS

Will you please ask each of your officers to be — 45
present at the special meeting of the old and new — 55
student councils on Thursday afternoon. The meeting — 65
will begin promptly at 3:45 in the cafeteria. — 75

DS

I'm looking forward to seeing everyone there. — 84

DS

Complimentary Close Sincerely — 85

In the block style, the date, salutation, and complimentary
close are typed at the left margin. The lines of the paragraphs are blocked. Open punctuation is used in this note
(no marks of punctuation follow the salutation or complimentary close).

LESSON 94

94a ● Keyboard Review

5 minutes

Directions: Keyboard each sentence three times SS. DS between 3-line groups.

alphabet   The jovial banquet speaker excited and amazed a large crowd of youths.

fig/sym   A total of 84 runners had cracked the 4-minute mile "barrier" by 1967.

adjacent keys   Roberta tried to remove their tire as we drew near on the return trip.

easy   The world does not owe you a living today; it is your duty to earn it.

| 1 | 2 | 3 | 4 | 5 | 6 | 7 | 8 | 9 | 10 | 11 | 12 | 13 | 14 |

7 minutes

94b ● Language Arts Skills: Punctuation Guides for Commas

Directions: The following are punctuation guides and sentences that illustrate the use of commas.

Study each guide; keyboard the sentence that illustrates the guide. Keyboard each sentence twice SS; DS between 2-line groups.

Use commas to set off interrupting words that are nonessential to the sentence.
All homework assignments, however, must be completed by next Thursday.

Use a comma to set off interjections (yes, no, well) if there is a break in continuity.
No, the Michael Jackson concert cannot be held in Chicago on that day.

Use commas to set off the name of the person addressed.
The meeting, Ted, was Thursday.   Carmelo, did you really see us there?

Use commas to separate dates from years and cities from states.
My twin sisters were born on July 8, 1985, in Los Angeles, California.

8 minutes

94c ● Speed Builder

Directions: **1.** Take a 1' writing. The last word typed will be your goal word.
2. Take a 5' writing with the return called after each minute. When the return is called, start the ¶ over again. Try to reach your goal each minute as the return is called.

sit erect;
feet flat
on the floor

all letters used   1.3 si

Just a few simple steps are required to keep your house a little
cooler on a hot summer day. In the evening and early morning hours,
open the windows to let in the cool breezes. Close up the house later
and keep the drapes closed during the day. Finally, shade windows that
are exposed to the sun.

25 minutes

94d ● Problem Typing

Directions: Continue keyboarding the leftbound report as directed in 92c, page 157. Keep margins and spacing uniform throughout the manuscript.

42d, continued

Directions: Problem 2

1. Set margins for a 60-space line.
2. On a half sheet of paper, keyboard the personal note below.

As you did in Problem 1, begin the date on the 7th line from the top edge of the paper and the salutation on the 4th line below the date.

words

Today's date   3

4 line spaces (return 4 times between date and salutation)

Dear Tami   5
DS

I must write a short paper for my English class on one of   17
our national parks. Since I have never been to any of our   28
parks, this is quite an order. I would like to write a good   41
paper.   42
DS

I recall your telling me that you camped in Yosemite last   54
summer. Do you have any booklets on Yosemite that you could   66
lend me? I shall be sure to return them to you.   76
DS

Sincerely   78

Sign your name

LESSON 43

60-space line

5 minutes   **43a ● Keyboard Review**

Directions: Keyboard each sentence 3 times SS. DS between 3-line groups.

strike each key with quick, sharp strokes

alphabet Bob Jade was given extra maps quickly as he was in a frenzy.

fig/sym We ordered 25 bicycles; 16 are 10-speeds and 9 are 3-speeds.

easy The right angle to use in solving problems is the try angle.

| 1 | 2 | 3 | 4 | 5 | 6 | 7 | 8 | 9 | 10 | 11 | 12 |

---

10 minutes   **43b ● Sentence Skill Builder from Script**

Directions: Take two 1' writings on each sentence. On the first writing, push for speed. On the second writing, drop back in speed and work for control.

words

Many fields require some sort of training after high school. 12
We all hope to find out where our talents and interests lie. 12
Quite a few of our class members now plan to attend college. 12
They have just begun to study the various careers available. 12

The title page contains the name of the report and its writer. The bibliography contains titles of references that have been consulted.

It will pay you to learn how to write clear, interest-holding papers. It's not an easy job, but with a plan to guide you and some practice, you can turn out good work on your typewriter.

[1]T. F. James, "Hemingway at Work," Cosmopolitan, August, 1957, p. 54.

[2]John E. Warriner and Sheila Laws Graham, English Grammar and Composition, Second Course, (New York: Harcourt Brace Jovanovich, Inc., 1977), p. 376.

[3]Ibid., p. 377.

LESSON 93

70-space line

93a ● Keyboard Review

5 minutes

Directions: Keyboard each sentence three times SS. DS between 3-line groups.

alphabet | Don is explaining why he believes I must acquire a jackal for the zoo.

fig/sym | Antonio got a 25% discount ($74.30) on a stereo he bought May 5, 1986.

eve | Have you ever realized that every member attends the evening meetings?

easy | Profit depends on whether you keep your mind or your feet on the desk.

| 1 | 2 | 3 | 4 | 5 | 6 | 7 | 8 | 9 | 10 | 11 | 12 | 13 | 14 |

93b ● Speed Builder

10 minutes

Alternate Procedure: Work for speed as you take one 5' writing on all three ¶s combined. Figure *gwam*.

Directions: Take two 1' writings on each ¶; try to increase speed on the second writing. Figure *gwam*.

all letters used   1.3 si   *gwam* 1' | 5'

	1'	5'
One of the biggest counting jobs in the world occurs every ten	13	3 | 36
years when the nation's census is taken. While the practice is as old	27	5 | 39
as collecting taxes and building an army, this country was the first	41	8 | 42
large one to plan such a count of its people. Since early times, the	55	11 | 45
census has been conducted in those years that ended in zero.	67	13 | 47
Today, the task is much more than just a head count and is used	13	16 | 50
for a lot of things other than finding out who will pay taxes or fight.	27	19 | 53
The data serve as the basis for the distribution of federal money to	41	22 | 55
states and cities. They are also used to help determine social trends	55	24 | 58
and the need for public services.	62	26 | 60
Most households, all except one in six, are given a form which	13	28 | 62
contains a series of questions to be answered. Census officials say an	27	31 | 65
eighth grader should be able to fill it out in much less than an hour.	41	34 | 68

gwam 1'	1	2	3	4	5	6	7	8	9	10	11	12	13	14
5'		1			2			3						

93c ● Problem Typing

30 minutes

Directions: Continue keyboarding the leftbound report in 92c, page 157.

43c ● Problem Typing: Personal Notes in Modified Block Style, Open Punctuation

Directions: Problem 1

1. Use a half sheet of paper and a 60-space line.

2. Keyboard the personal note below. Begin the dateline and the complimentary close at the horizontal center point of the paper. Begin the salutation on the 4th line below the date at the left margin.

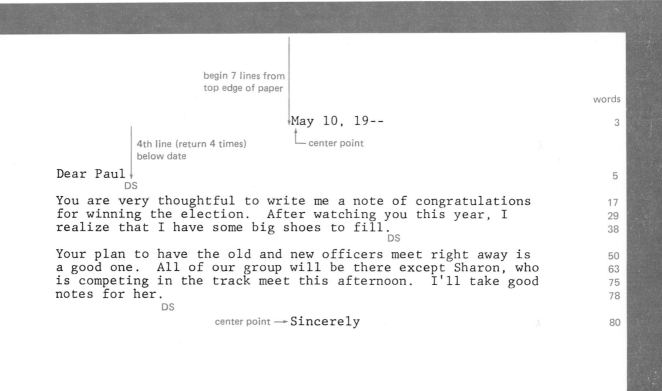

begin 7 lines from top edge of paper

words

↓May 10, 19--   3

↑— center point

4th line (return 4 times) below date

Dear Paul↓   5
      DS

You are very thoughtful to write me a note of congratulations   17
for winning the election. After watching you this year, I   29
realize that I have some big shoes to fill.   38
                                        DS

Your plan to have the old and new officers meet right away is   50
a good one. All of our group will be there except Sharon, who   63
is competing in the track meet this afternoon. I'll take good   75
notes for her.   78
      DS

center point → Sincerely   80

In the modified block style, the date and the complimentary close are started at the center point of the paper. The paragraphs may be blocked or indented.

Directions: Problem 2

1. Use a half sheet of paper and a 60-space line.

2. Keyboard the personal note at the top of page 74 in modified block style, open punctuation, with indented paragraphs. Space down for the date and the salutation the same as you did in Problem 1.

(continued on next page)

WRITING A REPORT
TS

"The test of a book," said Ernest Hemingway, "is how much good stuff you can throw away."[1] He added that anything that does not have the ring of hard truth, that seems the least bit overdone, must go into the wastebasket. Deep feelings about something written in words that stay with the reader--this is the goal of a good writer.

We can't all gain the fame that Hemingway knew as a writer. He worked hard and long at perfecting his skill. We can all learn how to write a short paper, however, long before we get into Hemingway's class. Almost all of us can learn to write a clear, interesting account about something we have read, heard, or seen. Let's see how you might go about this job.

Steps for Preparing a Report

Choose the right subject. To begin with, you need to select a subject you know something about. One authority says such a choice may be the most important decision you make in planning and writing your composition.[2] You can't write about the growing of figs unless you know how figs are grown. However, you can get information from books, from talks with fig growers, or from growing figs yourself.

Limit your subject. Don't try to cover too much ground in your paper. Young writers often butt their heads against this wall without getting anything more than a sore head for their trouble. As Warriner says, "Probably more student compositions turn out badly because their subjects are too broad than for any other reason."[3]

Narrow your subject down. Write about the kind of soil fig trees like or how figs are prepared for the market. You can't cover the whole life of a fig, from seedling to fig sauce, in two hundred words, no matter how skilled you become as a writer.

Prepare a preliminary outline. Jot down the major topics you expect to cover. This is the preliminary outline. It consists only of a number of topic headings. No subpoints need to be included.

Prepare bibliography cards. After you select a subject and prepare your preliminary outline, you must find out where you can obtain the information you need. For most students, books and articles will furnish the needed help.

As you find books and articles that appear to be helpful, write their titles on cards. On each card, write complete information about a single reference so the card can be used later to prepare the footnotes and bibliography for your paper.

Read and take notes. Start your reading. As you read, take notes. Record important facts, ideas, and quotations on note cards so that you can refer to them as you write your paper.

Each note card should be given a heading which describes the notes. Use one of the main headings of your preliminary outline, if you can, to identify each card. Write each note on a separate card. In every case, indicate the page number and reference from which the note was taken.

Prepare the final outline. When you have taken notes on all your readings, organize your cards in some order. This will usually be determined by the order of the points in the preliminary outline. You may find that some of the main points should now be changed. Try to group the cards under each major point into two or more subgroups. These will make up the subpoints of your outline.

Remember that an outline shows clearly what points are the most important as well as those that are less important. The Roman numerals show the chief ideas. The capital letters and Arabic numerals give details under the main points.

Steps for Writing a Report

Write the first draft. The first writing of a paper will usually not be the final one. Present the material you have collected. Don't worry too much about words, spelling, and typing mistakes.

Revise the first draft. When the first draft has been completed, check it for wording and mistakes. Mark your corrections with a pen or pencil. Careful writers read and correct their copy two or three times to make sure that their papers read well. It is recommended that you do this too.

Prepare the final copy. Good appearance in papers is important. Follow accepted rules for typing the final copy. Pay close attention to margins, placement of footnotes, and other similar details.

Prepare the title page and bibliography. Long, formal reports usually have a title page and bibliography.

(continued on next page)

words

December 3, 19-- 3

Note: To indent the first line of a ¶, space in 5 spaces from the left margin.

Dear Pam 5

I'm really looking forward to spending the holidays with 17
you and your family this year. If the weather forecasts are 29
correct, we should be able to give our skis a good workout. 41

Dad made reservations for me yesterday. I will arrive 52
December 18 on Flight 84 at 5:15 p.m. 60

Thanks a million for inviting me. I'll see you Sunday. 71

Sincerely 73

Directions: Problem 3

1. Use a half sheet of paper inserted lengthwise into your machine (short side up). Set a 40-space line.

2. Keyboard the note shown at the right. Begin the name and address of the writer (the return address) one-half inch from the top edge of the paper. Center each line of the return address.

3. Set off the return address by typing a line of hyphens from the left to the right edge of the paper, a line space or two below the return address.

4. Begin the date at the center point of the paper on the 3d line space below the hyphens under the return address. To find center point, refer to page 67; or fold your paper to bring the left and right edges together. Crease the paper lightly at the top.

5. Begin the salutation on the 4th line space below the date.

6. Begin the complimentary close at the center point of the paper a DS below the last ¶.

```
                KATHY MORENO
              175 Alameda Avenue
                   Topeka

- - - - - - - - - - - - - - - - - - - - - - - - - - - - - -

                    December 3, 19--


Dear Pam

     I'm really looking forward to spending
the holidays with you and your family this
year.  If the weather forecasts are correct,
we should be able to give our skis a good
workout.

     Dad made reservations for me yesterday.
I will arrive December 18 on Flight 84 at
5:15 p.m.

     Thanks a million for inviting me.  I'll
see you Sunday.

                    Sincerely
```

91e ● Compose at Your Typewriter

Directions: 1. Keyboard the following quotation and a short paragraph explaining what it means to you.
2. Using proofreader's marks, correct your copy.
3. Set a 60-space line. On a full sheet of paper, retype the paragraph; leave a 2″ top margin.

Mark Twain said, "Nothing so needs reforming as other people's habits."

LESSON 92

70-space line

5 minutes **92a ● Keyboard Review**

Directions: Keyboard each sentence three times SS. DS between 3-line groups.

alphabet Five or six big jet airliners flew quickly overhead at amazing speeds.

figure If I add 3,682 and 57, I certainly should not get 4,019 for an answer!

shift William A. Burt, Mount Vernon, Michigan, patented his machine in 1829.

easy The robot shown in the movies looked as if it came from another world.

| 1 | 2 | 3 | 4 | 5 | 6 | 7 | 8 | 9 | 10 | 11 | 12 | 13 | 14 |

---

10 minutes **92b ● Skill Builder**

Directions: 1. Take a 1′ writing on the ¶ below. The last word typed will be your goal word.
2. Take a 5′ writing with the return called after each minute. When the return is called, start the ¶ over again. Try to reach your goal each minute as the return is called.

1.3 si

keep a steady
flowing rhythm

   The value of a good mechanic is known by anybody who has ever owned a car. It is a trade that is often learned on the job. After working for a few years as a helper at a garage or gas station, one can make more complex repairs. A good way to start is by taking an auto repair class in high school.

---

30 minutes **92c ● Problem Typing: Writing a Report**

Directions: 1. Keyboard the report on pages 158 & 159 DS. Follow the directions given in 84b, page 145, for leftbound reports.
2. Refer to page 102 for assistance in formatting the two side headings in this report. The paragraph headings are indented 5 spaces and underlined. Format as shown in the report on page 158.
3. All pages are to be numbered.
4. Place footnotes at the bottom of the page in which reference is made to them.
5. Keyboard as much of the report as you can in the time given. You will be given time in Lessons 93 and 94 to complete the report.

(continued on next page)

44a ● Keyboard Review

7 minutes   Directions: Keyboard each sentence 3 times SS. DS between 3-line groups.

alphabet   Marvel Jackson was requested to pay a tax for the big prize.

fig/sym   At 9%, Daniel's monthly payment is $191; at 12%, it is $199.

adjacent keys She said there was a riot there just as the police returned.

hyphen   Sixty-two people heard the one-hour lecture on self-defense.

easy   It will pay you to learn what you are to do before you type.

| 1 | 2 | 3 | 4 | 5 | 6 | 7 | 8 | 9 | 10 | 11 | 12 |

15 minutes   ## 44b ● Paragraph Guided Writings

Directions: **1.** Take a 1' writing on ¶1. Figure *gwam*. Add four words to your *gwam* for a new goal.

2. Take two 1' writings. Try to reach your new goal on each writing.

3. Take a 1' writing on the same ¶. Drop back two to four *gwam*. Your goal is to keyboard the ¶ without errors.

4. Repeat Steps 1, 2, and 3 for the second and third ¶s.

all letters used   1.2 si   *gwam* 3'

The half-hour news broadcast which you watch each night   4 | 43

involves a lot more than the few people that you see on the 8 | 47

screen.   Nearly a hundred staff workers may be required to 11 | 51

plan just one network news program.   14 | 53

They have to decide which of the dozens of stories of 18 | 57

the day are the best ones for us to see.   Some writers work 22 | 61

on foreign news, some work on local news, and some work on 26 | 65

special features.   27 | 66

You will find that working with the news can be most 30 | 70

exciting.   It is not like most desk jobs because the hours 34 | 73

are often long, and you may have to work weekends and late 38 | 77

at night.   39 | 78

gwam 3' | 1 | 2 | 3 | 4 |

23 minutes   ## 44c ● Problem Typing: Personal Notes

Prepare to Format: Cut two sheets of 8½" by 11" paper in half. Beginning on line 4 (short side up), keyboard your name and address on each sheet. Use clever arrangement of your name and address if you wish. Set off the return address with a line of hyphens as you did in 43c, Problem 3, on page 74. You will use these sheets in keyboarding the following problems.

(continued on next page)

91c ● Speed Ladder Paragraphs

Directions: Take a 1' writing on ¶1 DS. When you complete ¶1 in 1', repeat the procedure on succeeding ¶s.

Take three 1' writings on any ¶ you do not finish in the time given.

Alternate Procedure: Work on control as you take a 1' writing on ¶1. Move to succeeding ¶s when you complete each one within the error limit specified by your teacher. If time allows, repeat any ¶s in which you exceeded the error limit.

all letters used   1.3 si   gwam 5'

Today it seems quite natural for us to shake hands when we greet   3 | 47

a person.   Like lots of things that we do without thinking, such an   5 | 49

action at one time likely symbolized something.   8 | 51

In primitive life the hand was probably a symbol of power.   It   10 | 54

was used to fight enemies and to make spears.   When extended, the hand 13 | 56

might have meant goodwill by showing that a person was not armed.   15 | 59

We know that the hand played a major role in early religions.   The   18 | 62

Greeks prayed to their gods with raised hands.   Presenting the hands,   21 | 65

palm to palm, was at one time how an inferior person paid homage to a   23 | 67

superior one.   24 | 68

In these days there are still a number of different ways to shake   27 | 71

hands throughout the world.   Certain groups of people rub their palms   29 | 73

together.   There are chiefs in some African tribes who snap the middle 32 | 76

finger three times when greeting.   34 | 77

We can easily see that the hand, and what was done with it, has   36 | 80

been full of meaning all through the ages.   Although today it is very   39 | 83

common for most of us to shake hands without even thinking, we are   42 | 86

really carrying on a custom handed down from ancient times.   44 | 88

gwam 5' | 1 | 2 | 3 |

---

5 minutes   **91d ● Correcting Errors: Spreading Letters**

Directions: **1.** Keyboard the sentence as it appears with the error in *extra*.

2. Erase the incorrect word. Move the carriage to the space where the *e* was typed in *exttra*. Depress and hold the space bar; strike the letter *e*. Release the space bar.

3. Repeat this procedure to type *tra*.

4. On an electric or electronic typewriter, use either the half-backspace mechanism or the incremental backspacer key which is on your machine.

Error: `Correct the exttra letter.`

Correction: `Correct the extra letter.`

44c, continued

Directions: Problem 1 Personal Note in Modified Block Style
1. Set margins for a 40-space line.
2. Keyboard the personal note below in modified block style with blocked paragraphs. Use today's date and place the salutation on the 4th line space below the date.

Note: The lines in the problems are not set line for line as you will type them. Set margin stops properly; listen for the bell to return your carriage.

Dear Ying

Will your school be sending any students to the District Fair next month? Mrs. Mendes, who is our club advisor, asked me to find out how many schools in our area will be sending students this year.

We thought it would be fun to have a picnic lunch together Friday at noon so we can get better acquainted before the activities begin.

Please let me know if any members from Sierra will be able to attend.

Sincerely

Directions: Problem 2 Personal Note in Block Style
1. Set margins for a 40-space line.
2. Keyboard the personal note below in block style. Use today's date.

Dear Andy

Thanks very much for sending me the information about stereo equipment. It was pretty easy to understand, even for a beginner like me.

I have to admit that the explanations about such things as watts per channel and total harmonic distortion were a little confusing, but I did learn a lot. I didn't realize how many different kinds of receivers there were.

With luck, I should have enough money saved to buy a pretty good system after Christmas. Get ready to share your record collection.

Sincerely

44d ● **Extra Credit**

Directions: Compose and keyboard a reply to the personal note in Problem 1. Use modified block style with indented paragraphs. Arrange your message neatly on the sheet; date the note three days from today.

LESSON 45

60-space line

5 minutes   **45a** ● **Keyboard Review**

Directions: Keyboard each sentence 3 times SS. DS between 3-line groups.

alphabet   Bud Roper may take this quiz next week if Jack will give it.
fig/sym   She paid $14.50 for the books and another $7.98 for pencils.
easy   He has to learn to handle those kinds of problems right now.

| 1 | 2 | 3 | 4 | 5 | 6 | 7 | 8 | 9 | 10 | 11 | 12 |

Note Card 2

Heading: Writing effectively
Notes: Descriptive paragraphs:
1. Concentrate on words that appeal to our senses.
2. Describe how things appear to us.
3. Let us sense what is being related.
4. Put us in touch with the physical world.
Reference: Conlin, p. 304.

Note Card 3

Heading: Prepare the final outline
Notes: An outline shows what points are most important and which are secondary. The Roman numerals show the main ideas. The capital letters and Arabic numerals give details under the main points.
Reference: Green, p. 251.

---

15 minutes **90c ● Timed Writings**

Directions: 1. Take one 1' writing on each ¶ of 86d, page 149. Circle errors.

2. Take one 5' writing on all four ¶s combined. Circle errors; figure *gwam*.

LESSON 91

70-space line

5 minutes **91a ● Keyboard Review**

Directions: Keyboard each sentence three times SS. DS between 3-line groups.

keep wrists and arms still

alphabet Kim was very excited to qualify for the bronze medal in the high jump.

fig/sym Miss Morse told the seventh grade students to add 5/6, 19/30, and 2/3.

adjacent keys Right after their retirement, other writers returned to the territory.

easy Your mind is like a good knife; it must be used often to remain sharp.

| 1 | 2 | 3 | 4 | 5 | 6 | 7 | 8 | 9 | 10 | 11 | 12 | 13 | 14 |

---

5 minutes **91b ● Language Arts Skills: Number Expression Guides**

Directions: The following are fraction number guides and sentences that illustrate those guides. Study each guide; then keyboard the sentence that illustrates the guide. Keyboard each sentence twice SS; DS between 2-line groups.

Made fractions are used when the fraction is not on the keyboard.
"Made" fractions should be typed in this way: 2/3, 1/5, 3/4, and 7/8.

Space between whole numbers and *made* fractions.
They needed 7 2/3 yards of wool and 6 1/2 yards of silk for their job.

Be uniform when you type fractions: ½ and ¼, but 1/2 and 2/5.
If all fractions you need are located on the keyboard, type: ½ and ¼.

45b ● **Timed Writings**

Directions: 1. Take two 3' writings on 44b, page 75. Proofread; circle errors.

2. Figure *gwam*; submit the better writing.

---

30 minutes **45c** ● **Problem Typing: Postal Cards**

Directions: Problem 1 Message

1. Insert a postal card or paper cut to size (5½" × 3¼") into your machine.

2. Set margin stops 4 spaces from each edge of the card. Set a tab stop at horizontal center.

3. Begin the date on line 3; then type the remaining lines as illustrated on the card.

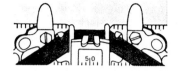

If using a manual typewriter, adjust the card holders, as shown above, and use the paper bail to keep the card from slipping.

```
 1
 2                      begin 3 lines from
                        top edge of card
 3                                    ↓April 13, 19--
 4                                    └center point        TS
 5    ┌4 spaces
 6    │ Dear Aunt Martha
 7                           DS
 8      The gold necklace you sent for my birthday is
 9      beautiful.  Thank you for being so thoughtful.
10                                                    DS
11      Mother said I should ask you to arrange your
12      vacation to include a visit at our house this
13      year.  Please try to come.
14                           TS
15
16            center point→Lauri
17
18
19
```

Directions: Problem 2 Address a Postal Card

1. Type the return address and the address of the recipient on the opposite side of the postal card you prepared in Problem 1.

2. Begin the return address on the second line from the top edge of the card and 3 spaces from the left edge.

3. Begin the address of the recipient about 2" from the top of the card and 2" from the left edge.

4. The 2-letter state abbreviations (typed in capital letters without a period or space between) may be used, standard abbreviations may be used, or state names may be typed in full.

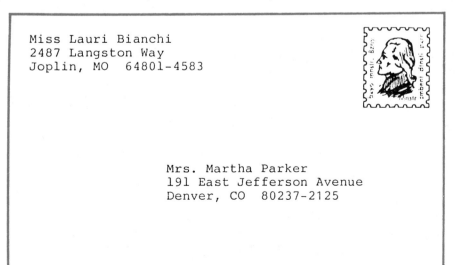

Miss Lauri Bianchi
2487 Langston Way
Joplin, MO 64801-4583

Mrs. Martha Parker
191 East Jefferson Avenue
Denver, CO 80237-2125

ZIP Code numbers are typed two spaces after the two-letter state abbreviation. The 2-letter state abbreviations are shown on page 116.

Bibliographical Card 2

Author:	Bartky, Joyce and Yvonne Kuhlman
Title:	Spectrum of English
Publisher:	Encino: Glencoe Publishing Company, Inc., 1979
Short Description:	Presents writing and speaking skills. Chapters include interviewing, discussion, and debating.
Library Call No.:	c 372.60 K658

Bibliographical Card 3

Author:	Fraier, Jacob J. and Flora Morris Brown
Title:	Effective English 7
Publisher:	Morristown: Silver Burdette Company, 1979
Short Description:	Content includes grammar, usage, composition, speaking and listening, mechanics and reference.
Library Call No.:	c 372.602 K658

LESSON 90

70-space line

5 minutes

90a ● Keyboard Review

Directions: Keyboard each sentence three times SS. DS between 3-line groups.

alphabet   I know it is an expensive job to organize and equip the men carefully.

figure   Approximately 1,074 girls and 826 boys were enrolled there after 1985.

4th finger   Paula, please play the part in the play. The play will open in April.

easy   Talk becomes cheap when there is a bigger supply than there is demand.

| 1 | 2 | 3 | 4 | 5 | 6 | 7 | 8 | 9 | 10 | 11 | 12 | 13 | 14 |

25 minutes

90b ● Problem Typing: Note Cards

Directions: 1. Prepare the following note cards on 5" × 3" cards or paper cut to size. Keyboard the first card from the illustration below, the second and third from the information that follows on page 155.
2. Begin the first entry a TS below the top edge of the card and 3 spaces from the left edge.

Note cards contain ideas, facts, and quotations to be used in preparing the body of a report.

heading   — 3 spaces   TS

Rules for making note cards

notes   A note card should carry only one idea.

The topic heading is placed in the upper left-hand corner and is usually taken from the preliminary outline.

Reference to the source is placed in the lower left-hand corner of the card.

reference   Sigband, pp. 39-40.

(continued on next page)

Directions: Problem 3 Postal Card in Modified Block Style

1. Prepare the following message on a postal card in modified block style. Use open punctuation (no punctuation after the salutation or complimentary close). SS the body of the message; use appropriate space between other message parts.

2. Use as the return address:

Jerry Bryan
814 North Tamara
Your city, state, ZIP Code

3. Address the card to:

Miss Karen Nelson
527 East Palm
Your city, state, ZIP Code

Current date

Dear Karen

Our annual barbecue will be held in O'Neal Park next Friday, (use next Friday's date) at 6 p.m.

Please remind all the students to bring their own dishes and silverware. All the food and soft drinks will be furnished.

Jerry Bryan
Student Body President

Directions: Problem 4 Postal Card in Block Style

1. Prepare the following message on a postal card in block style. Correct errors as indicated by the proofreader's marks.

2. Use as the return address:

David Statana
28 College Drive
Your city, state, ZIP Code

3. Address the card to:

Your name
Your street address
Your city, state, ZIP Code

Remember: When using the block style, begin the date and complimentary close at the left margin. Use open punctuation. SS the body of the message; use appropriate spacing between other parts of the message.

Use today's date

Dear *Use your name*

I ~~ha~~ was able to get five tickets to the rock concert for next saturday. At least ~~three~~ two new groups will be on the porgram, including the Seventh Dimensions and the Vagabonds. Several other poeple have ~~said~~ told me they would like to go, so I need to know your plans right away. I hope you can make it.

David Statana

45d ● Extra Credit

Directions: 1. Compose and type a reply to the message in Problem 4. Arrange the message neatly on a postal card.
2. Address the card to:

David Statana
28 College Drive
Your city, state, ZIP Code

3. Use your name and address for the return address.

89a ● Keyboard Review

5 minutes

Directions: Keyboard each sentence three times SS. DS between 3-line groups.

alphabet   Mickey won big prizes for diving in the last exciting junior aquatics.

fig/sym   The 1988 meeting (March 29-31) has been rescheduled for September 4-6.

long reaches   My brother Cecil gave my unlisted number to my Uncle Harvey yesterday.

easy   They tried to throw both of their keys down to us from an open window.

| 1 | 2 | 3 | 4 | 5 | 6 | 7 | 8 | 9 | 10 | 11 | 12 | 13 | 14 |

---

5 minutes

89b ● Speed Ladder Sentences

Directions: Keyboard each sentence for 1'. Your teacher will call the guide at 15", 12", or 10" intervals. As time permits, repeat sentences on which you were not able to complete a line with the call of the guide.

space quickly with down-and-in motion of thumb

		gwam	15" guide	12" guide	10" guide
1	Always use a quick, sharp stroke as you type.		36	45	54
2	Curve the fingers and hold them close to the keys.		40	50	60
3	Keep your wrists and elbows steady as you hit the keys.		44	55	66
4	Just try to think and type the short, easy words as a whole.		48	60	72

| 1 | 2 | 3 | 4 | 5 | 6 | 7 | 8 | 9 | 10 | 11 | 12 |

---

35 minutes

89c ● Problem Typing: Bibliographical Cards

Directions: 1. Prepare the following bibliographical cards on 5" × 3" cards or paper cut to size. Keyboard the first card from the illustration below, the second and third from the information that follows on page 154.

2. Begin the first entry a TS below the top edge of the card and 3 spaces from the left edge.

Bibliographical cards contain information about references you will use in a report. The illustration at the right shows the type of information included.

TS

author   — 3 spaces ↓ Glatthorn, Allan A.
DS

title   Composition Skills
DS

publication information   Chicago: Science Research Associates, Inc., 1980.
DS

short description   Explains composition process. Includes sentence and paragraph construction to writing the complete library paper.
TS

library call number   c 425.2028 G466

(continued on next page)

LESSON 46

46a ● Keyboard Review

5 minutes

Directions: Keyboard each sentence 3 times SS. DS between 3-line groups.

keep wrists
low and
still

alphabet	We might require five dozen packing boxes for our July crop.
fig/sym	Type distances in figures: I drove 837 miles in 1 3/4 days.
easy	Kate tossed the ball right to him as she ran down the court.

| 1 | 2 | 3 | 4 | 5 | 6 | 7 | 8 | 9 | 10 | 11 | 12 |

5 minutes

46b ● Language Arts Skills: Spelling and Proofreading Aid

Directions: Keyboard each line 3 times SS. Study carefully the spelling of each word as you type it.

keep fingers
deeply curved

1 remittance laboratory signature proposal eligible sufficient

2 via cooperate analysis definite capacity develop commitments

3 tremendous beautiful essential consequently survey recommend

15 minutes

46c ● Timed Writings

Directions: 1. Take a 3' writing on the ¶s below. Figure *gwam*.
2. Take two 1' writings on each ¶; take the first for speed, the second for control.
3. Take another 3' writing on the ¶s below. Figure *gwam*. Compare the *gwam* and number of errors on this writing with your first 3' writing.

all letters used   1.2 si   *gwam* 3'

There is little doubt that more and more people today	4	45
are concerned about keeping fit. We are being warned not to	8	49
gain too much weight or to let our blood pressure rise.	11	53
Some people lift weights in the executive suite, jog on	15	57
their lunch break, or work out with a rowing machine on the	19	61
back porch. They ride bikes, hike on trails, and swim laps	23	65
in greater numbers then ever before.	26	67
Whether you like to zoom down a roaring river on a raft	29	71
or whack a ball with a racquet, you will be wise to stay in	33	75
shape. If we sit behind a desk every day, we need some kind	37	79
of exercise to keep our bodies strong and our minds alert.	41	83

gwam 3' | 1 | 2 | 3 | 4 |

88c ● Problem Typing: Outlines

Starting with this lesson, you will prepare some of the materials needed for the left-bound report that you will keyboard in Lessons 92–95. A preliminary outline, bibliography cards, note cards, and a final outline are usually prepared before a report is written. Lessons 88, 89, and 90 will give you practice in preparing these items. With your teacher's approval, keep all items that pertain to this report until completion at the end of this unit.

Directions: Problem 1 Preliminary Outline (General Listing of Topics to be Used in a Report)

1. Set margins for a 40-space line.
2. On a full sheet of paper, keyboard the outline in exact vertical center.

3. Center the heading. TS below heading; DS all items.

STEPS FOR PREPARING A REPORT

Note: Since final outline will be bound with the report, use center point for leftbound report.

1. Choose subject.
2. Prepare preliminary outline.
3. Collect reading references.
4. Read and take notes.
5. Prepare final outline.

6. Prepare introduction.
7. Prepare first draft.
8. Correct and revise first draft.
9. Prepare final copy.
10. Prepare title page and bibliography.

Problem 2 Final Outline for a Leftbound Report

Use a 2″ top margin, 60-space line. Leave 1½″ left margin; 1″ right margin. Center the heading over the copy. Refer to 57d, page 100, if necessary.

WRITING A REPORT

I. STEPS TO TAKE BEFORE WRITING A REPORT
  A. Choose the right subject.
    1. Choose a topic that intrigues you.
    2. Choose a topic about which you know something.
  B. Limit your subject.
  C. Prepare a preliminary outline.
    1. Jot down the major points only.
    2. This outline acts as a guide in your search for information.
  D. Prepare bibliography cards.
    1. The cards should contain information on your readings.
    2. The data recorded should be complete and accurate.
  E. Read and take notes.
    1. Use note cards.
    2. Record important facts, opinions, and quotations.
  F. Prepare the final outline.
    1. Organize the information collected.
    2. Group note cards under topics used in the preliminary outline.

II. STEPS TO TAKE IN WRITING THE REPORT
  A. Write the first draft.
    1. The explanations should be clear, complete, to the point, and accurate.
    2. The sentences should be in logical order.
    3. Illustrate points by references to personal experiences.
    4. Compare your topic with one that is more familiar to the reader.
  B. Revise the first draft.
    1. Check the first draft for wording, spelling, and typographical errors.
    2. Make pencil or pen corrections.
  C. Prepare the final copy.
    1. Good appearance is important.
    2. Use standard rules on arrangement of report.
  D. Prepare the title page and bibliography.
    1. A title page contains the name of the report, the writer's name, and the date.
    2. The bibliography names the references consulted.

10 minutes | **46d** ● **Technique Builder: Carriage Return**

Directions: 1. Keyboard the first line of the ¶ 3 times as your teacher gives the signal each 20″. Return quickly; resume typing at once.

2. Repeat for lines 2, 3, and 4.
3. Take a 1′ writing on the entire ¶ DS without the call of the guide. Figure your *gwam*.

all letters used 1.2 si

	gwam 1′	20″ guide
One type of job you may wish to inquire about when	10	30
you get out of school is working for a temporary help firm.	22	35
Most towns of any size have such firms which hire both men	34	35
and women if they need extra help at certain times.	44	30

---

10 minutes | **46e** ● **Language Arts Skills: Capitalization Guides**

Directions: The following are capitalization guides and sentences that illustrate those guides.

Study each guide: then keyboard the line that illustrates the guide. Keyboard each sentence twice SS; DS between 2-line groups.

keep eyes and mind on copy as you keyboard

Capitalize the first word of a complete sentence.
Electronics is a growing field with many rich opportunities.

Capitalize the first word of a quoted sentence. (A period or comma is typed before the ending quotation mark.)
An old proverb says, "Kind words don't wear out the tongue."

The names of school subjects, except languages and numbered courses, are not capitalized.
Sheila is taking English, Music 2, Spanish, and bookkeeping.

Do not capitalize a quotation resumed within a sentence.
"The danger," an author said, "lies in giving up the chase."

Capitalize the pronoun *I*, both alone and in contractions.
Yes, I plan to go to the show, but I'll have to leave early.

Capitalize titles of organizations, institutions, and buildings.
The students of Westlake School saw a play at Ripon College.

LESSON 47

60-space line

5 minutes | **47a** ● **Keyboard Review**

Directions: Keyboard each sentence 3 times SS. DS between 3-line groups.

space quickly with down-and-in motion of thumb

alphabet | Ken Gumpy will acquire a deluxe razor just before he leaves.
fig/sym | <u>High Spirits</u> (Viking/Penguin) was $14.95 cloth, $5.95 paper.
easy | Please have them fix the sign on the left side of the field.

| 1 | 2 | 3 | 4 | 5 | 6 | 7 | 8 | 9 | 10 | 11 | 12 |

87c, continued   **Directions: Problem 2 Sentence Outline**
Set a 60-space line; set tab stops as in Problem 1. Leave a 2″ top margin.

SAFETY RULES FOR BICYCLES

I.   **WHAT ARE COMMON CAUSES OF ACCIDENTS?**
    A.   Two or more riders on a bicycle ranks first.
    B.   Bicycle hitchhiking ranks second.
    C.   Riding too closely behind other vehicles ranks third.

II.   **OBSERVE THESE COMMON-SENSE RULES**
    A.   Obey all traffic laws.
       1.   Make all necessary arm signals.
       2.   Use lights for night riding.
    B.   Do not be a show-off rider.
    C.   Avoid riding in heavy traffic.
    D.   Do not make sudden turns or stops.

LESSON 88
70-space line

5 minutes   **88a ● Keyboard Review**

Directions: Keyboard each sentence three times SS. DS between 3-line groups.

keep arms and wrists quiet

alphabet	Lee knew my expensive habits jeopardized chances for making the quota.
figure	In 1983, a record 1,055 U.S. corporations chose to change their names.
shift	Early typewriter inventors included Pratt, Sholes, Glidden, and Soule.
easy	Half of them think they slept more than eight hours during each night.

| 1 | 2 | 3 | 4 | 5 | 6 | 7 | 8 | 9 | 10 | 11 | 12 | 13 | 14 |

10 minutes   **88b ● Speed Builder**

Directions: Take two 1′ writings on each ¶; try to increase speed on the second writing. Figure *gwam*.

Alternate Procedure: Work for speed as you take one 5′ writing on all three ¶s combined. Figure *gwam*.

keep your eyes on the copy

all letters used   1.3 si   *gwam* 1′   5′

It is such a simple matter these days to hop on a giant jet and   13 | 3 | 35
zip from coast to coast in just a few hours. The vast plains, rushing   27 | 5 | 38
rivers, and rocky peaks below provide majestic views. Flying along   41 | 8 | 41
at top speeds, one can easily forget the hardships of early travel.   54 | 11 | 44

A century ago these wonders of nature caused major problems that   13 | 13 | 46
had to be solved if the country was to be linked by the iron horse. In   27 | 16 | 49
fact, many said the task of tying east to west with a ribbon of rails   41 | 19 | 52
was too great. Squabbles over the proposed route hindered progress.   55 | 22 | 55

The bulk of the work began after the Civil War. The job of laying   13 | 24 | 57
track across the vast expanse of land was finished in less than three   37 | 27 | 60
years. Thousands labored diligently for their meager dollar a day by   41 | 30 | 63
struggling over mountains and toiling in heat, cold, rain, and snow.   55 | 33 | 66

gwam 1′ | 1 | 2 | 3 | 4 | 5 | 6 | 7 | 8 | 9 | 10 | 11 | 12 | 13 | 14 |
     5′ | 1 | 2 | 3 |

5 minutes **47b ● Language Arts Skills: Keyboarding from Dictation and Spelling Checkup**

Directions: 1. Your teacher will dictate the words in 46b, page 79. Keyboard the words from dictation.

2. Check your work for correct spelling. Retype any words in which you made an error.

---

5 minutes **47c ● Continuity Practice from Rough Draft Copy**

Directions: Keyboard the ¶ at least twice DS. Make corrections as you work. Listen for the bell to know when to return your carriage (carrier).

	words
The personal letters you write should look neat and fresh.	12
make them ~~them~~ look as smart as you your self would like	22
to look when you meet your friends face to face. write clearly	35
and correctly, of course, but keep the ~~the~~ wording warm and	46
friendly.	48

---

5 minutes **47d ● Steps for Formatting Personal/Business Letters**

Directions: Read the steps for formatting personal/business letters below. You will need this information when you keyboard/format the personal/business letters in 47e.

Step 1 Set your machine for single spacing.

Step 2 Set your margins. The margins vary according to the length of the letter.

Step 3 Space down to begin the return address. (The number of lines to space down varies with the length of the letter. The longer the letter, the fewer the number of spaces.) For a modified block style letter, start the return address at the center point of the paper. For a block style letter, start the return address at the left margin.

Step 4 Space down 4 times below the return address to the letter address.

Step 5 Begin the salutation a double space below the letter address.

Step 6 Begin the body of the letter a double space below the salutation. Single space the paragraphs; double space between paragraphs.

Step 7 Begin the complimentary close a double space below the body of the letter. For a modified block style letter, start at the center point. For a block style letter, start at the left margin.

Step 8 Type the name of the writer on the 4th line space below the complimentary close. (The typewritten name of the writer is optional.)

---

25 minutes **47e ● Problem Typing: Personal/Business Letters in Modified Block Style**

Directions: Problem 1 Letter with Blocked Paragraphs, Open Punctuation

Keyboard/format the letter on page 82. Use a full sheet, 50-space line, open punctuation. Follow the formatting steps given above as well as the directions given on the model letter, page 82.

Directions: Problem 2 Letter with Indented Paragraphs, Open Punctuation

Using a full sheet, 50-space line, open punctuation, type the letter in Problem 1 again. Indent the first line of each paragraph 5 spaces. Listen for the bell to know when to return your carriage (carrier).

LESSON 87

5 minutes

87a ● Keyboard Review

Directions: Keyboard each sentence three times SS. DS between 3-line groups.

alphabet   Janice and David must take that final geography quiz before next week.

figure   Though 1,493 students took the 20 tests, only 76 scored more than 85%.

direct reaches   My uncle Myron brought my brother and aunt to Briton for the symphony.

easy   Both of them also spent their time working to aid others in the class.

| 1 | 2 | 3 | 4 | 5 | 6 | 7 | 8 | 9 | 10 | 11 | 12 | 13 | 14 |

10 minutes

87b ● Skill Builder

Directions: **1.** Take a 1' writing on the ¶ below. The last word typed will be your goal word.
2. Take a 5' writing with the return called after each minute. When the return is called, start the ¶ over again. Try to reach your goal each minute as the return is called.

use a quick carriage return

all letters used   1.3 si

Few things ever remain the same; the rise and fall of the corner drugstore is a good example of this truth. At very little expense a person could perch on a high stool, guzzle a soda, and just watch the world go by. Somehow the hamburger stand doing business there today doesn't quite do the trick.

30 minutes

87c ● Problem Typing: Formatting/Keyboarding Outlines

Directions: Problem 1 Topic Outline
1. Set a 60-space line. Clear all tab stops; set 3 tab stops of 4 spaces each beginning at the left margin.
2. Leave a 2" top margin; center the heading. If necessary, refer to 57d, page 100.

KEYBOARDING LEFTBOUND REPORTS

I.   MARGINS
   A.   Left Margin of 1 1/2 Inches
   B.   Right Margin of 1 Inch
   C.   Bottom Margin of 1 Inch
   D.   Top Margin of First Page of 2 Inches
   E.   Top Margin of Subsequent Pages of 1 Inch
      1.   At least 2 lines of paragraph at bottom of page
      2.   At least 2 lines of paragraph carried forward to new page

II.   SPACING
   A.   Triple Space Below Title
   B.   Double Space Contents of Report
   C.   Single Space Quoted Materials of 4 Lines or More, Footnotes, and Bibliographical Items

III.   PAGE NUMBERS
   A.   Centered 1/2 Inch from Bottom of First Page
   B.   Aligned with Right Margin 1/2 Inch (4 Line Spaces) from Top for All Other Pages

(continued on next page)

begin on line 18

words

return address   center point → 3502 Escondido Drive   4
Houston, TX 77083-5328   9
dateline → November 16, 19--   13

space down 4 times
(4 line spaces)

letter address   Mr. Armando Bolanos   17
Spectrum Business Systems   22
196 San Miguel Lane   26
Houston, TX 77060-7145   31
DS

salutation   Dear Mr. Bolanos   34
DS

body of   Your presentation at the James Madison School Career   45
letter   Center last Monday was very interesting to me. We   55
have been discussing several of these same topics in   65
our Computer Concepts class.   71
DS

My teacher, Ms. Anderson, suggested I write to you   82
for more information about the two films mentioned   92
in your talk. If possible, I would like to have a   102
copy of the brochure that describes the films and   112
explains where they may be obtained.   120
DS

Thank you for helping us learn more about job oppor-   130
tunities in the computer field.   137
DS

complimentary close   center point → Sincerely yours   140

space down 4 times
(4 line spaces)

typed name   Miss Jami Davies   143

This style, with minor variations, is used in many personal/business letters.
Open punctuation is used; no marks of punctuation are used after the salutation or complimentary close. A man need not use Mr. in his typed or
handwritten name at the end of a letter. A woman should use her personal
title (Miss, Ms., or Mrs.) with her typewritten name as a courtesy. This
allows a person to respond to a woman's letter using her preferred personal
title.

86d ● Speed Ladder Paragraphs

Directions: Take a 1' writing on ¶1 DS. When you complete ¶1 in 1', repeat procedure on succeeding ¶s.

Take three 1' writings on any ¶ you do not finish in the time given.

Alternate Procedure: Work on control as you take a 1' writing on ¶1. Move to succeeding ¶s when you complete each one within the error limit specified by your teacher. If time allows, repeat any ¶s in which you exceeded the error limit.

all letters used   1.3 si   *gwam* 5'

Minding one's manners is not an easy job these days. It is hard	3	47
to know the best way to handle someone who smokes without asking, or	5	49
how to get a neighbor to turn down the stereo.	7	51
What may be polite to one person can be rude to another. A man	10	54
might open the door for a woman only to find he has insulted her. A	13	57
woman might offend a man by offering to pick up the bill for lunch.	15	59
There can be little doubt that interest in this subject runs quite	18	62
high. Charm schools report long waiting lists. The corporate world now	21	65
realizes that many who are in the work force did not learn good manners	24	68
at home.	24	68
A lack of courtesy in business can ruin the chance for a sale if a	27	71
client feels that he or she has been offended in some way. It can slow	30	74
down or stop the chance for a raise when a top executive is treated	32	76
rudely by a person of lower rank.	34	78
The advent of the computer age has raised some new problems too.	36	80
Workers need to know when it's proper to send an electronic message to	39	83
the head of the firm. Also, they must resist taking a peek at what is	42	86
printed on the screen of one whom they are visiting.	44	88

gwam 5' | 1 | 2 | 3 |

86e ● Language Arts Skills: Number Expression Guides Review

Directions: The first sentence gives the rule; the other sentences illustrate the rule.   Keyboard each sentence twice SS. DS between 2-line groups.

1   You must type in full all numbers used at the beginning of a sentence.

2   Thirty-six of our states now grow choice eating apples for the market.

3   Twenty-five thousand carloads are shipped from Washington in one year.

LESSON 48

48a ● Keyboard Review

Directions: Keyboard each sentence 3 times SS. DS between 3-line groups.

alphabet Pete B. Mavy forgot he was required to sell six dozen jacks.

fig/sym John typed a 5-minute writing on page 127 with 98% accuracy.

easy I know she can see most of the fish if she sits on the dock.

| 1 | 2 | 3 | 4 | 5 | 6 | 7 | 8 | 9 | 10 | 11 | 12 |

48b ● Paragraph Guided Writings

Directions: 1. Take a 1' writing on the ¶ below. Note the last word you typed; make this your goal word.

2. Take three 1' writings on the ¶. Try to reach your goal word as time is called. Type no faster or slower than it takes to reach your goal word.

3. Raise your goal by 8 words. Take 3 additional 1' writings. Try to reach your new goal as time is called.

all letters used   1.3 si

                   .   4   .   8   .

We know that sizable numbers of people hold more than

12   .   16   .   20

one job these days. Two of every ten people who hold more

24   .   28   .   32

than one job do so because they like to work. The need for

36   .   40   .   44

extra cash is given as the reason more frequently, though.

48c ● Problem Typing: Preparing a Personal/Business Letter and Small Envelope

Directions: Problem 1 Letter with Blocked Paragraphs, Open Punctuation

Keyboard/format the letter below using a full sheet, 50-space line, open punctuation. Begin the return address on line 18; use today's date and your own address as the return address. Listen for the bell to determine line endings. Sign the letter.

words

When you supply the information, 11 words are counted for the return address and date.

	words
return address	11
Ms. Susan Barger	14
1295 Vista Drive	18
Your city, state, and ZIP Code	23
Dear Ms. Barger	26
As chairperson of Career Day, I want to thank you for coming	38
to Roosevelt School to speak on the subject of "Pharmacy as	50
a Career."	53
We especially appreciated learning about the educational re-	65
quirements for becoming a pharmacist and hearing your descrip-	77
tion of the trials and rewards of owning your own business.	89
I'm sure all of us now have a much greater understanding of	101
the field of pharmacy than we did before you talked to us.	113
Yours very truly	116

85c, continued

BIBLIOGRAPHY
TS

margin ↓

indent 5 spaces → Coon, George E., et al. American Book English. New York: American Book Company, 1980.
DS

Laughlin, R. M. "Fun in the Word Factory: Experiences with the Dictionary." Language Arts, (March, 1978), pp. 319-21.
DS

Maxwell, John C. Ginn Elements of English. Lexington: Ginn and Company, 1974.
DS

Pollock, Thomas Clark, and Richard L. Loughlin. The Macmillan English Series. New York: Macmillan, Inc., 1973.

LESSON 86

70-space line

5 minutes **86a ● Keyboard Review**

Directions: Keyboard each sentence three times SS. DS between 3-line groups.

alphabet We all realized that even an expert jockey must qualify before racing.

figure John Kennedy was President from January 20, 1961 to November 22, 1963.

double letters A need for referring all necessary letters for approval was discussed.

easy They made eight field goals and six free throws to win the title game.

| 1 | 2 | 3 | 4 | 5 | 6 | 7 | 8 | 9 | 10 | 11 | 12 | 13 | 14 |

8 minutes **86b ● Correcting Errors: Squeezing Letters**

Directions: **1.** Keyboard the first sentence as it appears below.

2. Erase the incorrect word and move the carriage to the space that follows *been*. Depress and hold the space bar; strike the letter o. Release the space bar. Repeat until the correction is completed.

3. Use the same procedure to correct the next sentence with an error.

4. On an electric or electronic typewriter, use either the half-backspace mechanism or the incremental backspacer which is on your machine.

Error: A letter has been mitted at the beginning of a word.
Correction: A letter has been omitted at the beginning of a word.

Error: A letter has bee omitted at the end of a word.
Correction: A letter has been omitted at the end of a word.

5 minutes **86c ● Speed Builder from Script**

Directions: Keyboard the ¶ below as many times as you can in the given time.

all letters used 1.3 si   words

What does it take to keep major league baseball teams going 12
these days? It requires top players, of course, and good fields 25
on which to play. But the teams need even more than that. 37
They must also have zealous fans who get excited and really 49
provide support with their attendance and their cheers. 60

48c, continued   **Directions: Problem 2 Addressing a Small Envelope**

1. Use a small envelope or paper cut to size (6½" x 3⅝").

2. Address the envelope for the letter you prepared in 47e, page 82. Follow the placement directions on the model

envelope illustrated below.

3. Fold the letter and insert it in the envelope (if you are using an envelope). Follow the procedures for folding letters illustrated below.

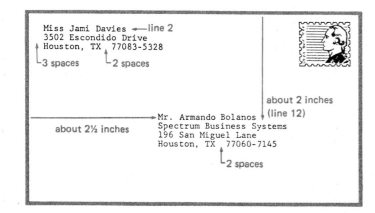

1. Type the writer's name and return address in the upper left corner as shown in the illustration. Begin on the second line space from the top edge and 3 spaces from the left edge.

2. Type the receiver's name about 2 inches (line 12) from the top of the envelope. Start about 2½ inches from the left edge.

3. Use block style and single spacing for all addresses. City and state names and ZIP Codes (see p. xv for ZIP Code abbreviations) must be placed on one line in that order.

4. The state name may be typed in full, or it may be abbreviated using the standard abbreviation or, preferably, the 2-letter state abbreviation.

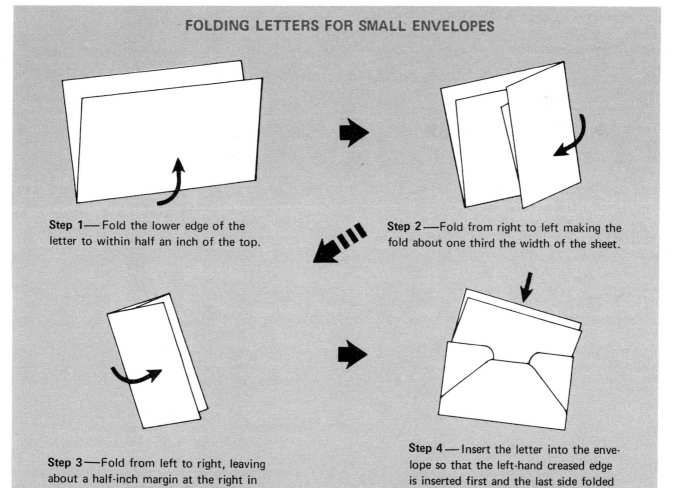

FOLDING LETTERS FOR SMALL ENVELOPES

Step 1—Fold the lower edge of the letter to within half an inch of the top.

Step 2—Fold from right to left making the fold about one third the width of the sheet.

Step 3—Fold from left to right, leaving about a half-inch margin at the right in order that the letter may be opened easily.

Step 4—Insert the letter into the envelope so that the left-hand creased edge is inserted first and the last side folded is toward the backside of the envelope.

85a ● Keyboard Review

5 minutes

Directions: Keyboard each sentence three times SS. DS between 3-line groups.

keep fingers
deeply curved

alphabet	The judge will request several dozen back copies of my deluxe edition.
figure	A total of 2,819,246 immigrants entered the country between 1955-1964.
4th finger	Paul and Polly were appalled by the opposite views of the politicians.
easy	It is usually better to keep your chin up than to stick your neck out.

| 1 | 2 | 3 | 4 | 5 | 6 | 7 | 8 | 9 | 10 | 11 | 12 | 13 | 14 |

15 minutes ## 85b ● Timed Writings

Directions: Take a 1' writing on each ¶ on 81d, page 140. Circle errors. Figure *gwam*.

Take one 5' writing on all five ¶s combined. Circle errors. Figure *gwam*.

25 minutes ## 85c ● Problem Typing

Directions: Problem 1 Title Page

1. Keyboard the title page for the report in 84c, page 146, as shown in the illustration at the right.

2. Center each line of the title page using the centerpoint you used for the leftbound report.

3. Follow all other spacing directions as given in the illustration at the right.

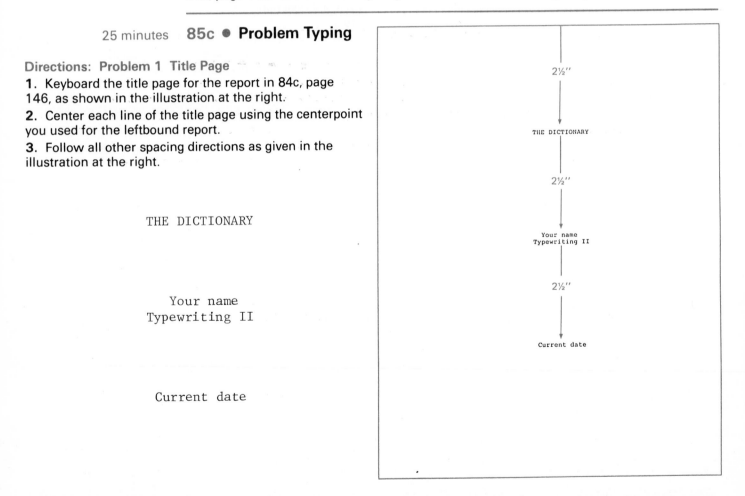

THE DICTIONARY

Your name
Typewriting II

Current date

Directions: Problem 2 Bibliography

1. Keyboard the bibliography on page 148 for the report you typed in 84c, page 146.

2. Use the same top and side margins used for page 1 of the report. Center the heading over the line of writing.

3. Start the first line of each reference at the left margin. Indent other lines 5 spaces. SS the entries; DS between entries.

4. Place the title page, report, and bibliography in the proper order. Staple together at the left side.

(continued on next page)

Directions: Problem 3 Addressing Small Envelopes

1. Address envelopes for the four names and addresses listed below. Use small envelopes or paper cut to size (6½″ x 3⅝″).

2. Use your name and address as sender. Follow the spacing directions given on the model envelope on page 84.

Ms. Eileen Houtzer
1608 Ridge Road
Cheyenne, WY 82001-4703

Custom Designers, Ltd.
84 Laurier E.
OTTAWA (ONTARIO)
CANADA
K1M 6N6

Mr. Kevin E. Lollar
25 Fulton Avenue
Birmingham, AL 35217-8846

Mrs. Joanne Sanchez
1924 Poplar Lane
Louisville, KY 40299-7043

LESSON 49

60-space line

5 minutes

49a ● Keyboard Review

Directions: Keyboard each sentence 3 times SS. DS between 3-line groups.

type with your fingers; keep wrists and arms still

alphabet Pamela gave Nick exquisite old jewelry for the bazaar today.

fig/sym The 269 3/4 acres of land sold for more than $1,875 an acre.

easy They came with the chain to see if we had made a first down.

| 1 | 2 | 3 | 4 | 5 | 6 | 7 | 8 | 9 | 10 | 11 | 12 |

10 minutes

49b ● Paragraph Guided Writings

Directions: 1. Take a 1′ writing on the ¶ below. Note the last word you typed; make this your goal word.

2. Take three 1′ writings on the ¶. Try to reach your goal word as time is called. Type no faster or slower than it takes to reach your goal word.

3. Raise your goal by 8 words. Take 3 additional 1′ writings. Try to reach your new goal as time is called.

all letters used   1.2 si

use quick, crisp, short strokes

Some people may not realize that flight attendants at
first were not women but were copilots on the flights. They
served· cold box lunches and poured drinks from thermos jugs.
After quite a long time, men are now hired for this type of
work.

Mixed Punctuation: When using mixed punctuation, type a colon after the salutation and a comma after the complimentary close. All other parts are punctuated the same as in open punctuation.

49c ● Problem Typing: Letters with Mixed Punctuation

30 minutes

Directions: Problem 1 Personal/Business Letter in Modified Block Style, Indented Paragraphs, Mixed punctuation

Keyboard/format the letter on page 86. Use a full sheet, 50-space line, modified block style with indented ¶s and mixed punctuation. Begin the return address on line 15. Address an envelope (or paper cut to size). If an envelope is used, fold and insert the letter.

Directions: Keyboard the 2-page leftbound report below DS. Refer to the directions in 84b and 84c, page 145, for assistance. (Do not number the first page of this report.)

Words

THE DICTIONARY   3
TS

Throughout our lives, the one book all of us will probably refer to more   18
often than any other is the dictionary. This invaluable reference book has to be   34
consulted again and again by everyone who speaks and writes English. It is one   50
of our most vital books for communicating ideas effectively.   62

While the English language dates back more than 1,500 years, the dictionary   78
we take for granted today has a considerable shorter history. The first English   94
dictionary was not written until the early 1600's. It was more than 200 years later,   111
in 1828, when Webster published his two-volume American Dictionary of the   131
English Language (Pollock and Loughlin, 1973, 23).   145

Although some people believe that dictionaries dictate rules for using words   160
correctly, such is not exactly the case. The dictionary describes how words are   176
used, not necessarily how they should be used. Before writing the entry for a   192
word, dictionary writers look at all the places the word has been used--in books,   208
newspapers, and speeches--and from these contexts determine the various ways a   224
word is used most often by most people (Maxwell, 1974, 214).   237

A dictionary provides a reliable way of getting answers to many different   251
kinds of questions about words. The major function of the dictionary, of course,   268
is to promote accuracy in spelling, pronunciation, and word division. In addition   284
to helping us spell, pronounce, and divide words properly, the dictionary offers   301
much other valuable information. The derivation of a word is often given, telling   319
from which language the word comes. If the object being looked up cannot easily   335
be described, an illustration may be shown. When words are not considered   350
appropriate for good usage, they are referred to as slang; when words are to be   367
used only in conversation or informal writing, they are noted as colloquial; when   386
words are no longer in common use, they are considered obsolete.   401
TS

REFERENCES   403
TS

Maxwell, John C. Ginn Elements of English. Lexington: Ginn and Company,   422
1974.   423
DS
Pollock, Thomas Clark, and Richard L. Loughlin. The Macmillan English   442
Series. New York: Macmillan, Inc., 1973.   452

1215 Norwich Road S.W.   5
Cedar Falls, IA 52404-6972   10
December 8, 19--   14

Ms. Julie Hardin, Manager   19
Central Savings & Loan   23
327 Chatham Road N.E.   28
Cedar Falls, IA 52404-2845   33

type a colon
after the
salutation

Dear Ms. Hardin: 37

Thank you for offering the facilities of your community service   50
rooms for the organizational meeting of Teens Against Muscular   62
Dystrophy.   65

We have scheduled the meeting for Wednesday, January 14,   76
from 7:30 to 10 p.m. About 20 people are expected to attend.   89

It is our understanding that there is no fee involved but that we   102
are responsible for leaving the rooms in good condition and locked 115
when we are finished.   120

If there is anything more I need to do, please call me at   131
378-4609 any time in the evening.   138

type a comma after
the complimentary
close

Very truly yours,   142

Marty Jon, President   146
Tioga Teens   148

Directions: Problem 2 Personal/Business Letter in Unarranged Form

Keyboard/format the letter below on a full sheet, 50 space line. Use modified block style, indented ¶s, mixed punctuation.

Begin the return address on line 16; use today's date. Address an envelope (or paper cut to size). Fold and insert the letter.

Return Address: Emerson School | Dallas, TX 75243-7738 | Today's   10
date | Letter Address: Mr. Larry Glandon | President, Hi-Y Club | 18
Clark School | Dallas, TX 75229-6572 | Dear Larry: 28

Plans are going ahead for the Hi-Y Conference to be held at   40
Bragg Park next weekend. Will you please send me the name of the   53
person in charge of the luncheon and the names of those who will be 67
helping with the games and other events planned for the afternoon.   80
We need this information for the printing of the program.   92

Six schools are now signed up to send delegates. Each one will   105
have at least eight members in attendance. It looks like a good   118
conference, and we all appreciate the time and work you are put-   131
ting into this meeting.   136

Sincerely, | Ms. Donna Nelson   141

LESSON 84

84a ● Keyboard Review

5 minutes   **Directions:** Keyboard each sentence three times SS. DS between 3-line groups.

sit erect;
keep feet
flat on floor

alphabet	The next evening Jack quickly scanned the horizon from Briarwood Peak.
fig/sym	The saving on Items #378 and #56-4 (on January 19) will be about 24%.
adjacent keys	We were sure that her partner's voice was barely heard over the noise.
easy	Turn to the division problems if you are through with your other work.

| 1 | 2 | 3 | 4 | 5 | 6 | 7 | 8 | 9 | 10 | 11 | 12 | 13 | 14 |

---

10 minutes   ## 84b ● Learn to Keyboard Two-Page Leftbound Reports

Directions: 1. For the first page of a leftbound report, leave a 2" top margin; leave a 1" top margin on all succeeding pages.

2. Leave a 1½" left margin and a 1" right margin. The bottom margin should be approximately 1".

3. Find your new center point by adding the figures at the left and right margins and dividing by 2. Backspace from this point to center the heading.

4. If the first page is numbered (optional), center the number one-half inch from the bottom. Other page numbers are placed on the fourth line from the top and aligned with the right margin.

5. At least 2 lines of a paragraph must appear at the bottom of a page, and at least 2 lines of a new paragraph should be carried forward to a new page.

84c ● Learn to Format/Keyboard Reference Citations   30 minutes

On page 143, you learned to document sources by using footnotes. The form of documentation shown here is the reference citation.

Step 1 After keyboarding the quoted material, place within parentheses the author's last name, date of publication, and page number of the cited material as shown in the example below.

Step 2 At the end of the report, TS and center the word "References." TS and keyboard in alphabetical order (by authors' last names) each complete reference.

```
16                                                                      51
15   give it to anyone.  It doesn't cost you a cent, but it is priceless to   52
14                                                                      53
13   a person who needs a listener" (Montgomery, 1981, 66).            54
12                                             TS                       55
11                                                                      56
10                          REFERENCES                                  57
 9                              TS                                      58
 8                                                                      59
 7   Montgomery, Robert L.  "Are You A Good Listener?"  Nation's Business,  60
 6        October, 1981, 66.                                            61
 5                                                                      62
 4                                                                      63
 3                                                                      64
 2                                                                      65
 1                                                                      66
```

(continued on next page)

LESSON 50

50a ● Keyboard Review

5 minutes

Directions: Keyboard each sentence 3 times SS. DS between 3-line groups.

type steadily;
do not pause
between letters
or words

alphabet Max delivered the wrong size pack to Jeff quite by accident.

fig/sym Use a diagonal for "made" fractions such as 2 7/8 or 15 3/4.

easy I asked them to print their names to the right of the title.

| 1 | 2 | 3 | 4 | 5 | 6 | 7 | 8 | 9 | 10 | 11 | 12 |

---

5 minutes

50b ● Addressing a Large Envelope and Folding Letters for Insertion

Directions: Read the directions and study the illustrations below for addressing large envelopes and folding and inserting letters into large envelopes. You will need this information to prepare evelopes for letters you type for 50c, p. 88.

A large envelope (9½" x 4⅛") is usually prepared for business letters or for letters of more than one page. Type the writer's name and return address as you did on a small envelope (and as directed on the model at the left). Begin the name and address of the receiver 2½" from the top and 4" from the left edge of the envelope. Use block style and single spacing as you did for a small envelope (see page 84).

```
Ms. Marcia Nagel ←— line 2
Student Body Secretary
Wolters School
Manhattan, KS  66502-8355
 └3 spaces      └2 spaces
```

about 2½ inches
(line 15)

about 4 inches →

```
Mr. Mike Garret
School Pictures, Inc.
487 Truman Road
Kansas City, MO  64106-3283
           └2 spaces
```

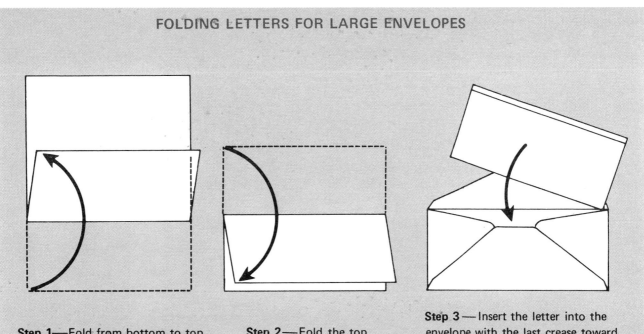

FOLDING LETTERS FOR LARGE ENVELOPES

Step 1—Fold from bottom to top, making the fold slightly less than one third the length of the sheet.

Step 2—Fold the top down to within one half inch of the bottom fold.

Step 3—Insert the letter into the envelope with the last crease toward the bottom of the envelope and with the last fold up.

LEARNING TO LISTEN
TS

The fact that communication is a two-way process means both people in a conversation must listen as well as talk before real understanding can be achieved.
DS

Experts in the field remind us that we spend more of our waking hours listening than we spend in any of the other basic communication activities. According to Miller, each of us can expect to spend more of our lives hearing and listening than doing anything else except breathing.[1]
DS

1″ left
margin

Listening is much more than just hearing, however. Hearing involves only the ears; listening requires the use of both the ears and the mind. Unless our minds are tuned in to what the other person is saying, communication will not take place.
DS

1″ right
margin

One of the keys to good listening is to learn to concentrate on the ideas the speaker is trying to convey and not be distracted by other sounds or thoughts. Because our minds are capable of going much faster than anyone can talk, we have to work at keeping our attention focused on what the other person is saying.
DS

We can help keep our minds from wandering off the subject by speaking to the point occasionally or by asking questions which will help the other person expand on some point which may not have been clear.
SS
_____
DS
[1]Dorothy Miller, *Ginn Elementary English* (Lexington: Ginn and Company, 1972), p. 55.

approximately 1″

50c ● Problem Typing: Personal Business Letters in Block Style

Directions: Problem 1

Keyboard/format the letter below using a full sheet, 50-space line, block style, open punctuation. Begin the return address on line 16 at the left margin. Sign the letter. Address a large envelope as shown on page 87.

Return Address: Wolters School | Manhattan, KS 66502-8355 | April 24, 19--**Letter Address:** Mr. Mike Garret | School Pictures, Inc. | 457 Truman Road | Kansas City, MO 64106-3283

Dear Mr. Garret

Ms. Taylor, our vice-principal, asked me to write to you regarding the arrangements for taking our school identification pictures.

As we understand it, our school will be able to use the pictures for school records, the yearbook, and the student body cards. Students may also buy a large packet for themselves by paying $4 at the time the pictures are taken.

We have scheduled students whose names begin with A-L for Tuesday, May 5, and students whose names begin with M-Z for Wednesday, May 6. Students will report to the gym beginning promptly at 9 a.m. each day.

Sincerely yours | Ms. Marcia Nagel | Student Body Secretary

begin return
address at
left margin

Wolters School
Manhattan, KS 66502-8355
April 24, 19--

Mr. Mike Garret
School Pictures, Inc.
487 Truman Road
Kansas City, MO 64106-3283

Dear Mr. Garret

Ms. Taylor, our vice-principal, asked me to write to you regarding the arrangements for taking our school identification pictures.

As we understand it, our school will be able to use the pictures for school records, the yearbook, and the student body cards. Students may also buy a large packet for themselves by paying $4 at the time the pictures are taken.

We have scheduled students whose names begin with A-L for Tuesday, May 5, and students whose names begin with M-Z for Wednesday, May 6. Students will report to the gym beginning promptly at 9 a.m. each day.

begin closing
lines at
left margin

Sincerely yours

Ms. Marcia Nagel
Student Body Secretary

Directions: Problem 2

Keyboard/format the letter below using a full sheet, 50-space line, block style, open punctuation. Begin the return address on line 16 at the left margin. Listen for the bell to determine line endings. Sign the letter; address a large envelope; fold and insert the letter.

Return Address: 406 Marker Road | Sioux Falls, SD 57103-6822 | May 10, 19-- | **Letter Address:** Mrs. Ruth Carr | 1634 Cottonwood Place | Sioux Falls, SD 57106-3380 | Dear Mrs. Carr

I am applying for a job at Woman Lake in Brainerd, Minnesota, for the summer months and need three letters of reference. Will you please write one of these letters for me.

Mr. Packard, manager of the lodge, said I should try to get someone to recommend me who was familiar with my dependability. Since I have been delivering the Sioux Falls News to your home for the past two years and have also been taking care of your yard during this time, I thought you would be well qualified to judge me.

The letter should be sent to Mr. Ron Packard, Manager, Woman Lake Lodge, Brainerd, MN 56501-8136. Thank you very much for your help.

Yours very truly | Bob Beckley

10 minutes

83b ● Learn to Keyboard Superscripts and Subscripts

Directions: 1. For placement of a superscript (superior number), use the automatic line finder (No. 6) and turn the platen knob one-half space toward you.
2. Keyboard the figure or symbol, and operate the automatic line finder and platen knob to return to original position.
3. Use the same procedure for a subscript, except turn the platen one-half space away from you.
4. Keyboard each sentence below two times SS. DS between 2-line groups.

```
Type superscripts one-half space above a line:  kg/m³, Wilson⁴.
```

```
Type subscripts one-half space below a line:  H₂O, Zn₃N₂, C₆H₆.
```

---

10 minutes

83c ● Steps in Formatting Reports with Footnotes

Note: Short quotations appear within the copy; long quotations of four lines or more are single-spaced and indented 5 spaces from each margin. DS the remainder of the report or manuscript.

Directions: Read the steps below for formatting reports with footnotes. You will need to include footnotes in a report if you use statements or direct quotations from books or articles. The traditional way to document sources is to type in footnote form complete information about the references from which the materials were taken.

Step 1 Type a superior number immediately following the material in the report which will be documented by a footnote.

Step 2 Draw a light pencil mark on your paper to mark the 1" bottom margin. Space up 2 or 3 lines from that mark for each footnote. If 2 or more footnotes will be on the page, leave an extra line space for a DS between each of the footnotes. Then space up an additional 2 lines and draw a second light pencil mark. This is where you will type the divider line that separates the footnotes from the body of the report.

Step 3 After completing the last line of the report that will appear on the page, change from double-spacing to single-spacing. SS, then use the underscore key to type a 1½" divider line (15 spaces pica; 18 spaces elite) at the point where you have your second pencil mark.

Step 4 After typing the divider line, DS, indent 5 spaces, and type the footnote reference. Type each footnote SS; DS between footnotes.

Step 5 On a partially filled page, the footnotes may appear at the bottom of the page, or they may begin a SS below the last line of the report.

```
 spend more of our lives hearing and listening than doing anything
                                                                   DS
 else except breathing.¹
                        SS
 _____
                       DS
   ¹Dorothy Miller, Ginn Elementary English (Lexington:  Ginn
 and Company, 1972), p. 55.
```

---

20 minutes

83d ● Unbound Report With Footnotes

Directions: Keyboard the first page of the unbound report as illustrated on page 144. Follow the directions on the illustration. If necessary, refer to page 94.

(continued on next page)

50d ● Timed Writings

Directions: 1. Take two 3' writings on all paragraphs. Figure *gwam*.
2. Take two 1' writings on each ¶; take the first for speed, the second for control.

3. Take another 3' writing on all the paragraphs. Figure *gwam*. Compare your *gwam* and number of errors on this writing to those of your first 3' writing.

all letters used   1.2 si   *gwam* 3'

Though many of us may not be aware of it, most hazards   4 | 46
to our health may be found in the home. Millions of people   8 | 50
are injured or killed in home accidents each year.   11 | 53

Falls are to blame for a great number of these mishaps.   15 | 57
They don't have to be from one level to another. They often   19 | 61
happen on the floor, ground, or sidewalk. Sometimes, people   23 | 65
fall off ladders because they try to reach too far.   27 | 69

The next leading cause of accidents around the home is   30 | 72
fire. To guard against fire danger, be sure never to leave   34 | 76
the house while something is cooking on the range. It is   38 | 80
also a good idea to equip your home with smoke detectors.   42 | 84

gwam 3' | 1 | 2 | 3 | 4 |

50e ● Extra-Credit Typing

Directions: Problem 1

1. Type the timed writing in 50d as a short report. Provide a title; type the title in all capital letters.

2. Use a 60-space line; center the entire report vertically on a full sheet; DS the body of the report.

Directions: Problem 2

1. Assume that you are Ruth Carr in the letter in 50c, Problem 2, page 88. Write the kind of letter about Bob Beckley (the writer of the letter in that problem) that you would like written about you if you were applying for the job.

2. Prepare the letter in modified block style, mixed punctuation. Date the letter May 15, 19--. Use personal titles as needed.

3. Address a small envelope (or paper cut to size.) Fold and insert the letter if you are using an envelope.

Directions: Problem 3

1. Address large envelopes (or paper cut to size) for each of the addresses given in 48c, Problem 3, page 85.

2. Type your name and address as the sender on all the envelopes.

Directions: Problem 2 Unbound Report with Indented Items

1. Keyboard the unbound report below on a 60-space line DS. Clear all tab stops; set a 5-space ¶ indention. Leave a 2″ top margin.

2. Indent numbered items 5 spaces from right and left margins SS. DS between items.

3. Use a spread heading.

IMPROMPTU SPEAKING

You will be called upon many times to give a talk on the spur of the moment. You might be asked to give a short report on a book, trip, or play. You might be called upon to make an announcement or present a gift to a teacher. If you found yourself in one of these spots, could you deliver?

A strategy for giving impromptu talks is always helpful. Here is such a strategy:

1. Make a statement that gets attention. If you can't think of anything else, tell your group that you are glad to tell them about your subject. Being glad in this situation is unique enough to draw some attention.

2. Explain why your subject is important to you.

3. Make two or three general statements about your subject. Illustrate each with a few examples. Cite interesting cases. Describe them vividly.

4. Summarize your ideas. Do this quickly. Don't let your talk drag --especially at the end.

The ability to give a brief talk on almost any subject on short notice can be very profitable to you. You will be envied by everyone. Practice giving this type of talk. Collect your wits; think fast; organize your ideas. Prepare your talk along the lines suggested in the plan just described.

Guide for Indented Items
Indent numbered items 5 spaces from each margin SS. DS between items.

Type Figure 1 at the ¶ indention point, type the period, space twice, and reset the left margin at this point. Move right margin five spaces to the left. Type the first numbered item.

After you complete the item, return carriage twice. Press the margin release and move to the left edge of the paper. Press tab, type Figure 2, type the period, space twice, and complete the item. Repeat the process for Items 3 and 4.

Return to original settings for margins and spacing to complete the report.

LESSON 83

70-space line

5 minutes   **83a ● Keyboard Review**

Directions: Keyboard each line three times SS. DS between 3-line groups.

alphabet   Joe believed that my trip from Arizona to New York was quite exciting.

figure   Mei actually delivered all 104 newspapers before 6:30 a.m. on July 24!

combination   for you, for trade, for him, for war, for pop, for fear, for a million

easy   The flies that make the loudest noise are the ones that get hit first.

| 1 | 2 | 3 | 4 | 5 | 6 | 7 | 8 | 9 | 10 | 11 | 12 | 13 | 14 |

Unit 8 ■ Keyboarding Reports and Outlines (Lessons 51-60)

General Directions Use a 60-space line, unless otherwise directed, for all lessons in this unit (center − 30; center + 30 + 5). SS sentences and drill lines; DS between repeated groups of lines. DS paragraph copy.
Your instructor will tell you if you are to correct errors on problem typing.

LESSON 51

5 minutes **51a ● Keyboard Review**

Directions: Keyboard each sentence three times SS. DS between 3-line groups.

keep fingers
deeply curved

alphabet Oakmont citizens have explored ways of quieting the big jet.

fig/sym I quoted three sources: Time, Newsweek, and The New Yorker.

easy They thought there should be goals at each end of the field.

| 1 | 2 | 3 | 4 | 5 | 6 | 7 | 8 | 9 | 10 | 11 | 12 |

5 minutes **51b ● Language Arts Skills: Spelling and Proofreading Aid**

Directions: Keyboard each line three times SS. DS between 3-line groups.

1 decision parcel ordinary maintenance canceled serious choose

2 belief familiar across wholly experience responsible visible

3 absence eighth congratulate immediate committee incidentally

5 minutes **51c ● Technique Builder: Stroking**

Directions: Keyboard each line three times SS. DS between 3-line groups.

use quick,
sharp stokes

one-hand we are│my grades│look upon│refer you│saw him│you are│we were

balanced-hand She does not know if the shelf is built at the right height.

direct reach Myron hoped that my Uncle Braxton brought my nylon umbrella.

| 1 | 2 | 3 | 4 | 5 | 6 | 7 | 8 | 9 | 10 | 11 | 12 |

10 minutes **51d ● Paragraph Guided Writings**

Directions: 1. Take a 1′ writing to establish a goal rate.
2. Take two additional 1′ writings, trying to reach your goal word just as time is called.

3. Add four words to your original goal. Take three 1′ writings, trying to reach your new goal on each timing. Your teacher may call the quarter- or half- minutes to guide you.

all letters used 1.2 si

keep your eyes
on the copy

One health hazard some of you can expect to face more now than in years past is that of noise. As workers insist on peace and quiet at their jobs, firms may have to give them earmuffs and muffle sounds of loud machines.

LESSON 82

82a ● Keyboard Review

5 minutes

Directions: Keyboard each sentence three times SS. DS between 3-line groups.

keep fingers
deeply curved

alphabet	Mr. Brown just received six dozen packages of quilts from the factory.
figure	Our address is 932 West 15th Street; our new phone number is 468-7038.
o,i	Most older pilots violently opposed revision of admission regulations.
easy	All eight of them were so tired they slept right on through the night.

| 1 | 2 | 3 | 4 | 5 | 6 | 7 | 8 | 9 | 10 | 11 | 12 | 13 | 14 |

82b ● Control Ladder Paragraphs

10 minutes

Directions: **1.** Take 1' writings on each ¶ in 81d, page 140. Circle errors and figure *gwam*.
2. When you keyboard a ¶ within the error limit specified by your teacher, move to the next ¶. Use control as you keyboard this exercise.

82c ● Problem Typing: Unbound Reports

30 minutes

Directions: Problem 1 One-Page Report
Keyboard the unbound report below on a 60-space line DS. Leave a 2" top margin (begin on line 13).

NEW RECORDS FOR THE RECORD BOOK

The GUINESS BOOK OF WORLD RECORDS, a publication that lists nearly every record ever set anywhere by anybody, has just set a couple of records of its own. It is now the world's all-time copyrighted best seller, having sold more than 50 million copies. It is also the book stolen most often from all public libraries throughout England.

Originally commissioned to settle arguments, this fascinating bit of reading contains 15,000 entries on a wide variety of subjects.

According to this book, somebody from Oxford, England, once talked nonstop for 150 hours. Interestingly enough, the longest political speech on record required only 33 hours and 5 minutes; and, luckily for the diners, the longest after-dinner talk was delivered in a mere 3 hours.

One record most of us wouldn't be too anxious to beat is held by a forest ranger who has been struck by lightning seven different times. Once he was hit on the head by a lightning bolt that ripped a hole in his hat and burned off his shoes.

Finally, you may be interested to know that the person who has lived to the oldest authenticated age--117 years and still counting--never slept on a bed in his life.

NEW RECORDS FOR THE RECORD BOOK

The GUINNESS BOOK OF WORLD RECORDS, a publication that lists nearly every record ever set anywhere by anybody, has just set a couple of records of its own. It is now the world's all-time copyrighted best seller, having sold more than 50 million copies. It is also the book stolen most often from all public libraries throughout England.

Originally commissioned to settle arguments, this fascinating bit of reading contains 15,000 entries on a wide variety of subjects.

According to this book, somebody from Oxford, England, once talked nonstop for 150 hours. Interestingly enough, the longest political speech on record required only 33 hours and 5 minutes; and, luckily for the diners, the longest after-dinner talk was delivered in a mere 3 hours.

One record most of us wouldn't be too anxious to beat is held by a forest ranger who has been struck by lightning seven different times. Once he was hit on the head by a lightning bolt that ripped a hole in his hat and burned off his shoes.

Finally, you may be interested to know that the person who has lived to the oldest authenticated age--117 years and still counting--never slept on a bed in his life.

(continued on next page)

51e ● Timed Writings

Directions: 1. Take two 1' writings on each ¶. Figure *gwam*.
2. Take 2' and 3'writings on all three ¶s combined. Compare your 2' rate to the longer writing.

If you complete a writing before time is called, retype the copy until you are told to stop. To figure *gwam,* add the last number in the column to the number of words in the second writing.

all letters used   1.3 si   *gwam* 2' | 3'

		2'	3'
No matter whether it is a trip of several miles or just		6	4
a jaunt to the local grocery store, many people are traveling		12	8
by bike these days. While kids still account for the greatest		18	12
share of all bike sales, quite a few adults now whiz around		24	16
on two wheels.		26	17
In a commuter race staged in one major city a few years		31	21
back, a bicycle rider covered a distance of four miles in less		38	25
time than two competitors. The cyclist beat a sports car by		44	29
one minute and a city bus by five.		47	31
Bicycle riding is one of the best ways to stay healthy		53	35
too. Some doctors prefer this type of exercise to jogging,		59	39
at least for those folks who are past middle age.		64	42

gwam 2' | 1 | 2 | 3 | 4 | 5 | 6 |
      3' | 1 | 2 | 3 | 4 |

---

5 minutes ## 51f ● Control Practice

Directions: Keyboard the last ¶ of 51e as many times as you can in the time that remains, striving for an error-free copy. Place a check mark in the margin of each ¶ in which you made no more than one error.

LESSON 52   60-space line

5 minutes ### 52a ● Keyboard Review

Directions: Keyboard each sentence three times SS. DS between 3-line groups.

keep wrists and elbows quiet

alphabet The quiz show Jack Palm entered had six girls and five boys.
fig/sym Mary claimed that 80.6% of all car trips are under 10 miles.
easy The profit you can make depends on both labor and materials.

| 1 | 2 | 3 | 4 | 5 | 6 | 7 | 8 | 9 | 10 | 11 | 12 |

5 minutes ### 52b ● Language Arts Skills: Typing from Dictation; Spelling Checkup

Directions: Keyboard the words in 51b, page 90, from your teacher's dictation. Check for correct spelling. Retype any words in which you made an error.

20 minutes **Directions: 1.** Take a 1' writing on ¶1 DS.
2. When you complete ¶1 in 1', continue
on to ¶2. Repeat this procedure as you try
to complete each of the five ¶s in the given
time.

3. Take three 1' writings on any ¶ you
cannot finish in the time given.

all letters used   1.3 si

gwam 5'

				gwam 5'
• 4 • 8 • 12				
Talking is one vital skill that most all of us pick up at quite an				3 | 47
• 16 • 20 • 24 • 28				
early age. It is something which we learn to do naturally, and we learn				6 | 50
• 32 • 36				
it with little or no formal instruction.				7 | 51
• 4 • 8 • 12				
Sending a message to someone by talking is a great deal easier				10 | 54
• 16 • 20 • 24 •				
than getting it there by writing. We don't have to worry about such				13 | 57
28 • 32 • 36 • 40				
matters as how to spell the hard words or where to place the commas.				15 | 60
• 4 • 8 • 12				
Some people have thought that we might not have needed to write				18 | 62
• 16 • 20 • 24 •				
very much at all if tape recorders had just been invented a few years				21 | 65
28 • 32 • 36 • 40				
sooner than they were. Paper and pencil beat them, though, and so did				23 | 67
• 44				
the typewriter.				24 | 68
• 4 • 8 • 12				
In fact, the keyboard was the first method we had for talking to				27 | 71
• 16 • 20 • 24 •				
computers. As the key you hit was the one the computer heard, there				29 | 73
28 • 32 • 36 • 40				
was no chance for misunderstanding that way. From there we moved to				32 | 76
• 44 • 48				
electronic mice and touching screens.				34 | 78
• 4 • 8 • 12				
Now it looks as though we might be coming full circle. While the				36 | 80
• 16 • 20 • 24 •				
problem is a complex one to solve, progress has been made in talking				39 | 83
28 • 32 • 36 • 40				
to computers. Once they can recognize the human voice, talking may yet				42 | 86
• 44 • 48 • 52				
win out as the best way to communicate with them too.				44 | 88

gwam 5' | 1 | 2 | 3 |

52c ● Paragraph Skill Builder from Rough Draft

Directions: Keyboard the ¶ once for practice; then take three 1' writings. Circle your errors. Figure *gwam*.

Compare your best rate with the highest rate reached in 51d, page 90.

all letters used 1.2 si

	gwam 1'
Schools of ten play not only for the victory but for	11 | 57
unique trophies that go to the victors. one well-known prize	24 | 70
is the little brown jug. Two famous football teams vie	36 | 82
each year for a peice of stel called the axe.	45 | 90

52d ● Vertical Centering: Backspace from Center Method

1. Insert paper to line 33 (vertical center of a piece of paper 11" long). Roll cylinder back (toward you) one line space for each two lines in the copy to be keyboarded. This will place the copy in exact vertical center.

2. To keyboard a problem off-center or in *reading position,* roll cylinder back two extra line spaces.

3. Another centering method is to fold the paper from top to bottom and make a slight crease at the right edge. The crease will be at the vertical center (line 33). Insert the paper to the crease; roll the cylinder back one line space for each two lines in the copy.

52e ● Problem Typing: Exact Vertical Center and Reading Position

Problem 1 Exact Vertical Centering

Directions: 1. Set a 40-space line.

2. Keyboard the poem line for line in exact vertical center position using a full sheet of paper.

3. Center the heading horizontally. Review horizontal centering on page 63 if necessary.

4. Place the author's name even with the right margin.

Problem 2 Reading Position

Directions: 1. Keyboard the poem in reading position.

2. All other directions are the same as in Problem 1.

TREES

TS

I think that I shall never see
A poem lovely as a tree.

DS

A tree whose hungry mouth is pressed
Against the earth's sweet flowing breast;

DS

A tree that looks to God all day,
And lifts her leafy arms to pray;

DS

A tree that may in summer wear
A nest of robins in her hair;

DS

Upon whose bosom snow has lain;
Who intimately lives with rain.

DS

Poems are made by fools like me,
But only God can make a tree.

DS

—Joyce Kilmer

Unit 11 ■ Keyboarding School Papers (Lessons 81–95)

General Directions.

Use a 70-space line for all lessons in this unit (center — 35; center + 35 + 5) unless otherwise directed. SS sentences and drill lines. DS paragraph copy.

Your teacher will tell you whether or not you are to correct errors on the problems in this unit and if you are to follow the procedures in this unit for correcting errors by "squeezing" and "spreading" letters and typing insertions.

LESSON 81

5 minutes **81a ● Keyboard Review**

Directions: Keyboard each sentence three times SS. DS between 3-line groups.

use quick,
sharp strokes

alphabet Jake realized that one quart of latex paint easily covers my big wall.

figure Mt. Everest, India, at 29,018 feet, is the highest point on the earth.

shift Jennifer and Luis Nelson, Dr. R. Norton, and M. Diaz live in New York.

easy We also wish to thank all eight of them for returning their own signs.

| 1 | 2 | 3 | 4 | 5 | 6 | 7 | 8 | 9 | 10 | 11 | 12 | 13 | 14 |

10 minutes **81b ● Alignment of Paper: Horizontal and Vertical**

It may be necessary to reinsert paper to correct an error. The following drill will help you align your paper correctly.

Directions: 1. Insert paper and keyboard this sentence:

I will align copy with skill.

2. Move the carriage or carrier so a word containing "i" or "l" is directly above a vertical line on the aligning scale (No. 21).
3. Note the relationship of the vertical line to the center of the letter. Note also the relationship of the top of the aligning scale to the bottom of the letters.
4. Remove paper; reinsert it. Use the variable line spacer (No. 3) to align the letters correctly in relation to the top of the aligning scale. Use the paper release lever (No. 18) to move the paper to the left or right until the lines on the scale are brought into alignment with the letters "i" and "l".
5. Retype the sentence over the first writing, making any necessary adjustments.
6. Repeat the problem if time permits.

10 minutes **81c ● Keyboarding "Spread" Headings**

Directions: 1. Backspace from center one space for each letter, character, or space in a spread heading. Do not backspace for the last character or space in the line.
2. Keyboard the heading. Space once between letters and three times between words.
3. The first heading below is formatted correctly. Center and spread each of the other headings.

S P R E A D   H E A D I N G S

WORKING WITH WOOD

TRAVELING THROUGH EUROPE

AIR POLLUTION

LESSON 53

60-space line

53a ● Keyboard Review

5 minutes

Directions: Keyboard each sentence three times SS. DS between 3-line groups.

return carriage
quickly

alphabet	Please pack my boxes with five dozen jugs of liquid varnish.
symbol	Place added information (such as a date) within parentheses.
easy	Most of the tires on the bus are worn down and out of shape.

| 1 | 2 | 3 | 4 | 5 | 6 | 7 | 8 | 9 | 10 | 11 | 12 |

10 minutes

53b ● Paragraph Guided Writings

Directions: 1. Take a 1' writing to establish a goal rate.
2. Take two additional 1' writings, trying to reach your goal word just as time is called.

3. Add four words to your original goal. Take three 1' writings, trying to reach your new goal on each timing. Your teacher may call the quarter- or half-minutes.

all letters used
1.2 si

Many health experts have a low opinion of what they
call junk food. They say that things like pop and chips
or crackers are a real health hazard because they fill us
up quickly and tend to crowd out good foods from our diet.

30 minutes

53c ● Problem Typing: One-Page Report

Directions: 1. Keyboard the report on page 94 using a 60-space line DS.
2. Begin on line 13; center the heading horizontally.

LESSON 54

60-space line

54a ● Keyboard Review

5 minutes

Directions: Keyboard each sentence three times SS. DS between 3-line groups.

alphabet	Max Cady just loves a big frozen pie after he quits working.
fig/sym	Even sums like $580 or $476 don't require decimals or zeros.
easy	Wait for your ship to come in only if you have sent one out.

| 1 | 2 | 3 | 4 | 5 | 6 | 7 | 8 | 9 | 10 | 11 | 12 |

5 minutes

54b ● Technique Builder: Stroking

Directions: Keyboard each line three times SS. DS between 3-line groups.

keep your eyes
on the copy

one-hand	John gave Lynn my extra red cards. We saw Barb waste water.
weak fingers	Pop quizzes, although appropriate, are always unappreciated.
double letters	Colleen takes bookkeeping and programming classes at school.

| 1 | 2 | 3 | 4 | 5 | 6 | 7 | 8 | 9 | 10 | 11 | 12 |

80a ● Keyboard Review

5 minutes

Directions: Keyboard each sentence three times SS. DS between 3-line groups.

alphabet   Jason knew exactly why he received a bad grade on that final map quiz.

fig/sym   The first ferris wheel (constructed in 1893) was over 20 stories high.

adjacent keys   Their newer engineers were prepared there before November or December.

easy   They kept their goals before them during the time they were in charge.

| 1 | 2 | 3 | 4 | 5 | 6 | 7 | 8 | 9 | 10 | 11 | 12 | 13 | 14 |

80b ● Timed Writings

15 minutes

Directions: **1.** Take a 1' writing on each ¶ in 76d, page 131. Circle errors. Figure *gwam*.

2. Take a 5' writing on all five ¶s combined as you work for control. Circle errors. Figure *gwam*.

80c ● Problem Typing: Club Schedule

25 minutes

Directions: Keyboard the club schedule below on a half sheet (long side up). Center the main heading 1" from the top. DS the entries. Leave eight spaces between columns.

You may need to review the steps for arranging tables, page 108, and the steps for centering columnar headings, page 117.

CURRENT EVENTS CLUB SCHEDULE

Month	Speaker	Topic
October	Angelina Cruz	Crisis in Education
November	F. Lee Hull	The Middle East
December	Kelly Black	Solar Energy
January	Jean Acevedo	Health Care
February	Irving Davis	A New China
March	Barbara Dodds	An Electronic Age
April	Ann Silveira	The Third World
May	G. L. Johnson	Nuclear Power

80d ● Extra Credit Typing

Directions: Problem 1
Assume that you were a weekend guest in a friend's home. On a half sheet of paper (short side up) compose/format a thank you note to your friend's parents.

Directions: Problem 2
Keyboard/format the letter in Problem 1, page 135, in modified block style with mixed punctuation on 8½" × 11" paper.

Directions: Problem 3
Keyboard/format the letter in Problem 1, page 133, in block style with open punctuation on a full sheet of paper.

TYPING A SHORT REPORT

TS

    Short reports of one page or less may be formatted with 15

a 60-space line. If the number of lines can be counted easily, 28

center the copy vertically; if not, use a standard margin of 40

2 inches (12 line spaces) at the top. 48

DS

    Double spacing is usually used for reports and book 58

reviews. Class notes and minutes are usually single spaced 70

to provide better groupings of information. 79

    Every report should have a heading which is keyboarded 90

in all capital letters. It is always separated from the body 102

by a triple space. 106

    Unbound or topbound reports or papers are usually for- 117

matted with side margins of 1 inch. When the paper is to be 129

bound at the left, however, an extra one-half inch must be 141

provided in the left margin for binding. 149

    The heading is placed 2 inches from the top of the first 160

page. All pages after the first have a top margin of 1 inch 172

except for topbound reports. If the report is to be topbound, 185

leave an extra one-half inch for binding. The bottom margin 197

should not be less than 1 inch. 203

One-page report

79c, continued

Enclosure Notation Guide: An enclosure notation is used when an attachment is sent with the letter. Type the enclosure notation at the left margin a double space below the typed name of the sender.

Use the plural *Enclosures* if two or more items will be enclosed.

Format/Type Totals: After typing a column of figures to be totaled, type an underline directly under the last line in the column.

Double space to type the word "Total"; indent three spaces from the left margin.

Directions: Problem 2 Order Letter in Block Style with Open Punctuation

1. Format/keyboard the letter below on a 50-space line. Begin the return address on line 15; leave four spaces between the date and the inside address.

2. Use a 40-space line for the table within the letter. (Indent five spaces from the right and left margins. To determine the tab stop for the second column, backspace 6 spaces from your new right margin.)

Return address: 450 Elwood Drive | Moorhead, MN 56560-8453 | November 5, 19--

Recipient's address: Weber and Byde, Inc. | 381 Hedman Way | St. Paul, MN 55110-6823 | Ladies and Gentlemen

(¶1) Please send me the following tools you have advertised in the December issue of Shop News. I understand that by ordering now I can be sure of having them in time for Christmas.

Crosscut saw	$14.95
Keyhole saw	5.65
Curved claw hammer	8.40
Deluxe hand drill	9.85
Total	$38.85

(¶2) Enclosed is a check for $38.85. According to your advertisement, the postage on these items will be prepaid. Sincerely yours | Andy Houtz | Enclosure

Directions: Problem 3 Order Form

1. Using the order form included in your workbook (WB, p 138), keyboard the copy below exactly as it appears in the illustration at the right.

2. Use the variable line spacer to adjust the paper correctly for each line of copy.

Alternate Suggestion: If a workbook is not available, order the items below by order letter similar to the one you typed in Problem 2.

Order No.: **102**   Ship via: **Express**

To: **Ceramic Supply House**
   2304 5th Avenue West
   Chicago, IL 60612-6732

Quantity	Cat. No.	Description	Price	Total
24	A106-F	Mugs	1.69	40.56
24	A107-F	Candle-holders	2.49	59.76
36	G801	Brushes	.89	32.04
				132.36

Date: **4/21/--**   Purchasing Agent: **Sandra Lee**

The Attic Shop
3724 Vine Street Lima, OH 45804-2985

419-242-3905

Order No. 102

To   Ceramic Supply House
2304 5th Avenue West
Chicago, IL 60612-6732

Ship via Express

Quantity	Cat. No.	Description	Price		Total	
24	A106-F	Mugs	1	69	40	56
24	A107-F	Candleholders	2	49	59	76
36	G801	Brushes		89	32	04
					132	36

Date 4/21/--   Purchasing Agent Sandra Lee

54c ● Language Arts Skills: Spelling and Proofreading Aid

Directions: Keyboard each line three times SS. DS between 3-line groups.

1 accept independent liable promptly appearance column fulfill

2 occasion explanation affect color vehicle budget unnecessary

3 summary guidance temporary favorable possibility approximate

---

54d ● Learn to Make Carbon Copies

Step 1 Place the carbon paper (with glossy side down) on a sheet of plain paper. The paper on which you will prepare the original is then laid on top of the carbon paper.

Step 2 Place the sheets between the cylinder and the paper table (glossy side of carbon facing you). Roll into the typewriter. The dull surface of the carbon should be facing you.

Step 3 Refer to page xi for erasing on carbon copies.

54e ● Problem Typing: Short Report With Carbon Copies

Directions: Keyboard the unbound report below on a 60-space line DS. Use a 2″ top margin (begin on line 13). Center the heading horizontally. Make one carbon copy.

sit erect;
keep your eyes
on the copy

words

HOW TO GET BETTER USE FROM YOUR PERSONAL COMPUTER | 10

TS

One of the most helpful computers available today is a | 21
personalized model that we carry along with us wherever we go. It's | 35
better in many ways than the most expensive electronic device, and its | 49
contents cannot be tapped by some mischievous hacker. | 60

This remarkable computer is our memory, a powerful machine | 72
that we seldom use efficiently to process information. | 83

One psychologist has pointed out that both humans and | 94
computers require the use of software as well as hardware. Our brain | 108
structure makes up the hardware; the processes we can control are the | 122
software. | 124

Here are two hints for developing the software of your memory. | 137
First, when you read, don't read the material several times and then | 151
underline it. Instead read it just once, stopping now and then to | 164
summarize the key points in your own words. Second, when you are | 177
introduced to someone for the first time, make sure you understand | 191
how to spell and pronounce the new name. Recall the name | 202
immediately and visualize its spelling. A few minutes later think of | 216
the name again, trying to associate it with other friends you know. | 230

Make the best possible use of your memory. It is your own | 242
personal computer, and you will still need it in the information age. | 256

LESSON 79

79a ● Keyboard Review

5 minutes

keep wrists and elbows quiet

Directions: Keyboard each sentence three times SS. DS between 3-line groups.

alphabet Seven plucky ushers quenched a major fire blazing in the western exit.

fig/sym Arabic numbers like 1, 2, and 3 are sometimes typed (1), (2), and (3).

long words The study of a file of correspondence will yield valuable information.

easy A few of the rogues had thrown rocks at the big signs outside of town.

| 1 | 2 | 3 | 4 | 5 | 6 | 7 | 8 | 9 | 10 | 11 | 12 | 13 | 14 |

79b ● Language Arts Skills: Punctuation Guides

10 minutes

Directions: The following are punctuation guides and sentences that illustrate those guides. Study each guide; then keyboard the line that illustrates the guide. Keyboard each sentence twice SS; DS between 2-line groups.

keep feet flat on the floor

Note: Do not use commas to separate groups of numbers when they are used as policy, year, page, room, telephone, or serial numbers.

Use a comma after each item in a series, except the last one.
Most of our players can hit, catch, and throw the ball extremely well.

Use a comma to separate consecutive adjectives when the *and* has been omitted.
You will enjoy this new, useful book Ted bought at the fair yesterday.

Use a comma to separate a dependent clause that precedes the main clause.
Whenever you type personal papers, you will want to type with control.

Use a comma to separate two complete clauses separated by and, but, for, or, so, yet.
Gayle worked the problems he assigned, but she did not write the poem.

Use a comma to set off day from year, city from state, and hundreds from thousands.
On May 5, 1989, a group of 1,743 students will meet in Houston, Texas.

Use a comma to set off a short direct quotation from the rest of the sentence.
I thought it was Franklin who said, "A penny saved is a penny earned."

79c ● Problem Typing

30 minutes

Directions: Problem 1 Typing on Ruled Lines

1. Keyboard three horizontal lines 30 spaces wide with the underline key DS. Pull paper release lever forward and remove the paper.
2. Reinsert paper and use the variable line spacer to align the paper.
3. Use the backspace-from-center method to center the first line. Set your left margin at the point where the backspacing is completed. Keyboard each line as shown below.
4. Compare your copy with the example to check alignment.

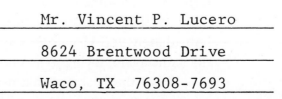

Mr. Vincent P. Lucero

8624 Brentwood Drive

Waco, TX 76308-7693

(continued on next page)

LESSON 55

55a ● Keyboard Review

5 minutes

Directions: Keyboard each sentence three times SS. DS between 3-line groups.

alphabet Jeff Long experienced a quick shave with my razor and brush.

fig/sym My new 4-door model had over 59.8 cubic feet of cargo space.

easy Their problem was to enter the figures right the first time.

| 1 | 2 | 3 | 4 | 5 | 6 | 7 | 8 | 9 | 10 | 11 | 12 |

---

15 minutes

55b ● Timed Writings

Directions: 1. Take two 1' writings on each ¶. Figure *gwam*.

2. Take 2' and 3' writings on all three ¶s combined. Compare your 2' rate to the longer writing.

If you complete a writing before time is called, retype the copy until you are told to stop. To figure *gwam,* add the last number in the column to the number of words on the second writing.

all letters used 1.3 si   *gwam* 2' | 3'

    After years of research, we now use robots to do some 6 | 4
jobs that used to require a human being. They have been used 12 | 8
for sentries along a track, for example. If its sensors pick 18 | 12
up an intruder, its sirens sound and quartz lights flash. 24 | 16

    You can even purchase a home robot that will move around 29 | 19
a smooth uncrowded floor and deliver a cart or tray to one 35 | 23
specified spot. If you want your dumb waiter to walk up a 41 | 27
flight of stairs, however, you are asking a little too much. 47 | 31

    Walking on two legs is one thing that no robots are yet 53 | 35
able to do. Nor can they recognize a face or understand a 59 | 39
natural language. While robots can do some types of work, 64 | 43
they must still learn to solve problems and make decisions 71 | 47
if they expect to mimic human skills. 74 | 49

gwam 2' | 1 | 2 | 3 | 4 | 5 | 6 |

3' | 1 | 2 | 3 | 4 |

---

25 minutes

55c ● Problem Typing: Two-Page Report

There are 10 pica spaces per inch; 12 elite spaces per inch.

Directions: 1. Keyboard the unbound report on page 97 DS (refer to page 94 for directions on preparing unbound reports).

2. Leave a 2" top margin above the heading on the first page (begin on line 13). Leave 1" bottom and side margins.

3. Center the heading horizontally (refer to 40c, page 67 to find center point).

4. Place the page number <u>2</u> at the right-hand margin on line 4 of the second page. Leave a 1" margin above the copy (begin on line 7).

78d ● **Problem Typing: Personal/Business Letters**

Directions: Problem 1 Block Style Application Letter with Open Punctuation

1. Keyboard the letter below as illustrated at the right. Use a full sheet, block style, open punctuation, 60-space line.

2. Begin the return address on line 15. Follow other spacing directions as shown on the model.

3. Address a small envelope (or paper cut to size). If an envelope is used, fold and insert the letter.

Return address: 1307 Bluff Drive | Fremont, NE 68025-6543 | May 10, 19--

Recipient's address: Ms. Ramona Trejo | The Fremont Bulletin | 289 North Elm Street | Fremont, NE 68025-5641 | Dear Ms. Trejo

Your advertisement in Sunday's issue of the Fremont Bulletin said you were looking for junior and senior high school age students to work part-time in the afternoons and evenings helping get new customers for your newspaper. I wish to apply for this job.

I am 15 years old and finishing the ninth grade at Carter Junior High School. I think a job such as the one explained in your ad would give me some excellent experience as well as help me earn money for my college education.

During the past school year I worked one hour a day in the attendance office at Carter. Mr. Albert Jensen, who is in charge of this office, will be glad to write a letter of recommendation for me. He has given me permission to use his name as a reference.

I can come in for an interview any day after school. My telephone number is 253-4879.

Sincerely yours | Kathy Miller

```
begin on
line 15   1307 Bluff Drive
          Fremont, NE  68025-6543
          May 10, 19--
                        space down
                        4 times
          Ms. Ramona Trejo
          The Fremont Bulletin
          289 North Elm Street
          Fremont, NE  68025-5641

          Dear Ms. Trejo  DS

          Your advertisement in Sunday's issue of the Fremont Bulletin
          said you were looking for junior and senior high school age
          students to work part-time in the afternoon and evenings help-
          ing get new customers for your newspaper.  I wish to apply
          for this job.  DS

          I am 15 years old and finishing the ninth grade at Carter
          Junior High School.  I think a job such as the one explained
          in your ad would give me some excellent experience as well as
          help me earn money for my college education.  DS

          During the past school year I worked one hour a day in the
          attendance office at Carter.  Mr. Albert Jensen, who is in
          charge of this office, will be glad to write a letter of
          recommendation for me.  He has given me permission to use his
          name as a reference.  DS

          I can come in for an interview any day after school.  My
          telephone number is 253-4879.  DS

          Sincerely yours
                            space down
          Kathy Miller      4 times

          Kathy Miller
```

Directions: Problem 2 Block Style Thank You Letter With Open Punctuation

1. Keyboard the letter below in block style, open punctuation, 50-space line.

2. Date the letter May 18, 19--. Begin the return address (use the return address given in Problem 1) on line 18. Also use recipient's address given in Problem 1. Follow other spacing directions as shown on the model above.

Dear Ms. Trejo | Thank you for the interview you gave me on Tuesday afternoon.

The job you described sounds very interesting. I like the fact that I would be working with kids my own age and also that I would have the opportunity to win trips or contests.

I can start working on June 5. My home telephone number is 253-4879.

Sincerely yours | Kathy Miller

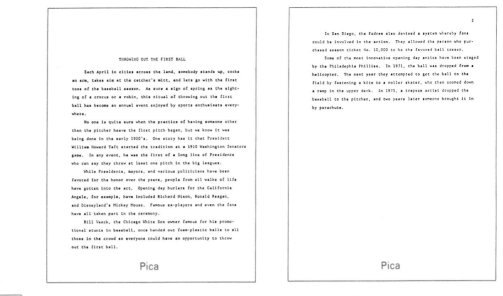

Pica

Pica

Elite

Elite

THROWING OUT THE FIRST BALL
TS

Each April in cities across the land, somebody stands up, cocks an arm, takes aim at the catcher's mitt, and lets go with the first toss of the baseball season. As sure a sign of spring as the sighting of a crocus or a robin, this ritual of throwing out the first ball has become an annual event enjoyed by sports enthusiasts everywhere.

No one is quite sure when the practice of having someone other than the pitcher heave the first pitch began, but we know it was being done in the early 1900's. One story has it that President William Howard Taft started the tradition at a 1910 Washington Senators game. In any event, he was the first of a long line of Presidents who can say they threw at least one pitch in the big leagues.

While Presidents, mayors, and various politicians have been favored for the honor over the years, people from all walks of life have gotten into the act. Opening day hurlers for the California Angels, for example, have included Richard Nixon, Ronald Reagan, and Disneyland's Mickey Mouse.

Even fans have taken part in the ceremony. Bill Veeck, the Chicago White Sox owner famous for his promotional stunts in baseball, once handed out foam-plastic balls to all those in the crowd so everyone could have an opportunity to throw out the first ball. In San Diego, the Padres also devised a system whereby fans could be involved in the action. They allowed the person who purchased Season Ticket No. 10,000 to be the favored ball tosser.

Some of the most innovative opening day antics have been staged by the Philadelphia Phillies. In 1971, the ball was dropped from a helicopter. The next year they attempted to get the ball to the field by fastening a kite to a roller skater, who then zoomed down a ramp in the upper deck. In 1975, a trapeze artist dropped the baseball to the pitcher, and two years later someone brought it in by parachute.

LESSON 78

78a ● Keyboard Review

5 minutes

Directions: Keyboard each sentence three times SS. DS between 3-line groups.

keep your eyes
on the copy

alphabet	They were required to save the jigsaw puzzles in the black box for me.
fig/sym	Ad #418-026 shows a reduction (on table models) from $9,263 to $7,450.
o,i	The anxious seniors outside noticed commotion coming from the offices.
easy	Forms for the maps in Problem Six are provided for you in Chapter Six.

| 1 | 2 | 3 | 4 | 5 | 6 | 7 | 8 | 9 | 10 | 11 | 12 | 13 | 14 |

---

10 minutes

78b ● Speed Builder

Directions: Take two 1' writings on each ¶; try to increase speed on the second writing. Figure *gwam*.

Alternate Procedure: Work for speed as you take one 5' writing on all three ¶s combined. Figure *gwam*.

keep fingers
deeply curved

all letters used   1.3 si

	gwam 1'	5'
Ever since the first typewriter was invented many years ago, most	13	3	37
of us have realized how vital good typing skill can be. To be able to	27	5	39
get one's thoughts down quickly and in a form that is easy to read has	42	8	42
long been a real advantage, both in the home as well as on the job.	55	11	45
In the computer world of today, however, typing skill is even more	13	14	48
helpful than it has been in the past. In fact, it is crucial. All who	28	17	51
work, from the top executives down to the lowest paid clerks, are now	42	19	53
likely to have to enter data at a keyboard of some kind.	53	22	56
Those who were once quite pleased if they could just hunt and peck	13	24	58
their way through some occasional typing task are in a bit of trouble.	28	27	61
They have found there is little use in having a machine that can process	42	30	64
words and numbers at lightning speeds if the information only trickles	57	33	67
into it in the first place.	62	34	68

gwam 1' | 1 | 2 | 3 | 4 | 5 | 6 | 7 | 8 | 9 | 10 | 11 | 12 | 13 | 14 |
5' | 1 | 2 | 3 |

---

5 minutes

78c ● Skill Builder

Directions: Take two 1' writings on each sentence. Figure *gwam*.

Work for speed as you keyboard this exercise.

keep arms and
wrists quiet

1 It is better to know where you are going than to get there in a hurry.
2 When you work in the right way, your typing skill is bound to improve.

| 1 | 2 | 3 | 4 | 5 | 6 | 7 | 8 | 9 | 10 | 11 | 12 | 13 | 14 |

LESSON 56

56a ● Keyboard Review

5 minutes

Directions: Keyboard each sentence three times SS. DS between 3-line groups.

alphabet Jerry Diamond packed the fine quartz in twelve larger boxes.

symbol Their boss shouted out, "Someone will have to pay for this."

easy It will pay you to learn what you are to do before you type.

| 1 | 2 | 3 | 4 | 5 | 6 | 7 | 8 | 9 | 10 | 11 | 12 |

56b ● Paragraph Guided Writings

10 minutes

Directions: 1. Take a 1' writing to establish a goal rate.

2. Take two additional 1' writings, trying to reach your goal word just as time is called.

3. Add four words to your original goal. Take three 1' writings, trying to reach your new goal on each timing. Your teacher may call the quarter- or half-minutes to guide you.

all letters used 1.3 si

In spite of all we read about the fitness craze, experts
say that most folks simply are not in very good shape. Though
you see joggers out running almost every day, it is a unique
adult who can climb one flight of stairs without becoming
short of breath.

56c ● Timed Writings

15 minutes

Directions: 1. Take two 1' writings on each ¶. Figure *gwam*.

2. Take 2' and 3' writings on both ¶s combined. If you complete a writing before

time is called, repeat until you are told to stop.

3. Figure *gwam*. Compare your 2' rate to the longer writing.

all letters used 1.2 si   *gwam* 2' | 3'

Most of us require a certain amount of physical activity   6 | 4
if we are to do our best in school or on the job. We need   12 | 8
some moderate exercise every day, and we should have a real 18 | 12
workout two or three times a week.   21 | 14

A good fitness program will help you build your strength   27 | 18
and endurance. You can count on exercise to supply a release 33 | 22
valve for stress and to put zip in your step. You will also 39 | 26
find friends for company in the gym or on the playing field. 45 | 30

| *gwam* 2' | 1 | 2 | 3 | 4 | 5 | 6 |
| 3' | 1 | 2 | 3 | 4 |

77c ● Problem Typing: Personal/Business Letters

Directions: Problem 1 Modified Block Style Letter with Open Punctuation

1. Keyboard the letter below as illustrated at the right. Use a full sheet, modified block style, open punctuation, 50-space line.

2. Begin the return address on line 18. Follow other spacing directions as shown on the model.

3. After you have finished, address a small envelope or paper cut to size (6½" × 3 ⅝") for the letter. Fold the letter and insert it in the envelope if you are using one. (Refer to 48c, page 84, for placement and folding instructions.)

Return address: 642 Hoover Road | Davenport, IA 52806-8778 | Today's date

Recipient's address: Ms. Ellen Medley | Federal Savings and Loan | 3948 Aspen Drive | Davenport, IA 52806-7634 | Dear Ms. Medley

My social studies teacher, Mr. Wayne Snell, suggested that I write to you for help with our class project. We are studying the various types of savings plans suitable for people who can save only a limited amount of money each month.

Will you please send me any materials you have that will help us understand the investment opportunities available at Federal Savings. My classmates and I are looking forward to hearing from you soon.

Sincerely yours | Miss Judy Miller

centerpoint

begin on line 18   642 Hoover Road
Davenport, IA 52806-8778
Current Date
space down
4 times

Ms. Ellen Medley
Federal Savings and Loan
3948 Aspen Drive
Davenport, IA 52806-7634

Dear Ms. Medley   DS

My social studies teacher, Mr. Wayne Snell, suggested that I write to you for help with our class
project. We are studying the various types of savings plans suitable for people who can save only a
limited amount of money each month. DS

Will you please send me any materials you have that
will help us understand the investment opportunities
available at Federal Savings. My classmates and I
are looking forward to hearing from you soon.   DS

Sincerely yours   space down
Judy Miller   4 times
Miss Judy Miller

Directions: Problem 2 Modified Block Style Letter with Open Punctuation

1. Keyboard the letter below in modified block, open punctuation. Use your own address and today's date in the return address.

2. Follow all other directions as given in Problem 1.

Return Address: Your address | Today's date | Recipient's address: Mr. Gary Davidson | 486 Arlie Circle | Monroe, LA 71203-5643 | Dear Mr. Davidson

An article in yesterday's Evening Herald stated that you have been named chairperson for the coming Super Olympics for the Hearing Impaired.

Last year, the members of our sign language class at Steinbeck Junior High School served as helpers for this event. We really enjoyed the experience and would like to volunteer again to help you and your committee in any way that we can. There are 22 of us in the class

If you could use our services for this year's Super Olympics, please write me at the above address.

Sincerely | Sign your name

56d ● Language Arts Skills: Composing at the Typewriter

Directions: Keyboard answers to each question below. Use complete sentences.

If time permits, correct any sentences in which you made errors.

Questions:

1. Name a nationally prominent person in politics and the office that person holds or has held.
2. Name one of the United States senators from your state.

3. Name the capital city of the state in which you are now living.
4. What nationally prominent person would you most like to meet in person? Why?

56e ● Language Arts Skills: Capitalization Guides

Directions: The following are capitalization guides and sentences that illustrate those guides. Study each guide.

Keyboard the sentences that illustrate the guides twice SS; DS between 2-line groups.

use a quick,
firm reach to
the shift key

Capitalize days, months, years, and holidays; but not seasons.
The Fourth of July falls on Monday this summer, does it not?

Capitalize names of rivers, oceans, and mountains.
Ralph crossed the Columbia River and soon saw Mount Rainier.

Capitalize North, South, etc., when they name particular parts of the country, but not when they refer to directions.
From Tacoma, I drove east on the Northwest's newest highway.

Capitalize names of religious groups, political parties, nations, nationalities, and races.
The Norwegian people gave the French books to the Democrats.

Capitalize all proper names.
I bought a Swiss watch, a Hawaiian shirt, and an Indian rug.

Capitalize the names of stars, planets, and constellations except sun, moon, or earth, unless they are used with astronomical names.
I saw Mercury and Mars in relation to the Earth and the Sun.

Capitalize a title when used with a person's name.
Senator Jones, Governor Brown, and Judge King spoke briefly.

LESSON 57

60-space line

57a ● Keyboard Review

Directions: Keyboard each sentence three times SS. DS between 3-line groups.

alphabet   Fay quoted six or seven major zoning laws checked by police.

symbol   We may wish to type "c/o" for the abbreviation "in care of."

easy   If you wish to think well of yourself, think well of others.

| 1 | 2 | 3 | 4 | 5 | 6 | 7 | 8 | 9 | 10 | 11 | 12 |

76e ● Language Arts Skills: Punctuation Guides
Period, Question Mark, and Exclamation Point

Directions: The following are punctuation guides and sentences that illustrate the use of periods, question marks, and exclamation points.

Study each guide; then keyboard the sentence that illustrates the guide. Keyboard each sentence twice SS. DS between 2-line groups.

Note: A space follows each period after initials.
No space is needed after a period within an abbreviation.
Space once after a period that ends an abbreviation unless that period ends a sentence, in which case, space twice.

Use a period after a sentence making a statment or giving a command.
Frank told the class that we bought Alaska for only two cents an acre.

Use a period after an initial.
The new members were J. L. Austin, Sally G. Costis, and Betty J. Dodd.

Do not use a period after a nickname.
Ed told me that he and Al would get together with Mary later that day.

Use a period after most abbreviations.
We will leave at 11:15 a.m. and arrive in Washington D.C. at 1:10 p.m.

Use a question mark after a question.
How many tickets have been sold for the variety show on Tuesday night?

Use a period after requests and indirect questions.
I question whether a report was mailed. Will you let me know at once.

Use an exclamation point to express strong or sudden feeling.
Hurrah! Your team won the game! Congratulations! What a great gang!

LESSON 77

70-space line

77a ● Keyboard Review

5 minutes

Directions: Keyboard each sentence three times SS. DS between 3-line groups.

keep feet flat
on the floor

alphabet The project was quickly moved by citizens anxious to avoid any fights.

fig/sym A crowd of 49,936 witnessed the 1966 All-Star game in 100-degree heat.

direct reach The mayor announced the results of the voting. An unknown doctor won.

easy It is true that one who does not drive the auto right may not be left.

| 1 | 2 | 3 | 4 | 5 | 6 | 7 | 8 | 9 | 10 | 11 | 12 | 13 | 14 |

77b ● Skill Builder

10 minutes

Directions: 1. Take a 1' writing. The last word typed will be your goal word.
2. Take a 5' writing with the return called after each minute. When the return is

called, start the paragraph over again. Try to reach your goal each minute as the return is called.

return carriage
quickly

1.3 si

                        •   4   •   8   •   12
Many will not know that the typical neckties we wear today are

    •   16   •   20   •   24   •
often called four-in-hand. They received this name from a group of

 28   •   32   •   36
nineteenth century carriage drivers who were noted for holding the

40   •   44   •   48   •   52
reins of four horses in one hand. When most people were wearing bow

 •   56   •   60
ties, the drivers wore long ones.

57b ● Language Arts Skills: Spelling and Proofreading Aid

Directions: Keyboard each line three times SS. DS between 3-line groups.

1 statue preparation foreign already quality listen economical
2 occupy receive piece dining judgment grateful emphasis loose
3 freight surprise competent weather language succeed campaign

---

5 minutes **57c ● Skill Comparison**

Directions: 1. Take a 1' writing on the goal sentence. Figure *gwam*.
2. Take a 1' writing on each of the other sentences.

3. Try to match or exceed your goal sentence *gwam* on each of the other sentences.

keep wrists and elbows still

words

goal sentence Those things you learn after you know it all count the most. 12

one-hand No test was graded. You sat on my seat. Sew my extra vest. 12

script *Folks who talk the most often seem to have the least to say.* 12

rough draft very few folks have good enough sight to see our own faults. 12

---

30 minutes **57d ● Learn to Format Outlines**

Problem 1 Sentence Outline

Always use complete sentences in a sentence outline. Each entry is followed by a period.

Directions: 1. Use a 60-space line. Clear all tab stops; set 3 tab stops of 4 spaces each beginning at the left margin.
2. Center the outline vertically in reading position (2 line spaces above center point).

Center the heading horizontally.
3. Keyboard the problem line for line; indent, space, capitalize, and punctuate exactly as shown.

GUIDES FOR STUDYING
TS

left margin → I. STUDYING IS A SKILL, LIKE READING AND WRITING.
2 spaces DS
1st tab stop → A. Learn how to study.
B. Develop correct study habits through practice.
DS
use margin release;
backspace one time → II. OBSERVE THESE GUIDES IN DEVELOPING STUDYING SKILLS.
DS
A. Set up a schedule with definite study periods.
2d tab stop → 1. Do not let anything change this schedule.
2. Find a quiet place to study.
3. Have needed materials available before you start.
4. Start at once; don't find excuses for delaying.
B. Study with a purpose.
1. Copy your assignments accurately; know what you
3d tab stop → are to do.
2. Search for ideas; think as you read or solve problems.
C. Practice remembering the main points of a lesson.
1. Ask yourself questions on what you have studied.
2. Take brief notes.

(continued on next page)

76c ● Technique Builder: Stroking

5 minutes   **Directions:** Keyboard each sentence 3 times SS. DS between 3-line groups.

quick return;
no pauses

1   Try never to confuse keeping your chin up with sticking your neck out.

2   Remember to borrow from pessimists, as they know they won't be repaid.

3   Someone once said that most hard-boiled people are usually half-baked.

4   It doesn't pay to brood--after all, only the chickens get paid for it.

| 1 | 2 | 3 | 4 | 5 | 6 | 7 | 8 | 9 | 10 | 11 | 12 | 13 | 14 |

---

15 minutes   ## 76d ● Speed Ladder Paragraphs

Directions: 1. Take 1' writings on ¶1 DS until you complete the ¶ in 1'.
2. When you complete ¶1 in 1', continue on to ¶2. Repeat this procedure as you try to complete each of the five ¶s in the given time.

keep your eyes
on the copy

all letters used   1.3 si   *gwam* 5'

	gwam 5'
One current concern of health experts is the amount of stress that	3 | 47
a worker must face on the job. They say stress can be a real threat to	6 | 50
a person's physical and mental condition.	7 | 51
If you had to guess which jobs place people under the greatest	10 | 54
pressure, you might choose those where danger is involved. Perhaps	12 | 56
the police would come to mind, or a window washer on a tall building.	15 | 59
You may think those who have to make hard decisions every day lead	18 | 62
the most stressful lives, but such is not the case. Studies suggest	21 | 65
that stress at the top levels is quite often offset by higher status	23 | 67
and better pay.	24 | 68
It seems that factors other than decision making or danger can turn	27 | 71
most any job into an ordeal for the person in it. Having a boss who	29 | 73
looks over your shoulder all day is one of them. Another is working at	32 | 76
tasks that are dull and boring.	34 | 78
There are some who now say that the increased use of computerized	36 | 80
equipment is one of the major causes of stress. If these people are	39 | 83
right, then secretaries and clerks are often placed under a great deal	42 | 86
of hidden stress because of the kinds of work they do.	44 | 88

gwam 5' | 1 | 2 | 3 |

Omit end-of-line periods when using the Topic Outline format.

Problem 2 Topic Outline

Directions: Keyboard the topic outline below on a 40-space line DS. TS after the heading. Refer to Problem 1 for formatting directions.

LEARNING TO WRITE SUMMARIES

I. REASONS FOR SUMMARIZING
   A. Getting Ideas From Your Lessons
   B. Expressing Ideas Concisely
II. GUIDES FOR WRITING SUMMARIES
   A. Reading the Lesson
   B. Finding the Central Idea
   C. Finding Supporting Ideas
   D. Writing Down Ideas
      1. Writing briefly
      2. Using nouns and verbs
      3. Using your own words
   E. Editing Your First Draft
      1. Eliminating minor details
      2. Arranging ideas in order
      3. Omitting your own opinions
   F. Writing Summary in Final Form
      1. Using proper form
      2. Writing or typing neatly

LESSON 58

60-space line

5 minutes

58a ● Keyboard Review

Directions: Keyboard each sentence three times SS. DS between 3-line groups.

alphabet Rex Fuji positively warned us smoking can be quite a hazard.
symbol   Tom delivered my papers (Los Angeles Times) in half an hour.
easy   He tried to learn to keep his eyes on the ball at all times.
        | 1 | 2 | 3 | 4 | 5 | 6 | 7 | 8 | 9 | 10 | 11 | 12 |

10 minutes

58b ● Paragraph Guided Writings

Directions: Take three 1' writings on each ¶ below. Try to make no more than three errors on the first writing; one error on the second; no errors on the third. Compare *gwam* on the three writings of each ¶.

all letters used 1.3 si   *gwam* 3'

keep your eyes on the copy

One sure method people can use to save both gasoline and   4 | 41
money is to crowd extra miles per gallon into their driving.   8 | 46
Good mileage depends on more than just the make and model of   12 | 50
a car. It is also a direct result of the grade of gas used,   16 | 54
the way the car is driven, and the condition of the engine.   20 | 58

Those who pay heed to these hints will be amazed at the   24 | 61
results. Avoid quick starts and jerky driving. Have the   28 | 65
engine tuned at regular intervals. Check tire pressure at   31 | 69
least once a month and watch the pattern of wear to see if   35 | 73
your wheels are properly aligned.   38 | 75

gwam 3' | 1 | 2 | 3 | 4 |

75c, continued   **Directions: Problem 2 Modified Block Style with Open Punctuation**

1. Set margins for a 40-space line.
2. On a half sheet of paper (short side up), keyboard the personal letter below.

3. As you did in Problem 1, follow spacing directions as given in the model.

Return address: 847 Highland Drive| Miami, FL 33181-5476| April 21, 19--

Recipient's address: Miss Roberta Potter | 2195 Ocean Court | Miami, FL 33139-2384| Dear Roberta

Congratulations to you upon your election as president of the North Miami High School Debating Club.

One of my final responsibilities as outgoing president is to make arrangements for our annual joint board meeting. This year we have scheduled a dinner meeting to be held in the school cafeteria on Tuesday, May 10, at 7:00 p.m.

I know you will have a most successful year. Please feel free to call upon me whenever you think I might be of assistance to you.

Sincerely| Sign your name

LESSON 76
70-space line

5 minutes   **76a ● Keyboard Review**

Directions: Keyboard each sentence three times SS. DS between 3-line groups.

alphabet Avis was quite upset after hearing crazy music from the old jukeboxes.

fig/sym Johnson, our 36th President, received 61.1% of the votes cast in 1964.

e,i Their retired neighbors tried hard to remain silent on certain issues.

easy When all their work is done, have them hand it in to the team captain.

| 1 | 2 | 3 | 4 | 5 | 6 | 7 | 8 | 9 | 10 | 11 | 12 | 13 | 14 |

10 minutes   **76b ● Speed Ladder Sentences**

Directions: Keyboard each sentence for 1'. Your teacher will call the guide at 15", 12", or 10" intervals. As time permits, repeat sentences on which you were not able to complete a line with the call of the guide.

	gwam	15" guide	12" guide	10" guide
1 You should think about the future today.		32	40	48
2 It will pay you to build strong study habits.		36	45	54
3 Choose all your classes with a great deal of care.		40	50	60
4 See if you can find where your own special talents lie.		44	55	66
5 Every student is a problem in search of some good solutions.		48	60	72
6 Learn all you can about those fields which interest you the most.		52	65	78
7 When you are older, you will be very glad that you heeded this advice.		56	70	84

| 1 | 2 | 3 | 4 | 5 | 6 | 7 | 8 | 9 | 10 | 11 | 12 | 13 | 14 |

58c ● **Learn to Format Class Notes**

Directions: 1. Keyboard the class notes below. Space as indicated by the colored notations on the copy.
2. Assume these notes will be placed in a notebook. Use leftbound report form.
3. Place the date even with the right margin on line 7. Center the heading 1″ below the date (center point will be three spaces to the right of the usual center point).
4. Clear all tab stops. Set two 4-space tab stops from the left margin.

Today's Date

TAKING NOTES
TS

left margin → Notes on What You Hear
                                        DS
1st tab stop ────────→ 1. Don't try to write everything down. Get only the
2 spaces ──────────┘   important facts and ideas.
                                        DS
                    2. Relate what you know to what you hear. In this way
2d tab stop ──────────→ you will get a better understanding of the topics
                        discussed.

                    3. If the speaker says something is important, put it
                        down.

                    4. If the speaker dwells on a fact or point, put it down.
                                                                        TS

Notes on What You Read

                    1. Get the major points in mind by reading an article
                        that gives you a broad view of the subject in which
                        you are interested.

                    2. Summarize. Don't try to copy everything you read.

                    3. If a statement is made that you wish to quote, put
                        quotation marks around it. Get the complete source.
                                                                        TS

Preparing Notes in Final Form

                    1. If you have taken the notes hurriedly, the sooner you
                        type them in final form, the better.

                    2. Type your notes in complete sentences. Add details
                        that you remember from your reading or from listening
                        to a discussion so that your notes will be meaningful
                        to you when you read them later.

                    3. Type your notes in good form. Space them so they will
                        be easy to read. Put a heading on them. Date them.

LESSON 75

75a ● Keyboard Review

5 minutes   **Directions:** Keyboard each line three times SS. DS between 3-line groups.

alphabet   Banjo players who balked were required to memorize five complex songs.

fig/sym   Yuki sent Check #6932 for $178 (dated November 15) to the stereo shop.

br   bright bray bring brought brace braid bread brain bran break brilliant

easy   You must have a goal in mind if you want to profit from your practice.

| 1 | 2 | 3 | 4 | 5 | 6 | 7 | 8 | 9 | 10 | 11 | 12 | 13 | 14 |

---

15 minutes   ## 75b ● Timed Writings

Directions: 1. Take one 1' writing on each ¶ on 71b, page 124. Circle errors.

2. Take one 5' writing on all four ¶s combined. Circle errors; figure *gwam*.

---

25 minutes   ## 75c ● Problem Typing: Personal Letters

Directions: Problem 1 Modified Block Style With Open Punctuation

1. Keyboard the letter below as illustrated at the right on half-size stationery (5½″ × 8½″), or use a half sheet of paper with the short side up. Set a 40-space line.

2. Use modified block style and open punctuation with 5-space paragraph indentions.

3. Begin the return address on line 9. Follow other spacing directions as shown on the model. Sign your name.

Return address: 1205 Evergreen Lane | Billings, MT 59105-3846 | November 28, 19--

Recipient's address: Mr. Kenneth Mitchell | 239 Cody Circle | Billings, MT 59105-3846 | Dear Mr. Mitchell

I am pleased to announce that the week of January 9-13 has been designated as Black History Week at Robinson School.

To celebrate this event, we plan to hold various activities during each school day and to present evening programs on Thursday and Friday.

If you have names of any speakers to suggest for either of those evenings, I should certainly appreciate receiving them.

Sincerely yours | Sign your name

```
                              ↓ centerpoint

begin on line 9  1205 Evergreen Lane
                 Billings, MT  59105-3846
                 November 28, 19--
                    space down
                    4 times

Mr. Kenneth Mitchell
239 Cody Circle
Billings, MT  59105-3846
                              DS
Dear Mr. Mitchell
                              DS
     I am pleased to announce that the
week of January 9-13 has been designated
as Black History Week at Robinson School.
                              DS
     To celebrate this event, we plan to
hold various activities during each school
day and to present evening programs on
Thursday and Friday.
                              DS
     If you have names of any speakers to
suggest for either of those evenings, I
should certainly appreciate receiving them.
                              DS
          Sincerely yours
```

continued on next page

LESSON 59

59a ● Keyboard Review

5 minutes

Directions: Keyboard each sentence three times SS. DS between 3-line groups.

type without
pauses

alphabet Four experts quickly amazed the crowd by juggling five axes.

fig/sym Barbara's score was 84%, Tim's was 89%, and Nancy's was 91%.

easy The folks to get even with are the ones who have helped you.

| 1 | 2 | 3 | 4 | 5 | 6 | 7 | 8 | 9 | 10 | 11 | 12 |

59b ● Language Arts Skills: Dictation and Spelling Checkup

5 minutes

Directions: **1.** Your teacher will dictate the words in 57b, page 100. Keyboard the words from dictation.

2. Check your work for correct spelling. Retype any words in which you made an error.

59c ● Skill Comparison

5 minutes

keep your fingers
deeply curved

Directions: **1.** Take a 1' writing on the easy sentence. Figure *gwam*.
2. Take a 1' writing on each of the other sentences.

3. Try to match or exceed your goal sentence *gwam* on each of the other sentences.

words

easy There is more than the usual risk when their firm is so big. 12

direct reach Brad wanted to bring music for my ceremony after the brunch. 12

script *The men and women who own land right near the lake are rich.* 12

rough draft It's it is tough to keep an open mind if you have an open mouth. 12

59d ● Language Arts Skills

30 minutes

Problem 1 Capitalization

Directions: **1.** Use a 60-space line and keyboard the problem below on a full sheet of paper DS.
2. Use a 2" top margin and center the heading horizontally.

3. Correct any word that needs capitalization (refer to rules on page xxi if necessary).

APPLYING THE CAPITALIZATION RULES

1 they plan to spend this fall and winter in phoenix, arizona.
2 robert visited miami junior high school on thursday morning.
3 she saw senator kennedy in a school in chicago on labor day.
4 three indians from asia stayed at the hilton hotel in omaha.
5 the danish reporters attended a noon meeting of republicans.
6 she will read a paper on venus and mars in my english class.
7 will major symthe tour damaged areas of the south this fall?
8 after leaving tulsa, i drove east until i crossed the river.
9 luis and anna banuelos belong to the national honor society.
10 the meeting is set for friday in the first methodist church.
11 will senator johnston study pollution in the atlantic ocean?
12 only the irish and french teams will meet on tuesday, may 1.

(continued on next page)

LESSON 74

74a ● Keyboard Review

5 minutes   Directions: Keyboard each line three times SS. DS between 3-line groups.

alphabet We quickly explained most of Mr. Beltzig's peculiar views to the jury.

fig/sym About 20% of the 370 students were making $45.00/month in March, 1986.

combination and the date, and the case, and the only, and the rest, and the faster

easy Write the names of all the machines you can in the blanks on the form.

| 1 | 2 | 3 | 4 | 5 | 6 | 7 | 8 | 9 | 10 | 11 | 12 | 13 | 14 |

5 minutes   ## 74b ● Control Builder

Directions: Take a 1' writing on each ¶ in 73b, page 126. Circle errors. Figure *gwam*.

2. Work for control as you keyboard this exercise.

5 minutes   ## 74c ● Language Arts Skills: Number Expression Guide

Directions: The following are examples of number expressions. The first line gives the rule; the remaining lines illustrate it.

Keyboard each sentence three times SS; DS between each 3-line group.

Note: When referring to the time of day, spell out the hour with *o'clock*; use figures with *a.m.* or *p.m.*

1 With "o'clock," spell out the hour.   Use figures with "a.m." or "p.m."

2 The bus will leave for the game sometime between nine and ten o'clock.

3 When it is 10:15 a.m. in Long Beach, it is 1:15 p.m. in New York City.

30 minutes   ## 74d ● Problem Typing: Postal Cards

Directions: Problem 1
1. Insert a postal card or paper cut to size (5½" × 3¼") into your machine.
2. Set margin stops 4 spaces from each edge of the card. Set a tab stop at

horizontal center.
3. Begin the date on line 3. TS below the date. DS between ¶s; TS to type name. Keyboard the address on the opposite side of the card.

April 28, 19--
TS
The next meeting of the International Club will be held on Friday, May 13, at Martin Luther King School. Our speakers will be Guenter Liesegang and Uthai Tanlamai, this year's foreign exchange students.
DS
The program will begin at 7:30 p.m. We look forward to seeing you there.
TS
Ms. Virginia Guerrero

Address the postal card to:
Mr. E. T. Hansen | 619 Canyon Road | Tulsa, OK 74131-4689

Directions: Problem 2
Keyboard the message in Problem 1 on

postal cards. Use an appropriate salutation. Address the postal cards to:

1. Mrs. Karlin Agao
   69 Carson Avenue
   Tulsa, OK 74119-4836

2. Dr. Sheri Morita
   3028 Waverly Drive
   Tulsa, OK 74104-6457

Problem 2 Topic Outline

Directions: 1. Keyboard the outline below on a 60-space line. Use a 2" top margin.

2. Follow the directions on the model outline. If necessary, refer to 57d, pages 100 and 101.

all Caps

~~*General*~~ Directions for Writing a Book Review)

I. Items to ~~be~~ Included in Review ┤ *all Caps*

and Name

   A. Title ∧of Author

   B. central Theme of Book

   c. Some of the Important People

   D. Setting for the Story

   E. Brief Summary of Some Incidents,

   F. Comments on and Opinion of the Book ~~Itself~~

II. General Guides ~~which are~~ to be Followed ┤ *all Caps*

   A. Should Arouse Reader's Interest

   B. Should be Well Written   *Support*

   C. Should Contain examples to∧ Comments

III. Typing Guides to be Observed ┤ *all Caps*

   A. Typed in Report Form∧ *at*

   B. Triple Space After ~~the~~ Title; all Other ~~Material~~ *Copy* Double Spaced

   C. center heading over copy

LESSON 60

5 minutes

60a ● Keyboard Review

Directions: Keyboard each sentence three times SS. DS between 3-line groups.

alphabet Joy Brave will squeeze six big limes for the drink of punch.

fig/sym Mr. Lang's 28 students collected $46.90 in their fund drive.

easy They paid for their eight chairs with the profits they made.

| 1 | 2 | 3 | 4 | 5 | 6 | 7 | 8 | 9 | 10 | 11 | 12 |

---

10 minutes

60b ● Timed Writings

Directions: Take two 3' writings on 58b, page 101. Figure *gwam*.

Submit the better writing.

---

30 minutes

60c ● Problem Typing: Book Review

Directions: 1. Keyboard the book review on page 105 in the format of a leftbound report DS.

2. Center the heading over the copy.

Use a 2" top margin. Follow the spacing as indicated in the model.

3. Clear all tab stops. Set a 5-space tab stop for indention.

(continued on next page)

Directions: Problem 1
Informal Invitation

1. Keyboard the informal invitation shown in the model illustration at the right on a half sheet of paper, (short side up). You may also use 4½" × 5½" stationery for personal notes such as informal invitations.

2. Leave a 2" top margin. Set a 40-space line and a 5-space tab stop for indented paragraphs.

3. Use modified block style, open punctuation. Begin the return address, dateline, and complimentary close at the horizontal center of the paper.

4. Begin the salutation on the 4th line space below the date. Sign the letter.

```
                          258 Wilder Street
                          Lowell, MA  01851-2364
                          April 2, 19--


Dear Virginia

     Jim and I are planning to attend the
spring concert of the Boston Symphony on
Friday evening, the fifteenth, at eight
o'clock.  Will you and Charles be able to
join us as our guests?

     We know how busy both of you usually
are, but we hope you will enjoy taking a
break for a fine musical performance.

                          Very sincerely
```

Directions: Problem 2 Informal Acceptance
Keyboard the informal acceptance below as directed in Problem 1.

Return Address: **123 Bay View Avenue**| **Lynn, MA 01902-6238**| Today's date|
Dear Sharon

Charles and I are delighted to accept your thoughtful invitation to attend the concert with you and Jim next Friday evening. We're especially anxious to hear the Symphony in the new convention center theater.

Thank you so much for thinking of us. We shall plan to meet you in the foyer before eight.

Very sincerely| **Virginia**

Directions: Problem 3 Thank You Note
Keyboard the thank you note below as directed in Problem 1.

Return Address: **18 San Jon Road**| **Ventura, CA 93001-4572**| Today's date|
Dear Christine

The weekend at your cabin on Shaver Lake was a real delight. It was just what I needed before heading back to Boston and another busy year of school and work.

I thoroughly enjoyed seeing the old gang again and catching up on all the news. Thanks a million for including me.

Sincerely| Sign your name

words

BOOK REVIEW: THE HOBBIT 5
TS

J. R. R. Tolkien (1892-1973) is probably best known for 16
writing a series of three books called THE LORD OF THE RINGS. 29
A prelude to this famous fantasy trilogy, THE HOBBIT is a 40
story of little people who inhabit a land located in the Middle 53
Earth. It is a story of delightful creatures who love peace 65
and quiet, have sharp ears and eyes, are handy with tools, 77
like to laugh and eat, and are inclined to be fat. 87

The main character is Bilbo Baggins, a Hobbit who is 98
talked into helping a group of dwarfs regain their kingdom 110
in a far-off land. Another interesting character in the story 122
is a magical wizard named Gandalf. His major role is to help 135
Mr. Baggins and his friends whenever they get into trouble, 147
which is most of the time. 153

During their journey, while trying to escape from a 163
creature called Gollum, Bilbo finds a ring which has the 174
amazing power to make him invisible. With the help of this 186
mysterious ring, he gets his friends out of several dangerous 199
situations. Once, when spiders entrap them in their webs, 211
Bilbo sets them free. Another time he uses the powers of the 223
ring to help his friends slay a fierce dragon. 233

The HOBBIT is both interesting and exciting. It is one 244
big adventure with no dull moments. Anyone who likes suspense 256
is bound to enjoy this book. 262

60d ● Extra Credit

Problem 1 Unbound Report
Directions: Keyboard the two ¶s in 58b, page 101 in unbound report form. Supply an appropriate heading.

Problem 2 Leftbound Report
Directions: Keyboard the two ¶s in 56c, page 98 in leftbound report form. Supply an appropriate heading.

72c, continued

Directions: Problem 2 Invitation
Keyboard the invitation below in exact vertical center using a half sheet of paper long side up.

Directions: Problem 3 Announcement
Keyboard the announcement below in reading position using a full sheet of paper.

DELEGATES TO STUDENT COUNCIL

you are invited to the advisor's home
for tea
Thursday, November 19, 4:15 p.m.
9900 Riverside Drive, Van Nuys

SPANISH CLUB BARBECUE

Saturday, June 1--4:00 p.m.
Ratcliffe Park Picnic Grounds
Tickets only $2 each
Sign up in Room 9 before Wednesday!

LESSON 73

5 minutes **73a ● Keyboard Review**

Directions: Keyboard each sentence three times SS. DS between 3-line groups.

alphabet Pat required them to wear extra heavy fur jackets during the blizzard.

fig/sym New subscriptions cost $4.87 for 39 weeks and only $6.10 for 52 weeks.

long words Andromeda is also the remotest heavenly body visible to the naked eye.

easy If you type right, you will be hitting those keys as if they were hot.

| 1 | 2 | 3 | 4 | 5 | 6 | 7 | 8 | 9 | 10 | 11 | 12 | 13 | 14 |

10 minutes **73b ● Speed Builder**

Directions: Take two 1' writings on each ¶; try to increase speed on the second writing. Figure *gwam*.

Alternate Procedure: Work for speed as you take one 5' writing on all three ¶s combined. Figure *gwam*.

keep fingers
curved and
upright

all letters used 1.3 si

	gwam 1'	5'
Some students and their parents seem to take it for granted today	13	3	35
that after high school comes college. This is quite sensible because	27	5	38
there is no doubt that a need exists for those persons who have been	41	8	41
college trained. We need them in key jobs throughout the nation.	54	11	43
Should everyone go to college? The answer to such a question is	13	13	46
clear. Many will realize that this is the last and perhaps worst place	27	16	49
for them to be. College is a place for people with good reasons for	41	19	51
wanting to be there and with sufficient talents to succeed.	53	21	54
Are you college material? You are if you're going to college for	13	24	56
the right reasons and if you have what it takes to succeed there. Go	27	27	59
because you want to go. Go to prepare yourself for a career. College	41	30	62
may be a place where you will discover what you really want in life.	55	32	65

gwam 1' | 1 | 2 | 3 | 4 | 5 | 6 | 7 | 8 | 9 | 10 | 11 | 12 | 13 | 14 |
5' | 1 | 2 | 3 |

Unit 9 ▪ Learning to Keyboard Tables (Lessons 61–70)

General Directions

Use a 60-space line, unless otherwise directed, for all lessons in this unit (center − 30; center + 30 + 5). SS sentences and drill lines. DS between repeated groups of lines and paragraph copy. Set tabulator for a 5-space paragraph indention. Your teacher will tell you whether or not to correct errors when keyboarding problems.

LESSON 61

5 minutes

61a ● Keyboard Review

Directions: Keyboard each sentence three times SS. DS between 3-line groups.

keep wrists and elbows quiet

alphabet	Ava Mudge will quickly explain the fire hazards on this job.
fig/sym	That company was in business there for 96 years (1890-1986).
easy	You win when you get your mind to stick to a job to the end.

| 1 | 2 | 3 | 4 | 5 | 6 | 7 | 8 | 9 | 10 | 11 | 12 |

5 minutes

61b ● Fluency Practice

Directions: Keyboard each line 3 times SS. DS between 3-line groups.

1 and he | and if he | and if he is | and if he is to | to do the work
2 and go | with us to | and go with us | and go with us to the right
3 if they | and if they | and if they go to | and if they go to this
4 and show | and to show | and to show it to | and to show it to the

| 1 | 2 | 3 | 4 | 5 | 6 | 7 | 8 | 9 | 10 | 11 | 12 |

10 minutes

61c ● Technique Builder: Stroking

Directions: Keyboard each line three times SS. DS between 3-line groups.

keep your eyes on the copy

hyphen	Their new Model LS-11 is a low-cost, letter-quality printer.
double letters	Keep that tall fellow from passing the football immediately.
direct reaches	Bradley may bring unusual play money for my younger brother.
one-hand	Fred's car starts faster in a garage. My car starts pokily.
balanced-hand	Elena may also fix the big oak chair and the worn throw rug.
combination	She saw Alan get the rare area award for the best race crew.

| 1 | 2 | 3 | 4 | 5 | 6 | 7 | 8 | 9 | 10 | 11 | 12 |

5 minutes

61d ● Skill Comparison

Directions: Keyboard 57c, page 100, as directed.

71d ● Language Arts Skills: Spacing Guides

Directions: The following are spacing guides and sentences that illustrate those guides.

Study the guides; keyboard each line two times that illustrates the guide SS. DS between 2-line groups.

keep your eyes on the copy

Space twice after a period at the end of a sentence.
Please pay attention.   Directions are not repeated.   Listen carefully.

Space once after a semicolon or comma.
Next Monday is the assembly; therefore, your schedule will be changed.

Space twice after a question mark at the end of a sentence.
What time is it?   Can I get there in an hour?   Who will drive the bus?

Space twice after a colon except when stating time.
You will need the following items: textbook, pencils, and calculator.

Space twice after an exclamation point that ends a sentence.
Watch where you are going!   That car is coming toward us!   Don't jump!

Keyboard the dash with two hyphens. Do not space before or after.
As prices keep getting higher, money doesn't talk--it merely whispers.

LESSON 72

70-space line

5 minutes **72a ● Keyboard Review**

Directions: Keyboard each sentence three times SS. DS between 3-line groups.

reach with your fingers

alphabet	We looked up at a majestic flag flying in the quiet breeze over Texas.
fig/sym	A 1964 Civil Rights Act filibuster took up 77 days (March 26-June 10).
shift key	Edmund Hillary and Tenzing Norkey scaled Mt. Everest in the Himalayas.
easy	Both of the men had to ride the bus to work in the busy city each day.

| 1 | 2 | 3 | 4 | 5 | 6 | 7 | 8 | 9 | 10 | 11 | 12 | 13 | 14 |

10 minutes **72b ● Control Ladder Paragraphs**

Directions: 1. Take 1' writings on each ¶ in 71c, page 124. Circle errors and figure *gwam*.

2. When you keyboard a ¶ within the error limit specified by your teacher, move to the next ¶. Use control as you keyboard this exercise.

30 minutes **72c ● Problem Typing**

Directions: Problem 1 Announcement
Keyboard the copy below in exact vertical center using a half sheet of paper (long

side up). TS below the heading; DS between all other lines.

FEBRUARY MEETING OF GIBSON SCHOOL PTA

Thursday, February 23, 7:30 p.m.

School Cafeteria

Discussion of Plans for Career Education Day

Mrs. Janet Pelton, President

(continued on next page)

61e ● Paragraph Guided Writings

Directions: 1. Take one 3' writing on the ¶s below. Circle errors; figure *gwam*.
2. Keyboard each circled word three times along with the words that precede and follow it.

3. Take two 1' writings on each ¶. Try to add 4 words to your 3' rate. Figure *gwam*.
4. Keyboard another 3' writing. Figure *gwam* and circle errors. Compare with your first 3' writing.

all letters used   1.3 si

strike each key with quick, sharp strokes

	gwam 3'
The subject of energy is now one of the hottest topics	4 / 54
around. Most experts think we are on the edge of a new era,	8 / 58
a new stage of history in which our wasteful way of living	12 / 62
will have to change.	13 / 63
To put it bluntly, all of us have been on one big energy	17 / 67
spree. As citizens, we have become used to a lifestyle which	21 / 71
consumes energy as though the supply will last forever. Our	25 / 75
entire stock of goods requires more and more power while the	29 / 79
sources of gas and oil are running low.	32 / 82
Here are several things that may happen in the next few	35 / 85
years. Our cars will be smaller, lighter in weight, and more	40 / 90
efficient. Houses will be built so as to reduce heating and	44 / 94
cooling costs. A shift from gas and oil to coal, nuclear, or	48 / 98
solar energy will need to be made.	50 / 100

gwam 3' | 1 | 2 | 3 | 4 |

---

5 minutes **61f ● Control Practice**

Directions: 1. Keyboard the last ¶ in 61e as many times as you can in the time that remains.

2. Circle your errors. Place a check mark in the margin of each ¶ in which you made no more than one error.

LESSON 62

60-space line

5 minutes **62a ● Keyboard Review**

Directions: Keyboard each sentence three times SS; DS between 3-line groups.

alphabet Jacqueline amazed everyone by fixing these packages of bows.

fig/sym Raul said, "To get the answer, add 9 1/3, 6 5/8, and 7 3/4."

easy Use well the gift of learning to add to the things you know.

| 1 | 2 | 3 | 4 | 5 | 6 | 7 | 8 | 9 | 10 | 11 | 12 |

71b ● Speed Ladder Paragraphs

Directions: 1. Take a 1' writing on ¶1 DS until you complete the ¶ in 1'.

2. When you complete ¶1 in 1', continue on to ¶2. Repeat this procedure as you try

to complete each of the four ¶s in the given time.

3. Take three 1' writings on any ¶ you cannot finish in the time given.

all letters used   1.3 si

use quick,
sharp strokes

			gwam 5'
In ancient times music was used to treat heart disease and help	3	36
those who couldn't sleep. Perhaps such a scheme can work even better	5	39
today because we have more noise to drown out.	7	41
Experts have known for quite some time that noise can be harmful	10	43
to one's health and general well being. In most cases, they say, people	13	46
are not actually aware of the ill effects it can have on them.	15	49
We're jarred out of bed by the ring of an alarm clock. The morning	18	52
news must be loud enough to be heard over the electric razor. The noisy	21	54
traffic on the freeway is only a prelude to more racket waiting for us	24	57
at work.	24	58
Maybe it's time again for us to try the remedy used in former days.	27	60
Because noise is sound that is out of order, we need to put orderly	30	63
sounds in its place. If you find yourself in a bad mood, replace the	32	66
noise around you with good music.	34	67

gwam 5' | 1 | 2 | 3 |

71c ● Learn to Divide Words

Beginning with this lesson, you will be formatting copy that appears in lines either longer or shorter than those for which your margin is set.

It will be necessary for you to listen for the bell and divide long words correctly to keep fairly even right margins.

Directions: 1. Read and study the word-division guides on page xxi.

2. As time permits, type a word which is an example of each guide given on the page but is *not* on the list. Divide each word correctly.

3. When dividing a word at the end of a line, use a hyphen and finish the word on the next line.

4. If you are uncertain about the division of a word, use a dictionary or a word-division manual.

62b ● Sentence Guided Writings

Directions: **1.** Take 1' writings on each sentence SS. Try to reach the end of the sentence as the guide is called.
2. Your instructor will call the return each 15" or 12" to guide you. If you complete each sentence as the guide is called, you will keyboard the sentence four times with the 15" call of the guide or five times with the 12" call of the guide.
3. Figure *gwam* and circle errors.

	gwam	15" guide	12" guide
1 Time will not wait for anyone.		24	30
2 Every day gives you another chance.		28	35
3 You are worth what you make of yourself.		32	40
4 Every time you speak, your mind is on parade.		36	45
5 Do not look for jobs that are equal to your skill.		40	50
6 Look, instead, for skills that are equal to your tasks.		44	55
7 The only time people dislike gossip is when it's about them.		48	60

| 1 | 2 | 3 | 4 | 5 | 6 | 7 | 8 | 9 | 10 | 11 | 12 |

62c ● Steps in Arranging Tables: Horizontal Placement

Step 1 Insert paper into the machine with left edge at "0."

Step 2 Move the left and right margin stops to the ends of the scale. Clear all tab stops.

Step 3 Move the carriage to the center of the paper.

Step 4 Determine spacing between the columns (if a specific number of spaces is not given).

Step 5 Spot the longest word or entry in each column.

Step 6 From the center of your paper, backspace once for each 2 letters, figures, spaces, or punctuation marks in each column. If you have an extra character in any column, add that character to the first character of the next column. If one space is left over after backspacing for all the columns, disregard it.

Step 7 Backspace once for every 2 spaces to be left between the columns. If one space is left over, disregard it.

Step 8 Set the left margin at the point at which you stop backspacing. This is the point where the first column will start.

Step 9 Space forward once for each letter, figure, space or punctuation mark in the longest entry in the first column and once for each space between Columns 1 and 2. Set a tab stop for the second column. Continue in this way until stops have been set for each column.

62d ● Problem Typing: Two-Column Tables

There are 33 line spaces on a half sheet of paper.

Directions: Problem 1
1. Center the table on page 109 horizontally and vertically on a half sheet of paper.
2. Vertical placement directions for this problem are given in the table. This table is placed in exact vertical center.

3. Center the heading over the columnar entries. Leave 12 spaces between columns. Set the left margin stop for the first column, as directed above.
4. Space forward once for each letter and space in Column 1. Then space forward 12 spaces for the space between columns. Set a tab stop.

(continued on next page)

Each Lesson in Cycle 3 provides materials to help you improve the basic skills you have learned in previous lessons. In addition, you may want to preview some of the problems you will prepare by using the following summary.

Announcements, invitations, and thank you notes, pages 125–128.
Letters in semibusiness form, pages 129–130.
Personal/business letters, pages 133–135.
Orders and order letters, page 137.
Themes and reports, including outlines, footnotes, title pages, bibliographies, and note cards, pages 141–161.
Agenda and minutes, pages 164–166.
Club tickets and membership cards, page 167.
Postal cards, pages 168–169.
Bar graphs, pages 171–172.
School organization budget, page 173.
Programs of meetings, pages 174–176.
Bulletin board notices, pages 178–179.
Articles and stories for the school newspaper, pages 180–182.
Student-writer's style guide, pages 183–187.

Basic Skills Improvement: One lesson in each group of five covers technique and skill building. These lessons are designed to help you improve your speed and accuracy.

Language Arts Development: Drills stressing capitalization, punctuation, and number expression guides appear throughout this cycle. These drills will help you improve the quality of all your written work.

Measurement: Timed writings are given in each lesson to aid you in checking your typing speed and accuracy. Use Unit 14 as a check on your understanding of the different types of problems in this cycle.

Extra-Credit Assignments: Problems are given at the end of units for students who finish early and wish extra credit.

Unit 10 ▪ Learning to Format Personal/Business Papers
(Lessons 71–80)

General Directions

Use a 70-space line for all lessons in this unit (center − 35; center + 35 + 5) unless otherwise directed. SS sentences and drill lines. DS paragraph copy. Set tabulator for a 5-space paragraph indention.

Your teacher will tell you whether or not to correct errors when formatting problems.

LESSON 71

5 minutes   71a ● **Keyboard Review**

Directions: Keyboard each sentence three times SS. DS between 3-line groups.

keep arms and wrists quiet

alphabet   They will be having Jose Sanchez speak on their new required tax form.

figures   As of September 1, 1983, the nation was importing only 28% of its oil.

adjacent keys   We said the captain was astonished to see several sailors fast asleep.

easy   To get to the top of the oak, do not merely sit on the acorn and wait.

| 1 | 2 | 3 | 4 | 5 | 6 | 7 | 8 | 9 | 10 | 11 | 12 | 13 | 14 |

```
 1
 2
 3
 4
 5
 6                          Begin on line 10
 7
 8
 9
10                        MUSIC AWARD WINNERS
11                                        TS
12
13        Mary Ellen Dunn           Piano
14                                     DS
15        Lynn Schramm              Alto Saxophone  Longest item
16
17        Gustavo Dominquez         Trumpet
18
19  Longest item  William A. Buzick, Jr.   Oboe
20
21        Diana Pollard             Clarinet
22
23        Barbara Garabedian        Trombone
24
25
26        Left margin               Tab
27
28
29              22            12          14
30
31
32
33
```

Simple two-column table

62d, continued   **Directions: Problem 2**

1. Keyboard the table in Problem 1. Add Mary Ann Wang, who plays the flute, to the list of award winners.

2. Place the table on a full sheet of paper in reading position. Use the backspace from center method for vertical centering. Refer to 52d, page 92, if necessary.

3. Center the heading. Leave 16 spaces between columns.

LESSON 63

5 minutes   **63a ● Keyboard Review**

Directions: Keyboard each sentence three times SS. DS between 3-line groups.

alphabet   The quiz kept Jim and Dick Law busy for six very long hours.

fig/sym   Send a check for $5.98 to 27 West 43rd Street, New York, NY.

easy   Those who were in good shape ran down the field at halftime.

| 1 | 2 | 3 | 4 | 5 | 6 | 7 | 8 | 9 | 10 | 11 | 12 |

CYCLE THREE

Preparing Personal Papers

63b ● Skill Comparison

Directions: **1.** Take two 1' writings on the easy sentence SS. Figure *gwam*.
2. Take two 1' writings on each of the other sentences.

3. Try to match or exceed your *easy* sentence *gwam* on each of the other sentences.

words

easy   She laid their keys down here so they would be out of sight.   12

fig/sym   A new 13-inch monitor (selling for $329) weighs 30.8 pounds.   12

script   *It takes much more than shined shoes to give someone polish.*   12

rough draft   one more spo̲r̲t onℓ a polka dot tie, w̶o̶n̶'̶t̶ *doesn't* realℓy mat̲ter much.   12

63c ● Language Arts Skills: Spelling and Proofreading Aid

Directions: Keyboard each line three times SS. DS between 3-line groups.

1   bureau February partial forty governor miscellaneous process

2   between niece participate battery ceiling graduate permanent

3   address lose recognize nephew courteous family exceed memory

---

63d ● Problem Typing: Centering Two-Column Tables

Directions: Problem 1
1. Keyboard the table below on a half sheet of paper SS. Use the exact vertical centering method.

2. Center the heading horizontally. Leave 20 spaces between columns.

TALLEST BUILDINGS IN TEN MAJOR U.S. CITIES
TS

Chicago	Sears Tower
New York	World Trade Center
Los Angeles	United California Bank
San Francisco	Transamerica Pyramid
Pittsburgh	U.S. Steel Headquarters
Boston	John Hancock Tower
Minneapolis	IDS Tower
Atlanta	Peachtree Plaza
Detroit	Detroit Plaza Hotel
Houston	One Shell Plaza
Dallas	First International

Directions: Problem 2
1. Keyboard the table in Problem 1 in reading position on a full sheet of paper.

2. DS the columnar entries. Leave 24 spaces between columns.

70d ● **Problem Typing: Report with Short Table**

Directions: 1. Keyboard the unbound report below on a 60-space line DS. Use a 2″ top margin. Center the heading over the copy. (Refer to page 94 if necessary.)

2. Leave 12 spaces between the columns of the table SS. TS before and after the heading and at the end of the table.

THE AUTOMOBILE IN AMERICA

Today more than 1 million cars compete for space on our nation's streets and highways. We have become so dependent upon automobiles that they now provide about 90% of our personal transportation needs.

Many different people have played important roles in the development of the auto industry in the United States. Here are just a few of them.

TS

AUTOMOBILE INDUSTRY LEADERS

TS

David Buick	Charles Kettering
Charles Duryea	George Selden
Henry Ford	Alfred Sloan

TS

While the earliest cars were powered by steam, the major source of power for automobiles has been the gasoline engine. In recent years, however, scarcity of oil and increasing concern over pollution have rekindled an interest in finding other types of fuel. Experiments with electric, atomic, and solar power will undoubtedly have to be speeded up if America's love affair with the automobile continues.

Another problem generated by the steadily increasing number of automobiles is that of finding places to park them. There are now more than 6 million spaces in 8,000 American cities where paid parking is available.

70e ● **Extra-Credit**

Directions: Problem 1
1. Keyboard the names of students in your typing class by rows.
2. Use your course title as the main heading; use Row 1, Row 2, etc. as column headings. Arrange the columns and center the table on a full sheet of paper.

Directions: Problem 2
1. Keyboard a summary of the report in 70d above. Do not use the table, but incorporate the ideas from it.
2. Use the directions in 70d for keyboarding your summary.

Directions: Problem 3
1. Keyboard the first ¶ in 70c, page 120 as many times as possible in the time that remains.
2. Submit the paragraph on which you made the fewest errors.

LESSON 64

64a ● Keyboard Review

5 minutes

Directions: Keyboard each sentence three times SS. DS between 3-line groups.

alphabet   Major taxes have clearly penalized quite a few bigger banks.

fig/sym   Hank is almost 5′8″, Mary is 5′10″, and Jose is nearly 6′2″.

easy   Try using your head at a job before you try your hand at it.

| 1 | 2 | 3 | 4 | 5 | 6 | 7 | 8 | 9 | 10 | 11 | 12 |

---

5 minutes

64b ● Language Arts Skills: Keyboarding from Dictation and Spelling Checkup

Directions: **1.** Your teacher will dictate the words in 63c, page 110. Keyboard the words from dictation.

2. Check your work for correct spelling. Retype any words in which you made an error.

---

10 minutes

64c ● Sentence Guided Writings

Directions: **1.** Try to keyboard each sentence in 62b, page 108, four times in 1′ without error.

2. Your teacher will call the return each 15″ to guide you.

---

25 minutes

64d ● Problem Typing: Tables With Subheadings

Directions: Problem 1
Keyboard the table directly below in exact vertical and horizontal center on a full sheet of paper. DS between main and subheadings; TS between subheading and body. SS entries in columns. Leave 18 spaces between columns.

Directions: Problem 2
Keyboard the table directly below in reading position. Center horizontally on a full sheet of paper. DS between main and subheadings; TS between subheadings and body. DS entries in columns. Leave 12 spaces between columns.

NATIVE STATES OF PRESIDENTS
DS
Since 1900
TS

Theodore Roosevelt	New York
William H. Taft	Ohio
Woodrow Wilson	Virginia
Warren G. Harding	Ohio
Calvin Coolidge	Vermont
Herbert C. Hoover	Iowa
Franklin D. Roosevelt	New York
Harry S. Truman	Missouri
Dwight D. Eisenhower	Texas
John F. Kennedy	Massachusetts
Lyndon B. Johnson	Texas
Richard M. Nixon	California
Gerald Ford	Nebraska
Jimmy Carter	Georgia
Ronald Reagan	Illinois

STATE NICKNAMES
DS
Fifteen Largest U.S. States
TS

Alaska	Last Frontier
Arizona	Grand Canyon
California	Golden
Colorado	Centennial
Idaho	Gem
Kansas	Sunflower
Nebraska	Cornhusker
Nevada	Sagebrush
New Mexico	Sunshine
Minnesota	Gopher
Montana	Treasure
Oregon	Beaver
Texas	Lone Star
Utah	Beehive
Wyoming	Equality

70b ● Sentence Guided Writings

Directions: 1. Take 1' writings on each sentence. Try to keyboard the sentence four times within the minute.

2. Your instructor will call the return each 15 seconds to guide you.

3. Figure *gwam* and circle errors.

	15" guide	*gwam*	words
1 Do you sit poised and erect as you type?		32	8
2 Do you type without pauses between the words?		36	9
3 Do you strike each key with a quick, sharp stroke?		40	10
4 Do you think and type the short, easy words as a whole?		44	11
5 Do you hold the wrists low and quiet as you strike the keys?		48	12

| 1 | 2 | 3 | 4 | 5 | 6 | 7 | 8 | 9 | 10 | 11 | 12 |

70c ● Timed Writings

Directions: 1. Keyboard two 1' writings on each ¶ DS. Check the one on which you made your best rate; then check the one on which you made the fewest errors.

2. Take two 3' writings on all three ¶s combined. Circle errors. Figure *gwam*. Submit the better of the two writings.

all letters used   1.3 si   *gwam* 3'

Do you know why many people fail in their jobs? Their	4	54
spelling, poor as it often is, is not the reason. They get	8	58
by in figuring too. The reports of many studies show that	12	62
they fail because they do not work with one another as well	16	66
as they should.	17	67
We ask much of other people but give little in return.	20	70
We stress their mistakes with the same zest we use in hiding	24	74
our own. We are being neither fair to them nor honest with	28	78
ourselves. When we do these things, we cannot work as well	32	82
as we should.	33	83
Good teamwork comes, first of all, from handling our	37	87
duties well. It comes, too, from using kind words when we	41	91
refer to those with whom we work. Adopt the rule never to	45	95
say anything about someone else that you would not like to	49	99
have said about you.	50	100

gwam 3' | 1 | 2 | 3 | 4 |

65a ● Keyboard Review

5 minutes

Directions: Keyboard each sentence three times SS. DS between 3-line groups.

alphabet Gary Wells put five dozen quarts of jam in the box for Jack.

fig/sym Since the tickets sell for $3.50 each, two will cost you $7.

easy Rosa took the lead early in the race and thus won the title.

| 1 | 2 | 3 | 4 | 5 | 6 | 7 | 8 | 9 | 10 | 11 | 12 |

10 minutes

65b ● Technique Builder: Stroking

Directions: Keyboard each sentence 3 times SS. DS between 3-line groups.

home row Dashing Sir Galahad, with sword and half a flag, flashed by.

1st finger You can try to hunt with my gun if you cannot get a new one.

2d finger Did Dick decide to check Cindy's deck to locate any defects?

3d finger Wilma Swanson followed Lolita to Oslo with sixty-six others.

double letters We agreed to call a committee meeting to discuss the matter.

| 1 | 2 | 3 | 4 | 5 | 6 | 7 | 8 | 9 | 10 | 11 | 12 |

10 minutes

65c ● Timed Writings

Directions: Take two 3' writings on all three ¶s combined. Circle errors. Figure *gwam*. Submit the better of the two writings.

all letters used   1.3 si   *gwam* 3'

keep wrists and arms still

As more and more of us work in white collar jobs each   4 | 50
year, we hear increased concern being expressed about real   8 | 54
health hazards which we may face in the office. Two factors   12 | 58
often mentioned are eyestrain and stress.   14 | 61

The fact that so many people must look at their computer   18 | 64
screens all day long has raised questions about the role of   22 | 68
computer screens in causing eyestrain. Some say they think   26 | 72
that computer terminals make their eyes tired and sore.   30 | 76

A few workers even blame the modern office for their back   33 | 80
pains, heart diseases, and other ills that can be caused by   37 | 84
stress. These critics point out that the worst health hazards   42 | 88
of the factory have now been brought to workers who sit behind   46 | 92
a desk.   46 | 92

gwam 3' | 1 | 2 | 3 | 4 |

69c ● Problem Typing: Table with Columnar Headings

Directions: Problem 1
1. Keyboard the table below in reading position on a full sheet of paper.
2. DS columnar entries; leave six spaces between columns.
3. Center the columnar headings over the columns.

JOBS HELD BY FAMOUS PEOPLE

Name	Latest Job	Former Job
Debbie Allen	Producer	Dancer/Singer
Jim Brown	Actor	Football Player
Carol Burnett	Comedian	Usher
Johnny Carson	TV Personality	Magician
Sean Connery	Actor	Bricklayer
Howard Cosell	Sports Announcer	Lawyer
Albert Einstein	Physicist	Patent Clerk
William Faulkner	Author	House Painter
Althea Gibson	Tennis Player	Teacher
Adolph Hitler	Dictator	Poster Painter
Barbara Jordan	Professor	Representative
Dean Martin	Entertainer	Steelworker
Golda Meir	Prime Minister	School Teacher
Marilyn Monroe	Actress	Factory Worker
O. Henry	Author	Cowboy
Sandra O'Connor	U.S. Justice	Lawyer
Elvis Presley	Singer	Truck Driver
Babe Ruth	Baseball Player	Bartender
Shirley Temple	Ambassador	Actress
Harry S. Truman	President	Haberdasher

Directions: Problem 2
1. Keyboard the table above in exact vertical center on a half sheet of paper.
2. SS columnar entries; leave eight spaces between columns.
3. Center the columnar headings over the entries.

LESSON 70

60-space line

70a ● Keyboard Review

Directions: Keyboard each sentence three times SS. DS between 3-line groups.

alphabet Mavis Grable will quickly explain what John made for prizes.

fig/sym Leave 18 spaces (elite) for the left margin of 1 1/2 inches.

easy He will throw the rocks out of sight at the end of the lane.

| 1 | 2 | 3 | 4 | 5 | 6 | 7 | 8 | 9 | 10 | 11 | 12 |

65d ● Problem Typing: Tables

Directions: Problem 1 Three-Column Table

1. Keyboard the table below in reading position on a full sheet of paper.
2. DS columnar entries; leave six spaces between the columns.
3. Refer to page 108, if necessary.

GREAT INVENTIONS AND SCIENTIFIC DISCOVERIES

Selected Items

Bifocal Lens	Benjamin Franklin	1760
Parachute	Louis S. Lenormand	1783
Cotton Gin	Eli Whitney	1793
Eau de Cologne	Jean Marie Farina	1850
Dynamite	Alfred Nobel	1867
Phonograph	Thomas A. Edison	1877
Radium	Marie Curie	1898
Tractor	Benjamin Holt	1900
Xerography	Chester Carlson	1938
Helicopter	Igor Sikorsky	1939
Nuclear Reactor	Enrico Fermi	1942
Ball Point Pen	Lazio Biro	1944

Directions: Problem 2 Two-Column Table from Script

Space the main and subheadings as you did in previous problems.

1. Keyboard the table below in exact vertical center on a half sheet of paper.
2. SS the columnar entries; leave 18 spaces between columns.

LARGEST U.S. CITIES

Ranked Per Population

New York	New York
Los Angeles	California
Chicago	Illinois
Houston	Texas
Philadelphia	Pennsylvania
Detroit	Michigan
Dallas	Texas
San Diego	California
Phoenix	Arizona
San Antonio	Texas

68e, continued

Directions: Problem 2 Table with Columnar Headings

1. Keyboard the table below in exact vertical center on a half sheet of paper. Center horizontally.

2. SS the columnar entries, as shown. Leave 12 spaces between columns.

3. TS between the subheading and columnar headings. Center the columnar headings over the entries. Refer to 68d, page 117 if necessary.

Note: Space the main and subheading as you did in previous problems.

JEFFERSON CAMERA CLUB
DS
Program Assignments
TS

Date	Chairperson
	DS
October 3	Jeff Herron
October 17	Craig Johnson
November 14	Rosemary Papagni
November 28	Valerie Fender
December 12	Orlando Gomez
January 9	Susan Anderson
January 23	Nancy Brock

LESSON 69

60-space line

5 minutes

69a ● Keyboard Review

Directions: Keyboard each sentence three times SS. DS between 3-line groups.

use quick,
sharp strokes

alphabet Tammy Planck will squeeze five or six juicy oranges by hand.

fig/sym Prices -- except on 1986 and older models -- will increase 6.8%.

easy See if they can do most of their work on these new machines.

| 1 | 2 | 3 | 4 | 5 | 6 | 7 | 8 | 9 | 10 | 11 | 12 |

---

10 minutes

69b ● Language Arts Skills: Composing at the Typewriter

Directions: Compose answers to as many of the questions below as time permits. Use complete sentences as you keyboard your answers.

1. What is your favorite song?
2. Which singer do you like best?
3. What is your favorite subject in school?
4. What is the capital of your state?
5. What do you enjoy doing most in your spare time?
6. What event is celebrated on July 4?
7. Who is the governor of your state?
8. What was the event that made Charles Lindbergh famous?

66a ● Keyboard Review

5 minutes

Directions: Keyboard each sentence three times SS. DS between 3-line groups.

alphabet   May Dick will give the puzzle to Jess Quinn for the old box.

fig/sym   Asia's Mount Everest (5 1/2 miles high) was climbed in 1953.

easy   Most of us show what we are by what we do with what we have.

| 1 | 2 | 3 | 4 | 5 | 6 | 7 | 8 | 9 | 10 | 11 | 12 |

---

5 minutes

66b ● Language Arts Skills: Capitalization Guides

Directions: The following are capitalization guides and sentences that illustrate those guides. Study each guide.   Keyboard the sentences that illustrate the guides twice SS; DS between 2-line groups.

Capitalize the principal words in titles of publications, except short prepositions, conjunctions, or articles.

Nina will play a small part in the musical "Sound of Music."

I took the notes from the article "Africa's Garden of Eden."

Capitalize or underscore the complete title of a book.

DELOS is the name of Nelson's book on the islands of Greece.

Carole reviewed Durrell's book Birds, Beasts, and Relatives.

---

15 minutes

66c ● Sentence Guided Writings

Directions: 1. Take 1' writings on each sentence SS. Try to keyboard each sentence four times within the minute without error.   **2.** Your instructor will call the return each 15" to guide you.
3. Figure *gwam* and circle errors.

gwam   15" guide

1 We live in an information age.   24

2 Computers are used for many things.   28

3 Some people are worried about eyestrain.   32

4 A few factories are now making use of robots.   36

5 Most machines are now becoming more user-friendly.   40

6 *In some instances you can do your banking by telephone.*   44

7 Skill in keyboarding is really important for all of us.   44

8 *Persons of every age group are being affected by technology.*   48

9 Not everybody will adjust easily to this new computer world.   48

LESSON 68

68a ● Keyboard Review

5 minutes

Directions: Keyboard each sentence three times SS. DS between 3-line groups.

alphabet Hal G. Kumpf also said it was just six above zero in Quincy.

fig/sym Martie ran the 100-yard dash (91.4 meters) in less than 15".

easy Fix the handle so tight that he will not be able to turn it.

| 1 | 2 | 3 | 4 | 5 | 6 | 7 | 8 | 9 | 10 | 11 | 12 |

68b ● Skill Comparison

5 minutes

Directions: **1.** Take a 1' writing on the *easy* sentence. Figure *gwam*.
2. Take a 1' writing on each of the other sentences.

3. Try to match or exceed your *easy* sentence *gwam* on each of the other sentences.

words

do not pause between words

easy He is to make a pair of signs to hang on the end of the bus. 12

script *Don't think you are generous simply because you give advice.* 12

rough draft I think it is better to be a has been than den who never was. 12

68c ● Language Arts Skills: Keyboarding from Dictation and Spelling Checkup

5 minutes

Directions: **1.** Your teacher will dictate the words in 67b, page 116. Keyboard the words from dictation.

2. Check your work for correct spelling. Retype any words in which you made an error.

68d ● Centering Column Headings

5 minutes

Directions: Study these steps for centering headings over columns in a table.

Step 1 Set the carriage at the point a column is to begin.

Step 2 Space forward 1 space for each 2 spaces in the longest line in that column.

Step 3 From that point, backspace once for each 2 spaces in the columnar heading.

Step 4 Keyboard the heading. It will be centered over the column.

Note: If a column heading is longer than any item in the column, use the heading as the longest item in the column to figure the point to begin the column.

68e ● Problem Typing: Learn to Center Column Headings

25 minutes

Directions: Problem 1 Practice Problem

1. Insert a sheet of practice paper. The two entries below are the longest items in each of two columns in a table.

2. Center the longest entries horizontally on your paper, leaving six spaces between the columns.

3. Following the steps given in 68d above, center the headings two spaces above the entries.

4. Then keyboard the entries under the column headings.

Column Headings	Date DS	Chairperson DS
Longest entries	November 14	Rosemary Papagni

continued on next page

66d ● **Paragraph Guided Writings**

Directions: **1.** Take one 3' writing on the ¶s below. Circle all errors. Figure *gwam*.
2. Keyboard each circled word three times with the word that precedes and follows it.

3. Take two 1' writings on each ¶. Try to increase your speed. Figure *gwam* and circle errors. Compare with your first 3' writing.

all letters used   1.3 si

gwam 3'

keep your wrists
low and still

			4			8		

Down through the years, humans have always found a need   4 | 50
12   16   20
to exchange written messages with those who live some distance   8 | 54
24   28   32   36
away.   The first record of a system for doing this goes back   12 | 58
40   44
to the days of bronze tablets carried on horseback.   16 | 62

Our own mail service has evolved from the era of the   19 | 65
12   16   20
pony express to the jet age.   To handle the expanding volume,   23 | 70
24   28   32
equipment is used that reads zip codes to direct a piece of   27 | 74
36   40   44
mail to one section of a block or one certain building.   31 | 77

No one knows how we will be sending written notes to   34 | 81
12   16   20
each other in the future.   Today many firms use some form of   38 | 85
24   28   32
electronic mail, where their letters are sent by means of   42 | 89
36   40   44
telephone lines and no written copies are transported at all.   46 | 93

gwam 3' | 1 | 2 | 3 | 4 |

---

5 minutes   **66e** ● **Control Practice**

Directions: **1.** Keyboard the last ¶ in 66d, above, as many times as you can in the time that remains.

2. Circle your errors. Place a check mark in the margin of each ¶ in which you made no more than one error.

LESSON 67

60-space line

5 minutes   **67a** ● **Keyboard Review**

Directions: Keyboard each sentence three times SS. DS between 3-line groups.

alphabet   Fred Vasquez again explained why he objected to the remarks.

figure   On July 1 their extension will be changed from 2983 to 6745.

easy   She thinks he will be there to see her when the plane lands.

| 1 | 2 | 3 | 4 | 5 | 6 | 7 | 8 | 9 | 10 | 11 | 12 |

67b ● Language Arts Skills: Spelling and Proofreading Aid

Directions: Keyboard each line three times SS. DS between 3-line groups.

keep arms and
wrists quiet

1 machinery endeavor faculty assistant ninth necessity equally

2 appropriate ninety knowledge career truly pamphlet Wednesday

3 doctor completely enthusiasm since occur accurate beneficial

5 minutes

67c ● Paragraph Guided Writings

Directions: **1.** Take a 1' writing on ¶1, 66d, page 115. Figure *gwam*. Add four words to your *gwam* for a new goal. **2.** Take three 1' writings on the same ¶.

Try to reach your goal on each writing. The quarter- or half-minutes will be called to guide you.

30 minutes

67d ● Problem Typing: Four-Column Table

Refer to page 108 for setting the left margin stop for the first column and tab stops for the second, third, and fourth columns.

Directions: **1.** Keyboard the table below in reading position on a full sheet of paper. **2.** SS the columnar entries; leave six spaces between the columns.

TWO-LETTER ABBREVIATIONS FOR THE STATES

Recommended by the U.S. Postal Service

Alabama	AL	Montana	MT
Alaska	AK	Nebraska	NE
Arizona	AZ	Nevada	NV
Arkansas	AR	New Hampshire	NH
California	CA	New Jersey	NJ
Colorado	CO	New Mexico	NM
Connecticut	CT	New York	NY
Delaware	DE	North Carolina	NC
Florida	FL	North Dakota	ND
Georgia	GA	Ohio	OH
Hawaii	HI	Oklahoma	OK
Idaho	ID	Oregon	OR
Illinois	IL	Pennsylvania	PA
Indiana	IN	Rhode Island	RI
Iowa	IA	South Carolina	SC
Kansas	KS	South Dakota	SD
Kentucky	KY	Tennessee	TN
Louisiana	LA	Texas	TX
Maine	ME	Utah	UT
Maryland	MD	Vermont	VT
Massachusetts	MA	Virginia	VA
Michigan	MI	Washington	WA
Minnesota	MN	West Virginia	WV
Mississippi	MS	Wisconsin	WI
Missouri	MO	Wyoming	WY